Rupert D. V. Glasgow

*Minimal Selfhood and
the Origins of Consciousness*

Rupert D. V. Glasgow
Minimal Selfhood and the Origins of Consciousness

Impressum

Julius-Maximilians-Universität Würzburg
Würzburg University Press
Universitätsbibliothek Würzburg
Am Hubland
D-97074 Würzburg
www.wup.uni-wuerzburg.de

©2018 Würzburg University Press
Print on Demand

Coverdesign & Illustrationen: Christina Nath

ISBN: 978-3-95826-078-8 (print)
ISBN: 978-3-95286-079-5 (online)
URN: urn:nbn:de:bvb:20-opus-157470

 Except otherwise noted, this document – excluding the cover –
is licensed under the Creative Commons License
Attribution-ShareAlike 4.0 International (CC BY-SA 4.0):
https://creativecommons.org/licenses/by-sa/4.0/

 The cover page is licensed under the Creative Commons License
Attribution-NonCommercial-NoDerivatives 4.0 International
(CC BY-NC-ND 4.0):
http://creativecommons.org/licenses/by-nc-nd/4.0/

Acknowledgements

The present book originally formed a rather long final chapter of a PhD dissertation entitled *The Minimal Self*. Once again, I owe a great debt of gratitude to Roland Borgards, Martin Heisenberg and Karl Mertens of Würzburg University for their generous guidance and encouragement throughout that project. Together with Bertram Gerber of the Leibniz Institute of Neurobiology in Magdeburg, moreover, it was their idea that I should turn that long, final chapter into a book in its own right. Given the stamina that would have been required of readers of *The Minimal Self* to reach that long, final chapter, I think that the advice was absolutely spot-on.

As with *The Minimal Self*, special thanks go to Bertram, who has provided invaluable criticism and feedback as well as support and friendship. It was Bertram who first encouraged me to pursue my thinking on 'selfhood', and without his influence I doubt whether the book would have even been conceived (at least by me), let alone written. It goes without saying that I bear full responsibility for the mistakes and shortcomings.

Again, I should like to thank the organizers and participants in the various courses and talks I have given on the 'The Phylogeny of the Self'. In particular, I thank (in alphabetical order) Mirjam Appel, Achim Engelhorn, Alex Gómez Marín, Apollonia Heisenberg, Manos Paissios, Alois Palmetshofer, Teiichi Tanimura and Ayse Yarali. Many thanks also go to Christina Nath for contributing the beautiful illustrations, to the team at Würzburg University Press for their great care and skill in preparing the book and to Christina Kolbe for helping me to track down some of the research material. I am very grateful, once more, to Bertram Gerber for making the illustrations possible.

A special mention also goes to my lovely friends in Zaragoza and elsewhere. Carmen Canales, Las Peñas Altamira and Los Helechos, and Winni

Schindler and Sarah Lothian have all coped admirably with my even more than usually idiosyncratic behaviour, as have Barbara Glasgow in Berkhamsted and Faith Glasgow and Tony and Mattie Doubleday in Stoke Newington.

RDVG
Zaragoza, Spain

Contents

I.
A Brief Introduction to Minimal Selfhood

Minimal Selfhood 13

II.
Consciousness: Preliminary Considerations

Consciousness and Behaviour 23
A Scale of Consciousness 32
Consciousness, Meta-Mental States and Tacit Selfhood 37
Consciousness and Brains 42

III.
From Motionlessness to Directed Motility

Non-Movers and the Almost Immobile 51
The Sessility of Plants 57
Plant-like and Animal-like Unicellulars 60
Motile Bacteria: *Escherichia coli* and Company 66
Motile Protozoa: *Oxyrrhis marina* and Company 73

IV.
Appetite and Tacit Selfhood

Hunger, Satiety and Siesta 81
Recognizing Hunger: Some Doubts 86
Appetite, Motivation and Pleasure 92
Further Aspects of Tacit Selfhood: Pain and Emotion 102
Attention, Arousal and Their Absence: Sleep and Anaesthesia 109

V.
Where Consciousness is Superfluous

Taxis and Reflexes 121
Metazoan Cells 129

VI.
Limits to Claims about Rudimentary Consciousness

A World of Objects 135
Choice and Freedom 142
Future and Past 147
Knowledge, Thought and Morality 155

VII.
Epilogue: Consciousness in Simple Animals

Three Questions 165
Sponges and Other Filter Feeders 169
The Non-Directional Movement of Placozoans 172
'Hungry' Cnidarians 174
Two Worms 179

Glossary..191
List of Figures..199
Endnotes..201
Bibliography..243

I.

*A Brief Introduction
to Minimal Selfhood*

Minimal Selfhood

The present treatise seeks to ground rudimentary forms of consciousness in what I have elsewhere referred to as the 'minimal self'. This concept has been explored at length in a book of the same name.[1] The idea underlying the present treatise is that consciousness is logically dependent not, as is commonly assumed, on ownership of an anatomical brain or nervous system (as happens to be the mammalian paradigm), but on the intrinsic reflexivity characteristic of minimal selfhood. While minimal selfhood need not in itself imply consciousness, it provides the foundation for its possible appearance. I hope to trace the logical path by which basalmost consciousness can be presumed to have emerged from minimal selfhood and thereby to pinpoint the sort of empirical questions we should ask when trying to decide whether or not to ascribe consciousness to any *particular* type of organism.[2] Possibly counterintuitively, it will be proposed that consciousness can in certain circumstances be meaningfully attributed to a subset of single-celled organisms such as amoebae and dinoflagellates, as well as to some – but not all – of the simpler animals. Before unfolding this argument, however, we must recapitulate the basic features associated with a concept of minimal selfhood based on *intrinsic reflexivity*. The aim of this brief introduction, therefore, is to spare readers unacquainted with *The Minimal Self* the trouble of having to plough through it in order to make full sense of the present argument about rudimentary consciousness.

So what is reflexivity? Consider our everyday use of the word 'self' as a pronoun in a simple reflexive proposition such as 'I wash myself'.[3] The identity of the grammatical subject with the grammatical object of the sentence suggests an activity that is in some sense *turned back* on itself,[4] resulting in a relationship of something to itself. By defining a self in terms of *intrinsic* reflexivity, the reflexive activity is pinpointed as constitutive of the self that performs such activity. Well-known examples of intrinsic reflexivity are self-organization and self-production (often referred to as *autopoiesis*). By contrast with the extrinsic or contingent reflexivity of washing oneself, the reflexivity of self-organization or self-production is judged to be essential to the entity engaged in the activity. The claim is that a self is the sort of entity that engages in and is constituted by intrinsically reflexive processes such as self-organization or self-production, and if it ceases to undertake these intrinsically reflexive activities (e.g. if it ceases to organize or produce itself), it will cease to be.

Entities constituted by such intrinsically reflexive processes necessarily embody two underlying features: reflexivity and continuity in time. To the extent that I engage in such processes (say, by producing or creating myself), *reflexivity* comes to light in the duality of subject and object, cause and effect. Through the process of self-creation, I become my own creator and my own creation. The *continuity* of the process is logically guaranteed by the use of the first person for both constituents of the duality: *I* create *myself*, or self creates self. There is a logical and a causal link between the self that creates itself and the self that is created by this process of self-creation. Conceived in these terms, selfhood is inherently processual, involving the continuity of an intrinsically reflexive process, not merely the persistence of the product of such a process. It is the self-producing system that persists, not the self-produced product. This is illustrated by the distinction between *self-organization*, which is founded on energy-driven flow and produces dynamic phenomena such as whirlpools or whirlwinds, and *self-assembly*, which generally occurs without any input of energy and produces structures that are stable or metastable, such as crystals[5]. Insofar as it is processual, selfhood can never be 'complete'; completion would imply stasis and the end of the self in question.

Such a notion may be felt to reduce the mysteries of living selfhood to an empty formalism.[6] As a result of its processual nature, however, the grounding of selfhood in intrinsic reflexivity gives rise to a conception of selfhood that is dependent upon energetic flow and the dictates of thermodynamics; a self-maintaining self requires an input of energy to keep on maintaining itself as the self that it is. An intrinsically reflexive self is thus a *thermodynamic* self. Far from being reductionistic, such a definition is appropriately circular. What emerges is that a self is an entity constituted by an intrinsically reflexive relationship to itself, or that converts itself from a pre-existing self into a post-existing self. What remains undetermined is *what* a self that is constituted in this way actually *is*. Such an understanding of selfhood does not specify whether we are dealing with a controlled flow of energy, a unit of genetic material, an organism, a living individual, a human being, a super-organism or community of individuals, a biosphere or even a universe.[7] In fact, any of these things (and more) may be selves, or at least self-like, depending on how they 'delimit' themselves.

In *The Minimal Self* three overall categories of intrinsic reflexivity were distinguished: self-maintenance, self-reproduction and self-containment. All three are required for 'full' minimal selfhood to be present, whereas to show just one or two of the three categories is to be merely *self-like*.

The first category, *self-maintenance*, incorporates concepts such as self-organization (as exhibited by whirlpools and whirlwinds), self-propagation (as exhibited by forest fires) and self-production (as exhibited by *autopoietic* or biological systems). Varying degrees of self-change are also implied by the concept of self-maintenance, embodied in processes such as self-adaptation and even self-transformation. Noteworthy, again, is that such notions embrace the twin features of reflexivity and continuity in time. However radical the reflexive process of self-transformation may be, it presupposes the continuity of the pre-existing self with the self that emerges from the process of transformation. Self-transformation is the activity of a self at time *a* transforming itself into itself at time *b*.

The second category, *self-reproduction*, refers to various forms of self-multiplication and includes both the self-division of cells and the replication of genetic macromolecules. It happens to be the case that these two phenomena are intricately associated with one another in the present-day biology of our planet, yet this intimate association is not logically pre-ordained and it may *de facto* not always have prevailed. Here too we find the twin features of reflexivity and continuity in time.[8] The key difference with respect to the first category is that, notwithstanding the *continuity* between parent and offspring, there occurs an infringement of numerical identity, exemplified by a single amoeba undergoing fission to become two. The crux of self-multiplication is that over time one self turns itself into multiple selves. These first two categories of intrinsic reflexivity correspond neatly to the two most widespread conceptions of the underlying nature of life: on the one hand, as a metabolic process typified by activities such as eating and excretion, growth and decay; on the other, as an evolutionary or (self-) transformational process grounded in the propensity of a population of entities to undergo natural selection.[9]

The third category of intrinsic reflexivity, *self-containment*, subsumes two distinct but closely related ideas. The first idea is that the entity in question is held within a boundary or limit that is of its own manufacture and is intrinsic to that entity. Whether existing singly as a unicellular organism or cooperating with thousands, millions or even billions of other cells to form a multicellular organism such as an animal, each individual cell is enclosed within its own self-generated phospholipid membrane. In turn, each and every multicellular animal sports its own epithelium, which in many cases includes not only the outer boundary provided by the skin but also the mucous membrane that forms an internalized boundary running through us from mouth to bum. Self-containment may further be understood to encompass mechanisms of self/non-self discrimination such as the immune system. The unit of self-containment may thus be designated not merely an individual (in the sense of an object endowed with a physical boundary), but a biological individual (in that it is an individual that *constructs* the very boundaries that separate self from non-self).

The second idea subsumed within the concept of self-containment relates to the functional integration of the entity. The point here is that the various component parts of a self-containing self, whether the mitochondria of a cell or the heart and liver of an animal, cannot simply jump ship and pursue an autonomous existence; nor can the self-containing self exist without its component parts. The diverse parts of a self can be conceived as collectively embracing one another in a hug of mutual interdependence. Indeed, they have no option but to hold themselves together. In this sense the unit of self-containment may be designated an organism, i.e. a composite entity whose parts are causally integrated into a single functional unit. In the case of both biological individuals and organisms, the unit of self-containment can be taken to be coterminous with the unit of selfhood, and by extension with the unit of selfishness, self-care or self-interest.[10]

An underlying assumption of this approach to selfhood is that multi-celled organisms as well as free-living single-celled organisms exhibit the three forms of intrinsic reflexivity considered necessary and sufficient for the ascription of full minimal selfhood: self-maintenance, self-reproduction and self-containment.[11] Understood thus, full minimal selfhood is a term that can be applied not just to the simplest or foundational biological unit (the free-living cell), but also to more complex organisms insofar as they too are characterized by all three forms of intrinsic reflexivity. Unicellular organisms such as bacteria and protozoa represent a paradigm of minimal selfhood: they maintain themselves through an ongoing process of metabolic self-production; they reproduce themselves, for example by periodically splitting into two; and they contain themselves by generating their own membrane and forming functionally integrated bodies. By analogous arguments, animals ranging from sponges and placozoans to cetaceans and primates can also be regarded as embodying minimal selfhood.[12] It goes without saying that this is not an exhaustive description of the selfhood of humans or complex animals. However, more sophisticated forms of animal or human selfhood are grounded in and presuppose this foundation.

In particular, the parallelisms and correspondences between their respective forms of self-containment – their physical boundaries and functional integration – cast light both on free-living single-celled organisms and on multicellular selves such as animals and plants. In neither the unicellular nor the multicellular case is self-containment merely a matter of enclosure or autonomy. Self-contained though it may be, any particular self is always reliant on the environment that sustains it with a flow of energy and matter. The boundary implied by self-containment must thus always allow nutrients in and waste out, while keeping the internal environment strictly separate from the external environment. Indeed, there is a sense in which a boundary or limit is in essence *ambiguous*, for it cannot help but link what it separates (in this case self and non-self). To the extent that the boundary represents the point at which self coincides with non-self, it is necessarily Janus-faced, infringing the law of identity, and the notion of self-delimitation or self-containment is inextricably bound up with that of self-transcendence. Given this inherent ambiguity, a self-containing self is also a self-transcending self. This is crucial to the possibility of directed self-movement and, by extension, consciousness.

The best-known illustration at the unicellular level is perhaps provided by the model bacterium *Escherichia coli*, where this 'openness' specifically takes the form of transmembrane receptor proteins that can be conceived as gateways or windows traversing the boundary between self and non-self. As we shall see below, these membrane-spanning receptors 'recognize' certain molecules (amino acids or toxins) on the outside of the cell and in turn activate the biochemical circuitry on the inside.[13] This is what makes it possible for the cell to direct its locomotion towards what is good for itself and away from what is bad for itself. Activated by the transmembrane protein, a protein-based signal pathway involving the addition or removal of phosphates from a small protein called CheY regulates the rotary motor activity of the bacterium's locomotory flagella, causing the cell either to 'tumble' (i.e. change direction in search of food) or to continue swimming in the same direction. *E. coli* has some ten thousand such membrane-spanning receptors clustered mainly at one end of the organism, thanks to which it inhabits a chemical universe comprising over fifty attractants and repellents. As a consequence of this sensitivity, even the 'slightest whiff' of its preferred amino acid will elicit a change in its swimming activity.[14]

It is this openness to its environment that permits a hungry organism not just to stumble or grope around at random, but to engage in intentional, directed behaviour, i.e. to go after what is good (for itself). By sensing environmental non-self, the organism can be said to reach out beyond its boundaries. To the extent that a self-containing self thus also transcends itself, it is able to behave (i.e. to move itself) in a manner that conforms with its interests and fosters its self-perpetuation. Such self-transcendence can also be conceived in terms of indexicality. While the concept of 'self-containment' entails that I am always here now (this is tautologically true of the first-person perspective associated with selfhood: here is where I always am; now is the time it always is), my self-transcendence allows for me to be there and then (i.e. to be intentionally directed towards wherever my next meal is likely to be in the future).

In a multicellular context, this openness manifests itself immediately in our sense of touch. Our skin is not just a container that holds us in, but one of the 'main sensory portals'[15] by which we open onto the world. The human dermis contains a variety of specialized receptor cells that communicate with the central nervous system about the external world and the state of the skin. These include mechanical pressure receptors, temperature receptors and diverse pain sensors that alert us to the presence of potentially harmful physical stimuli and to inflammation and injury, prompting us to recoil from what might threaten our bodily integrity and to protect areas where damage has already occurred. Yet even the single-celled *Paramecium* has something akin to a sense of touch, reacting to a bump from behind by speeding up its swimming and to a thump at the front by swimming off in a new direction. These responses are mediated by movements of charged ions through special channels in the cellular membrane that cause changes in the beating of the organism's cilia. Such ion channels, it is thought,[16] would have originally provided cells with a means of adapting to osmotic variability in the environment, but they have subsequently been co-opted for the regulation of swimming behaviour.

Much greater distances are opened up by light-sensitivity, but the same principle is at work, namely the coupling of 'outside' and 'inside'. In this case, the membrane-spanning protein *rhodopsin* plays the central role. The eye is thought to have evolved independently as many as forty times in various parts of the animal kingdom,[17] yet across the whole range it is rhodopsin that is responsible for the absorption of photons. This applies equally to the single photosensitive cells of certain cnidarians and the complex camera-like lenses of vertebrates, where an image is projected onto a whole sheet of photoreceptors. Rhodopsin consists of the light-sensitive protein opsin linked to a form of vitamin A called retinal. The light-induced isomerisation of the molecule results in a change of shape both in the retinal itself and the protein surrounding it. It is this conformational switch in the transmembrane protein that transmits the signal from outside to inside, triggering the cascade of biochemical events in the organism's neural circuitry that in turn gives rise to behaviour appropriate to the changing environment around it. This in turn serves the interests of the self in question.

Such behaviour is typified by the well-known 'shadow reflex' of the barnacle, a sessile arthropod commonly found encrusted on tidal rocks on coastal beaches. The barnacle's simple eyes, each of which comprises just a few rhodopsin-containing photoreceptor cells, are not equipped with a lens capable of forming an 'image'. However, they are acutely sensitive to a sudden drop in light intensity, which can be taken as a reliable indicator of the shadow cast by a potential predator and promptly causes the animal to withdraw into its protective shell.[18] Though not ubiquitous, rhodopsins are also present in unicellular light-sensitive organisms, where some varieties govern the phototactic locomotion of cells towards sources of light (and thus energy), and others function as proton pumps.[19] A particularly remarkable case among single-celled organisms is provided by the warnowiids, a family of dinoflagellates that feed largely on other dinoflagellates rather than the energy of the sun. Warnowiids are endowed with a photoreceptor system called an 'ocelloid' that is no less complex than a metazoan eye in its structure and organization and that incorporates cornea, iris, lens and retina.[20] The mechanisms by which this single cell transmits signals from its 'eye' to its flagellum and thus guides its locomotion – if this is indeed what happens – are yet to be established.

A number of forms of intrinsic reflexivity converge in the above cases of self-transcendence. At issue is a self-maintaining self that may be said to 'care' for itself and whose concern is to pursue its own interests, i.e. to orient itself towards what is good for itself rather than what is less good. This active pursuit of one's own interests involves a manner of self-adaptation that manifests itself as self-movement. Furthermore, it presupposes a mechanism of self-containment that at the same time opens out onto the world, generating a world imbued with value or valence, in which non-self may be better (for self) or worse (for self) and where the rational option is always to head for the better and shun the worse. It is self-transcendence in this sense that enables the self-caring self to identify *where its interests lie* and to *pursue* these interests by moving itself in the appropriate direction.

II.

Consciousness: Preliminary Considerations

Consciousness and Behaviour

The preceding recapitulation of minimal selfhood pinpointed the 'openness' of the senses – spanning the boundary between self and non-self – as a crucial feature of self-containment, providing the basis for self-movement that is not merely random but directed, in effect at least. It is thanks to an ability to sense what is in the vicinity that imbalances in the inner environment of the organism can be rectified not only by means of internal physiological or biochemical mechanisms but also by outward *behaviour* or *action*. So-called homeostatic sensations such as hunger, thirst or discomfort thus tend to generate appropriate locomotive action such as a search for nutrition or liquid or a self-displacement towards more suitable or less harmful surroundings.

In other words, a sensation of hunger – an appetite – motivates behaviour that is in the interest of the self in question (the procurement and ingestion of food), indirectly maintaining the constancy of the body's internal milieu. Once a state of satiety has been reached (signalling the imminent[21] restoration of inner balance), the pleasure taken in the food wanes and the motivation to eat ceases. By the same token, a sensation of pain leads to a response of immediate withdrawal from whatever threatens to breach or undermine our integrated self-containment. This ability both to sense relevant non-self and to move oneself (to move one's self) in accordance with one's interests hinges on the nature of self-containment as intrinsically reflexive, in other words on the fact that the self is contained by *itself* and not by a vessel that is extrinsic or extraneous. Containment by what is 'other', i.e. *allo*- rather than *auto*-containment, is tantamount to imprisonment and precludes or at least restricts the possibility of self-movement.[22]

The aim of this brief treatise is to show that such minimal selfhood – as embodied in the threefold intrinsic reflexivity of self-maintenance, self-reproduction and self-containment[23] – grounds the possibility of consciousness. It will seek to do so first by arguing that the minimal selfhood of single-celled protozoa such as amoebae, ciliates and flagellates[24] may in certain (but not all) cases beget an elementary or rudimentary[25] form of consciousness. It will then proceed to apply this same analysis to a number of the simplest multicellular animals. The converse of these claims is that the rudimentary consciousness of these protozoans and simple metazoans – like the more complex forms of consciousness for which such rudimentary consciousness provides the foundation – in turn presupposes minimal selfhood. In experiential terms, this will be seen to manifest itself as what has been termed 'tacit' selfhood (or sometimes 'pre-reflective self-awareness'). This refers to an implicit bodily self-familiarity: the appetites and aversions, drives[26] and dispositions that shape and structure a selfish perspective on the world.

The argument, however, is not that all minimal selves exhibit consciousness all the time, and the underlying task will be to distinguish selfhood that does from selfhood that does not. Certainly, a conception of selfhood in terms of the intrinsically reflexive relationship that a self has to itself also implies an intrinsic relationship to the non-self to which it is structurally coupled.[27] The deep dependence of any metabolic entity upon meaningful non-self for energy and nutrition thus prompted the philosophical biologist Hans Jonas to propose that 'world' is there from 'the earliest beginning',[28] thereby including passively drifting micro-organisms or sedentary plants within the realm of sentience. There is a sense indeed in which all living selves – and even merely 'self-like' phenomena such as self-organizing dissipative structures – must necessarily be open or responsive to the changing environmental non-self around them in order to perpetuate themselves. The self-concern or care that is essential to selfhood is wed to the presence of a 'world' upon which the self depends for energy and sustenance but that constantly threatens, one way or another, to put an end to its striving to maintain itself.

This striving may manifest itself as various forms of self-adaptation, ranging from homeostatic self-regulation in the face of environmental fluctuation to the phenotypic plasticity shown by organisms able to modify their internal physiology or morphology so as to cope with variations in external conditions. The form of self-adaptation that is relevant to consciousness, however, is self-movement or behaviour, i.e. the locomotion that permits a self to get from 'here' to 'there', where 'there' can be taken as synonymous with 'good for self' or 'better for self'. The distinction in question is not between internal, chemical self-regulation and movement *in itself*. Organisms are constantly engaging in rhythmical, cyclical movements such as breathing, pumping blood and moving food along the digestive tract. Locomotion itself tends to be a rhythmic behaviour, as exemplified by the cadences of walking or running, swimming or flying.[29] At issue is the modulation of such rhythmic motions into self-movement towards a target.[30] Consciousness is conceived, in its origins, as serving an essential role within the functional armoury of the sort of self-concerned, self-adapting self that is also capable of directional self-movement. The function of basalmost consciousness is to ensure, as far as possible, that this self-movement successfully complies with the interests of the self in question, i.e. that 'there' does indeed coincide with 'good/better for self' and not with 'bad/worse for self'.

The present account is functionalist, therefore, in the sense of assuming that the origin of consciousness can be explained in terms of its function. The idea is that consciousness is a Darwinian adaptation and that as such it confers an advantage upon those organisms that happen to be endowed with it: in concrete terms, the advantage of being able to propel oneself in a direction that is aligned with one's interests rather than just remaining motionless or moving at random. This ability to align self-caused self-movement with self-interest is what consciousness, in this primitive sense, *is*. Of course, functions may morph over time, just as the feathers that originally played a role in thermoregulation subsequently gave rise to the possibility of flight. In this way, what initially enabled a motile organism to move itself in the direction of some nutritious feature of its environment has now transformed itself (in humans) into an ability not only to procure and ingest a meal but to remember, plan, share and generally reflect upon the process.[31]

With various caveats that we shall encounter below, this primal function of consciousness thus consists in enabling the self to go in the right direction, which – at a most elementary level – means moving towards wherever there is food or water, or perhaps mates for reproduction, and moving away from predators and potentially damaging or noxious conditions. In these terms, consciousness is grounded in the need to satisfy appetites (for sustenance) or drives (to reproduce) and to avoid what is harmful in a context where there is no guarantee that one's interests are best served by simply sitting still and waiting. An implication is that consciousness did not suddenly and inexplicably bootstrap itself into existence in enlightened mammals or primates – an evolutionary afterthought or belated gift bestowed upon one or a few privileged species while all the 'lower' creatures continued to flounder and fumble about in literal and metaphorical obscurity – but has been present from simple beginnings, gradually evolving in tandem with self-moving selfhood. Let me reiterate: this should not be understood to imply that human consciousness is not unique. Human consciousness is characterized by a manifold of features that would be utterly pointless in a microbial context.

The present tract will begin by defending this view against traditional dismissals of microbial consciousness in the hope that the reader will at least start out agnostic in the matter. It will analyse various modes of adaptability and various forms of nutrient acquisition available to unicellular organisms, with the aim of distinguishing those likely to be associated with consciousness from those that are not. The proposed ascription of 'hunger' to certain single-celled eukaryotic predators such as amoebae or dinoflagellates forms the central pivot of the argument. This will in turn lead to an analysis of the possible association of certain other attributes such as 'pain', 'emotion' and 'wakefulness' with consciousness in its basalmost manifestations. The chapter 'Where Consciousness is Superfluous' will look more closely at examples of selfhood and movement where the ascription of elementary consciousness would arguably be misguided, this emphasis on possible mis-attributions serving to shed further light on the appropriate attribution of consciousness.

The focus will then shift to a number of more doubtful – though not absurd or empirically empty – claims about microbial consciousness, claims about whether and in what sense consciousness of this sort can meaningfully be said to embrace features such as choice, freedom, learning and an awareness of the future. This will also provide an opportunity to sketch a brief outline of the claims that I am emphatically *not* making about unicellular consciousness: these relate, in particular, to the unique properties of human consciousness. The differences between human consciousness (or even that of primates, cetaceans and birds) and consciousness in its most minimal manifestations help illustrate the way in which the former build upon and logically presuppose the latter. The final chapter will attempt to apply this minimal-self-based exploration of consciousness to some of the basalmost metazoans, animals such as sponges, placozoans, jellyfish, and planarian and nematode worms. The conclusion will be that sometimes it makes sense to ascribe consciousness to these relatively simple animals and sometimes it does not.

*

The idea of microbial consciousness is probably aberrant to most people. Yet it is compatible with venerable traditions of philosophical thought that have associated mind or soul[32] with behaviour, movement or activity. The pre-Socratic and Platonic equation of soul with self-movement[33] made no explicit provision for disqualifying certain self-movers simply on the grounds that they were too small to see. For Aristotle too, soul inhered in an organism's ability to be active. The Aristotelian tradition saw all living things as 'ensouled', ranging from plants – endowed with a merely nutritive or vegetative soul – at the bottom of the *scala naturae* through to human beings possessed of an intellective or rational soul at the pinnacle.[34] Animals are positioned 'above' lowly plants precisely to the extent that they have not only a nutritive soul but also a sensitive soul capable of perception and a volitional soul capable of locomotion.

The tiny 'animalcules' whose existence was revealed with the invention of the microscope initially represented a taxonomic conundrum, generating protracted debate on whether they were to be assigned to the animal or plant kingdom or whether a new kingdom was required. Eighteenth-century thought on the matter was dominated by the prolific Berlin-based naturalist and microscopist Christian Gottfried Ehrenberg, renowned among other things for coining the term 'bacteria'. Ehrenberg insisted that, like 'higher' organisms, protozoa had complete systems of organs and comprised a multiplicity of cells.[35] It was not until the third quarter of the 19th century that the 'unicellular' nature of many of these animalcules was definitively established and single-celled organisms acquired a kingdom of their own.

In the following years, eminent zoologists and physiologists such as Ernst Haeckel, Max Verworn and Alfred Binet regarded it as a natural consequence of evolutionary theory that all organic matter – each and every cell – was 'ensouled' *(beseelt)*. By this they meant that it was endowed with a psyche or *Zellseele* that displayed the basic properties of psychological life, though not necessarily consciousness.[36] The trailblazing protozoologist Herbert S. Jennings, who had studied under Verworn at Jena, argued that even though there was no way of providing an objective demonstration of the presence or absence of consciousness in either animals or protozoa, a helpful strategy was to ask whether their behaviour was as we might expect it to be if they *did* have limited forms of consciousness – a question to which he replied in the affirmative.[37] Yet despite the rigour of his scientific work and the tentative tone of his speculations, Jennings' views were subject to scathing criticism. Since the first decade of the 20th century only a few lone voices such as the maverick biologist Lynn Margulis[38] have ventured to speak of microbial consciousness.

Nonetheless, empirically oriented philosophies have insisted on the close association between mind and behaviour. The doctrine of logical behaviourism – a theory about the meanings of psychological concepts[39] – claims that any proposition about minds can be translated, without loss of meaning, into a proposition about publicly observable behaviour. On this view, to be in a such-and-such a state of mind is to be in a particular *behavioural* state, which means either to behave in such-and-such a way or to have a complex disposition to behave in this way. Such behaviour, or such a disposition, is what mind *is*. The doctrine of philosophical functionalism – which may overlap with but is not identical with the evolutionary functionalism sketched above[40] – likewise associates mind with behaviour, but this time the relationship is not one of logical identity but of causality. For functionalists, mind is defined not as behaviour but as the *cause* of behaviour; it is what brings behaviour about.[41] On this view, to be in a particular mental state is to be in a particular *functional* state, which means a state individuated by its causal relations, for example its relations with the sensory input that gives rise to it and the behavioural output to which it leads.[42] Functionalism is notably indifferent to the details of the physical structures that realize mental processes, for – as philosopher Daniel Dennett puts it – what makes something a mind 'is not what it is made of, but what it *can do*'.[43] Providing that these structures are physically capable of fulfilling the functions that define a mental state (i.e. generating behaviour), it does not matter whether they are realized in the neural circuits of a brain, the electronic circuits of a computer or (one might add) the phosphoprotein circuits of a unicellular organism.

Both logical behaviourism and functionalism define 'mind' in terms of behaviour, the relationship being either of identity or causality. In this respect, they are attempts to delimit mind to what can be observed in public, dispensing with the troublesome first-person perspective of subjectivity and with the introspective 'privacy' that is by definition out of bounds to science. In the present unicellular context, behaviour is certainly all there is to go on. Moreover, with behaviour arguably reduced to minimal variability and complexity (pursuit and ingestion of prey; escape from harm), there is a sense in which this presents us with mind not only in its most ancestral or 'primitive' but also in its most fundamental guise.

The first counterclaim, of course, is that what single-celled organisms do cannot genuinely be classified as 'behaviour', or at least not as behaviour in the proper sense. This has probably been the consensus – when the matter has been given any attention at all. Yet the assertion that protozoan self-movement is not behaviour seems dogmatic, to say the least. So far as it is visible to us, it certainly *resembles* behaviour. Take the following short description of the day-to-day doings of the unicellular ciliate *Paramecium* by neurobiologist Ralph Greenspan: '*Paramecia* live in ponds, streams, and stagnant pools where they swim, consume bacteria, avoid predators, and occasionally mate. This short list of activities encompasses the vast majority of animal behavior and therefore most of what nervous systems have evolved to perform'.[44] If all such behaviour-like activity is indeed to be excluded from the realm of 'genuine' behaviour, the onus is on the counterclaimant to find a very good reason for this exclusion.

One of the best-known attempts to provide such a reason is owed to the philosopher Jerry Fodor, who starts by severing the association between apparent 'behaviour' and the possession of mental states. 'Whereas behaving – at least in the sense of producing adaptive movements – is a pervasive achievement at all levels of the phylogenetic continuum', he notes, 'possessing mental states is presumably not. ... It would, for example, be preposterous to attribute mental representations to paramecia; where would they keep them?'[45] The implication that mental representations require 'storage' in a spatially determinate entity is perhaps only half-serious, but it is typical of the sort of logical muddle riddling discourse about 'mind' and 'mental' entities such as states and representations. Ruling out the possession by paramecia of mental states or representations on the grounds of their diminutive stature, Fodor follows this up by reducing all their putative behaviour to what he calls 'tropism' (a form of movement now technically known as taxis),[46] as exemplified by their phototactic activity. His argument is that the movement of a paramecium towards the light can be explained without remainder as a merely lawful or 'nomic' relationship between a stimulus (the light) and a response (the movement).[47] The difference between paramecia and organisms endowed with somewhere to keep their mental states and representations is that, unlike the former, the latter are able to respond 'selectively' to 'non-nomic' stimulus properties. According to Fodor, this capacity to produce a behavioural response unlinked by a 'lawful relation' to a stimulus property is what characterizes a system as 'intentional'.[48]

It is true that there tends to be an element of invariability – the 'lawful co-variation of a property of the stimulus with a property of the response'[49] – about locomotion based on taxis or tropism. Even so, there is no guarantee that one form of taxis, say phototaxis, may not conflict with other forms of taxis such as chemotaxis (caused by a chemical stimulus) or thigmotaxis (caused by physical contact). In such cases, the relative strengths of the opposed taxes will have to be weighed against one another, introducing a degree of variability into the response to any particular stimulus. In itself, this does not alter the logic of Fodor's argument, for the invariance can now be understood to exist between the *conjunction of stimuli* and the response. More importantly, however, Fodor's argument relies on a wholesale reduction of *all* paramecium behaviour to such invariance. As it happens, certain eukaryotic organisms are capable of reacting to a particular property in a stimulus, or set of stimuli, in one way on one occasion and in another way on another occasion. In what follows, I shall argue that although a great deal of unicellular activity may indeed be interpreted as a mere response to a stimulus or set of stimuli (i.e. as wholly determined by environmental input), there are other sorts of activity that really are *behaviour* – where 'behaviour' implies that the self-movement of the organism in question is not determined solely by forces external to itself but also by its own inner state, by forces endogenous to it, in other words by its *self*. In this respect, behaviour is activity that is at least partly *self*-caused.[50] One might refer to behaviour in this sense as 'action', where taking an action contrasts with merely responding invariably to a stimulus or conjunction of stimuli.

A second strategy for countering the disconcerting extension of consciousness to unicellular organisms is to follow Fodor in denying that the association between behaviour and consciousness (or mind) really holds. Descartes was the most radical advocate of this view, explicitly rejecting the Aristotelian notion of distinct categories of soul (vegetative, sensitive and rational) on the grounds that the powers of growth and movement were faculties that man shared with the 'brutes' and were '*toto genere* different from mind'.[51] The specifically human faculty of reason was what distinguished man from the rest of the animal kingdom, whose movements – whether microscopic or macroscopic – were performed mechanically and without the aid of a 'mind'.

More recently, philosopher John Searle has espoused what he calls 'the principle of the independence of consciousness and behavior', according to which there is no 'conceptual or logical connection between conscious mental phenomena and external behavior'.[52] This principle is grounded in the perfectly licit realization that certain sorts of behaviour, such as pain behaviour, can be feigned, whereas conversely certain sorts of mental states, such as genuine pain, can be concealed. Yet both simulation and dissimulation are themselves categories of behaviour. The fact that behavioural strategies may be highly complex (especially once they incorporate the dimension of intersubjectivity, i.e. the capacity of one self to view itself from the perspective of another self, with the concomitant opportunities for deceiving that other self)[53] does not invalidate the close logical connection between mental phenomena and the behaviour through which they come to expression. It simply means that the correlation between them may not always be straightforward, and considerable interpretative expertise may be required to decipher the mental phenomenon underlying any particular behaviour. By the same token, *pathologies* such as locked-in syndrome (where there is consciousness more or less completely without movement) in no way disprove that consciousness is conceptually or causally bound up with its behavioural manifestations. The fact is simply that behaviour can break down.[54] It will be argued in the following pages that appropriately directed, self-caused self-movement (i.e. behaviour in the sense of 'action') and the consciousness it both presupposes and expresses exist in such a tight logical embrace that neither can be conceived without the possibility of the other.

A Scale of Consciousness

Yet there are other arguments that can be drawn upon to deny consciousness to unicellular organisms. Perhaps the most extreme such argument is that consciousness does not exist anyway. This was a claim made by the psychological behaviourist John Watson,[55] who held the behaviour of all living things to be a product merely of conditioning. Maintaining that we do not consciously act but merely *react* to stimuli, Watson extended to the whole of the human and non-human animal kingdom the sort of argument normally reserved for micro-organisms or 'lower' animals. Indeed, his declaration that the behaviourist recognized 'no dividing line between man and brute'[56] could have been rephrased to proclaim the continuity between 'man and amoeba'. Watson's asseveration that consciousness was a metaphysical fiction might have been felt by some to be liberatingly egalitarian in divesting the 'high' and the 'low' alike of any pretensions to mindedness. Yet it is of course a metaphysical claim in itself[57] and a supremely counterintuitive one at that.

A more common approach to denying the possibility of single-celled consciousness has been to regard the phylogenetic 'scale'[58] as in some sense coincident with a 'scale' of consciousness. As we descend towards the 'lowlier' forms of life, there comes a point in the hierarchy where the 'light' of consciousness flutters and is eventually extinguished. Philosopher of mind Michael Tye thus opens his paper 'The Problem of Simple Minds' with a sequence of questions: 'Are frogs conscious? Or fish? What about honey bees? Do paramecia have experiences? Somewhere down the phylogenetic scale consciousness ceases. But where?'[59] Not surprisingly, Tye's answer is that consciousness has already 'ceased' long before we reach the depths represented by paramecia, which are considered bereft of all flexibility in their behaviour. 'Tropistic' organisms, which here seem to include the ranks of plants, protozoa and rigidly phototactic animals such as caterpillars, 'feel and experience nothing'; they are 'full-fledged unconscious automata or zombies'.[60] Yet Tye's argument, like Fodor's, relies on the assumption that *all* the behaviour of *all* such 'lower' organisms can be interpreted as a mere reflex, a tropistic or tactic response to a stimulus. It can accordingly be refuted by showing that the behavioural repertoire of certain organisms includes just *one* mode of activity that *cannot* be reduced to reflex or taxis. This is what the present argument will attempt.

However, the notion of a 'scale' – perhaps of body size, brain size or complexity – remains appealing to common sense. The idea that paramecia or dinoflagellates are philosophical 'zombies'[61] is certainly less disconcerting to the modern-day sensibility than the idea that one's lover, child or dog is a zombie. Cetaceans and great apes also seem privileged with subjectivity, whereas amphibians and fish – expressionless as they are – appear to reside somewhere in between.[62] Most people, I suspect, would not hesitate long in flushing insects and arachnids down the plughole of zombiehood, whereas rotifers and nematode worms, if given a second thought, would surely be deemed too small to harbour a mind (after all, where would they keep it?). But what is so special about size? Certain large unicellular organisms are bigger than a whole range of small multicellular animals. Ciliates such as *Stentor* or *Neobursaridium* may attain sizes of around a millimetre, overlapping in range with metazoans such as rotifers, gastrotrichs, nematodes and tardigrades.[63] Amoebae may be similar in size, dwarfing the more Lilliputian of insects: not only the diminutive parasitic wasps known as fairyflies, which are blind and wingless and are scarcely likely to require much in the way of consciousness anyway, but even the 170 μm-long hymenopterans of the genus *Megaphragma*, which exhibit behaviours such as flight, feeding and the ability to search for hosts for oviposition.[64] H. S. Jennings drew attention to the size chauvinism implicit in our customary dismissals of amoeban consciousness, noting that if an amoeba were the size of a whale we would not think twice about granting it states such as pleasure and pain, hunger and desire. We would be foolish to do otherwise in the presence of a whale-sized 'beast of prey'.[65]

Equally, what is so special about complexity? The philosophers M. R. Bennett and P. M. S. Hacker describe our tendency to be led astray by the picture or image of 'mental representations', which – as with Fodor – somehow require a specific degree of complexity in the brain or mind they have to 'fit' into:

> *Of course, we shall want to say that consciousness, experience, emerges only when phenomena in the physical world have evolved a certain degree of complexity. For we do not ascribe consciousness to plants, or experience to amoebas. ... [But how] can something so unlike mere matter and its properties emerge from what is just a more complex arrangement of material particles? How could 'subjectivity' spring into existence through nothing more than an increase in the complexity of the nervous system? How could the 'realm of consciousness' be created? But this is the wrong way to think about the matter. We need to jettison the picture.*[66]

In fact, they contend, consciousness is ascribed to a creature 'on the grounds of its behaviour in the circumstances of its life', not in virtue of it possessing some sort of mental picture of its environment. Consciousness does not 'emerge' miraculously at a particular point in the evolutionary scale once brains are complex enough to 'house' mental representations, but is generally ascribable to living animals capable of movement and behaviour. There is 'no sharp divide in nature between creatures to which it makes sense and creatures to which it makes no sense to ascribe consciousness or experience in one or other of their many forms'.[67]

Even when life is regarded as more or less coterminous with mind or consciousness, however, one tends to find a persistent terminological squeamishness where unicellulars are concerned. Talk of 'consciousness' is scrupulously avoided. Hans Jonas thus speculates that as we 'ascend' the 'scale' of morphological, experiential and behavioural sophistication, the 'mirroring' of the world 'becomes ever more distinct and self-rewarding, beginning with the most obscure sensation somewhere on the lowest rungs of animality, even with the most elementary stimulation of organic irritability as such'.[68] Rather than being endowed with true consciousness or even proto-consciousness, micro-organisms and simple metazoans are thus reduced to mere *irritability*, a notion that misleadingly evokes behaviour that is little more than the scratching of an itch or an automatic response to a mechanical or chemical insult. In fact, 'irritability' is a concept with rich connotations and a notable history stretching back to the 17th-century anatomist and physiologist Francis Glisson.[69] It was subsequently taken up by the philosopher F. W. J. Schelling, who understood the twin features of 'sensibility' and 'irritability' as denoting the fundamental receptivity of organic beings to their environment and the resulting drive to activity and movement.[70]

By the late 19th century, however, isolated voices were starting to take exception to the way the term had come to be used. Rather like tropism, it now suggested a merely passive reaction to exterior forces, failing to do justice to the complexity of cellular psychology. The movements of micro-organisms, wrote Alfred Binet, 'are not in most instances simple reflex motions; they are movements adapted to an end'. Such movements, he insisted, 'are not explained by the simple phenomenon of cellular irritability'. Binet was not denying the existence of irritability, but disputing the view of contemporaries such as Charles Richet that 'cellular psychology is represented wholly and solely by the laws of irritability'.[71] In particular, Binet lamented the less than felicitous choice of the term, which, though 'long in use', remained highly ambiguous and lacked an 'exact signification'.[72] Despite his admonitions, the concept continues to be employed to denote the limited class of reflex movements of which unicellulars are thought to be capable, conjuring up something rather *less* than behaviour in the sense of an *action*.[73]

At the same time, the defective quasi-consciousness of micro-organisms tends to be depicted in terms of 'dimness' or 'dullness', by contrast presumably with the implacable lucidity of human consciousness. Yet perhaps it might be amoeban consciousness which, though simple, shows the limpidity that comes with being uncluttered by 'concepts'? A recurrent literary and philosophical leitmotif – the coherence of which need not concern us here – is how words and ideas distort and misrepresent 'bare' experience and how the baggage of human intellectuality precludes any genuine perception of things as they really are. Admittedly, protozoa are not normally portrayed as the model from which warped human consciousness has deviated. But then again, this may in part be because they are not normally considered to be conscious anyway.

Musing on whether an amoeba might possess, 'in an extremely reduced and primitive form, some of the mechanisms that mediate the sense of environment and self in humans', cell biologist Dennis Bray thus asks: 'Is it completely dark in there, a black space full of blind molecular machinations? Or might that watery slurry contain an ember of emotion, a prototype of sentience?'[74] The emphasis on metaphors from the visual sphere is understandable, especially given the privileged role of human vision in perception *at a distance*. Yet it should be borne in mind that dogs too live in a world that is visually 'dull' and 'dim', but that is a vibrant cornucopia of olfactory diversity and nuance. The unicellular world too, if it exists, is likely to be primarily an olfactory and a gustatory space. The absence of vision,[75] moreover, should not be understood as implying obscurity, deprivation or disruption – just as blind people cannot be taken to experience their sightlessness as akin to darkness. In this sense, the non-visual eukaryotic world is neither light *nor* dark. However, it may be very smelly and very tasty.

Ultimately, the point is that there is very little – but not nothing, I believe – that can be predicated of amoeban consciousness, or what it is like to be an amoeba. Nonetheless, the tiny creature can be assumed to be exquisitely attuned to its medium. Insofar as it does perceive the world, it perceives just as much and as little as it needs to in order to seek the opportunities and avoid the perils of its life and thus pass on its genes to the next generation.

Consciousness, Meta-Mental States and Tacit Selfhood

Even though thinkers such as Jonas may have entertained a notion of consciousness (in however dim or irritable a guise) as coterminous with life, the prevalent view remains that there are specific cut-off points in the ascending evolutionary scale above which consciousness can be ascribed to living creatures and below which it cannot. Two cut-off points have been particularly influential in thinking about how far 'down' consciousness goes.

The more drastic cut-off – Cartesian in orientation – comes directly below humans. This is generally justified by making consciousness dependent upon language or a linguistically structured system of internal representations.[76] On this view, consciousness involves not just a perception or feeling (relating to world or self), but requires that this first-order perception or feeling[77] should become the object of a *higher-order* linguistically or symbolically structured thought, i.e. a belief *about* the first-order perception or feeling. At one fell swoop this view denies consciousness to neonates and young children prior to the acquisition of a certain level of language skill, as well as to the rest of the animal kingdom, not to mention lowly micro-organisms. The answer to the question of what it is like to be a bat or a baby (or an amoeba) is 'nothing at all', for perceptions and feelings only enter consciousness if one can think about them in higher-order linguistic thought.

Of course, the possession of language is crucial to the emergence of characteristically *human* consciousness. Few would deny this. However, this does not entail it being a precondition for consciousness as such. Such flagrant anthropocentrism, aptly described as 'species solipsism',[78] is at least partly a result of certain philosophers being misled by the fact that whenever they *reflect on* their consciousness, their consciousness necessarily assumes the form of a *reflective* consciousness, couched in the form of an internalized dialogue.[79] In reflecting on this reflective process, such philosophers have thus shown a recurrent tendency to forget that consciousness is not primarily an attribute of reflective philosophers. By contrast with such higher-order theories, a first-order theory of the sort I am advocating holds that mental states or processes can be described as 'conscious' not on account of the subject's higher-order awareness of them, but because the states or processes in themselves make the subject aware of – and able to behave in – the external environment.[80]

In fact, not all 'higher-order' theories of consciousness require linguistic thought. A divisive issue among the proponents of such models has been whether the higher-order, meta-mental states that transform an unconscious first-order mental state into a conscious one should be considered thought-like or perception-like.[81] On the latter view, perceptions and feelings become conscious if they are the object not of a higher-order linguistic thought, but of some form of higher-order *inner* sense or perception. Although this view is not necessarily so radical in its exclusivity (in that it does not presuppose linguistic ability), in both cases consciousness is understood as arising when the mind directs its attention upon its own states and processes. Both cases, however, overlook the logical problem raised by a scenario in which one mental state takes another, different mental state as its object, where this implies the occurrence of two mental states that are necessarily distinct from one another – and yet the one has to 'recognize' the other as pertaining to the same 'self'.[82] The unanswered question is how to account for the self-recognition that such models require for a mind to be able to focus on its own mental states *as its own*.

Meta-mental theories fail to get to the bottom of consciousness because any such recognition of self by self logically *presupposes* and is thus *derivative* upon the intrinsic reflexivity of a self that is in some sense already familiar with itself, the tacit selfhood or pre-reflective self-awareness broached above. In the course of the present treatise, we shall look more closely at some of the diverse forms of this non-representational, non-reflective self-awareness that provides the logical underpinning for consciousness. We shall examine below how it expresses itself, for example, in the appetites, emotions, pains and immediate self-familiarity of the body that one *is*. Appetite in particular will be seen to reside at the very heart of elementary consciousness.

In the present rather more general context, however, one especially relevant manifestation of tacit selfhood is a phenomenon termed 'corollary discharge'. This refers to our normally unquestioned and unnoticed ability to distinguish whether changes in our sensory input result from occurrences in the environment or from our own movements: for example, whether a change in the signal from my retina is caused by my own eye movements or by an event within my field of vision.[83] To produce a coherent picture of what is around me and of my position within it, it is essential that I should be able to distinguish the sensory effects of movements of my own perceptual apparatus from those of movements that may occur in the external world. As a modality of self/non-self discrimination, this facility of implicit differentiation between self-caused sensory input ('reafference') and non-self-caused sensory input ('exafference') is perhaps best considered an aspect of self-containment, albeit one that only pertains to selves capable of moving themselves, or moving a part of themselves.

In a recent account of consciousness, neuroscientist Björn Merker[84] clearly has corollary discharge in mind when he describes consciousness as the synthesis of a coherent and stable 'world-space' or 'reality space', a representation of the environment from which the 'contamination' of self-caused sensory information has to be 'subtracted'. A precondition for successful decision-making, he suggests, is access to such information in a form 'stripped of the confounding effects of self-produced motion'.[85] Whether or not representation is indeed viewed as a defining feature of consciousness, Merker has certainly expressed a deep point about the nature of representational consciousness. A tacit distinction between self and non-self is logically *presupposed by* the ability of a self-moving self to represent the world around it, and to this extent the pre-reflective self-familiarity of corollary discharge is a fundamental component of consciousness understood in terms of 'representation'. Indeed, it is (more or less)[86] impossible to conceive of coherent representational consciousness *without* such a distinction. This of course throws up the question of how such a pre-representational distinction between self and non-self is possible in the first place. One answer might be to invoke some sort of Kantian transcendental argument, affirming as an *a priori* truth that a precondition for representational consciousness (as we know it) is an ability to draw this distinction between sensory input that is caused by self and sensory input that is caused by non-self. But this is really just repeating the same thing in grander terms.

An alternative answer is to focus upon the nature of corollary discharge as a modality of self/non-self discrimination, in other words self-containment. As with the capacity of the immune system to distinguish self from non-self, it is at bottom a question of *what works*, or what fosters the successful self-perpetuation of an intrinsically reflexive self. Ultimately, self-moving selves that fail to make this distinction will be just as unlikely to flourish as organisms whose immune system fails to detect a pathogen or a parasite; they will be compromised in their capacity for self-containment.

A relatively straightforward illustration of the principle involved is provided by sea-slugs, whose ability to feed depends upon their capacity to distinguish self-caused from non-self-caused sensory input. This is because these slow-moving marine gastropods generally retreat whenever contact is made with the highly sensitive tactile mechanoreceptors of their 'oral veil' or mouth. During feeding, a signal must thus be channelled via 'corollary discharge interneurons' to inhibit the withdrawal response.[87] If the sea-slugs failed to suppress this reflex, the predisposition to draw back from the food that touches their oral veil would prevent them from nourishing themselves and they would rapidly come to a hungry end. So by implicitly signalling 'I'm feeding' (effectively: 'I'm the one causing the stimulation to my mouth; no need to be jumpy'), corollary discharge provides a simple mechanism that enables an organism to fuel itself in a complex environment comprising both predators and food, thereby increasing its chances of perpetuating itself through the generations.

Tacit self-awareness grounds the possibility of representational or reflective consciousness of oneself as oneself, and lays the foundations for consciousness of non-self in ways that go beyond corollary discharge (as will emerge below). In itself, however, it is not representational, reflective, introspective, linguistic or higher-order. Rather, it is a manifestation of the intrinsically reflexive relationship of a self to itself. By contrast with such tacit selfhood, self-representation – whether by language or any other sort of mental reflection or neural isomorphism – is precisely *not* a form of intrinsic reflexivity, for the relationship between the representation and the self that is represented is by definition *extrinsic* or contingent: generally speaking, the whole point of a representation is that it is not actually the same as what it represents. This is exemplified by the fact that the constituent propositions of my autobiographical or narrative self – a derived function available to certain sorts of linguistic consciousness – can be either true or false, accurate or inaccurate (possibly without me even knowing, as when my memory lets me down). By contrast, intrinsic reflexivity, in the form of my tacit awareness of hunger or toothache, is not a relationship that can be specified in terms of truth conditions or accuracy.

Even so, the idea that the difference between conscious and non-conscious mental states can be pinpointed in terms of whether or not they are the object of a meta-mental perception or thought continues to be beguiling. In his fine exposition and development of autopoietic theory, philosopher Evan Thompson thus argues against unicellular consciousness on the grounds of there being 'no good reason ... for thinking that autopoietic selfhood of the minimal cellular sort involves any kind of intentional access on the part of the organism to its sense-making'.[88] In other words, single cells lack an *awareness* of their own valenced awareness of the world as better or worse; they are without meta-mental access to their first-order awareness. Thompson also believes that such minimal selves lack the 'prereflective self-awareness constitutive of a phenomenal first-person perspective'. The explanation he gives for this is telling: 'this sort of awareness', he suggests, 'would seem to require (in ways we do not yet fully understand) the reflexive elaboration and interpretation of life processes provided by the nervous system'.[89]

Consciousness and Brains

Thompson's point is itself indicative of the other major cut-off in the 'ascent' that leads to human consciousness as its most glorious expression. This is the distinction between multicellular animals – endowed with a brain – and 'brainless' single-celled organisms. Of course, the cut-off is not a clean one. Not all animals have brains. Ancestral metazoans such as sponges and jellyfish either do without neurons altogether or have diffuse neural nets rather than brains, whereas other metazoans seem to have evolved and then 'lost' their brain in the process of natural selection.[90]

Again, however, our tendency to privilege the brain makes intuitive good sense, given the close relationship between consciousness and the brain in humans (evidenced by the effects of brain damage and the workings of drugs) and the remarkable structural and biochemical similarities between how human and non-human brains respond to environmental contingencies. Such similarities are lacking in our relationship with single-celled organisms, which are decidedly more *alien* to us. In his account of the evolution of mind, neurophysiologist Rodolfo Llinás thus writes that 'neurons arose within the space between sensing and moving: this space mushroomed to become the brain',[91] endowing us with flexibility and adaptability rather than restricting us to an invariant spatial relay of information between stimulus and response. Yet unicellular prokaryotes and eukaryotes are likewise equipped with a logical space between sensing and self-movement: in this case it is the reversible phosphorylation of proteins that allows these proteins to act as molecular 'switches', guiding cellular processes in one direction or another according to whether they are phosphorylated or not.[92] Such phosphoprotein networks can be considered functionally analogous to the neural networks of the brain.

In spite of what is now known about the biocomputational workings of single cells, a residual cerebrocentrism tempts us to assume an intrinsic relationship between the brain and consciousness, indeed even to ascribe consciousness to the brain itself. As Ludwig Wittgenstein notes in the *Philosophical Investigations*, however, this constitutes a profound logical error: 'only of a human being and what resembles (behaves like) a living human being can one say: it has sensations; it sees, is blind; hears, is deaf; is conscious or unconscious'.[93] A brain cannot be conscious, in other words, but only the self-moving self whose brain it is. Wittgenstein's remark is aimed at a conceptual confusion, yet there is also an empirical dimension. The human brain *cannot* behave, for it is tucked away in its cranial exoskeleton; it *cannot* feel pain, not only because it cannot exhibit pain behaviour, but also because – unlike other organs – it has no pain receptors. Yet selves do not have to be designed in the way that ours happens to be, with this strange 'blind spot' in the logical space between sense and self-movement. The contrast with an amoeba is illuminating, for an amoeba *is* its brain; the organism as a whole constitutes a biocomputational unity incorporating not only its sensors but the pseudopods by virtue of which it moves. Indeed, an amoeba is a brain that *behaves*, a motile or self-moving brain that shows appetites, aversions and motivations. In this respect, it bears a much more marked resemblance than a human brain to Wittgenstein's 'living human being'.[94]

Recent neuroscience has attempted to 'localize' consciousness by focusing on its 'neural correlates', i.e. patterns of firings in a specific set of neurons or a specific part of the brain that are taken to be the 'physical' counterpart to the 'mental' phenomenon of consciousness. What has struck researchers as remarkable is that despite the range of candidates for such neural correlates – despite the multitude of distinct neuronal populations that seem to be involved in generating our consciousness – our perception of the world is nonetheless characterized by its seamless unity and coherence. The question has thus become how the brain synthesizes these discrete modules of sensory processing to engender experiences that are unified. This has come to be known as the 'binding problem', where 'binding' refers to the process by which separately represented items of information about a particular perceived entity or situation are brought together, as when information about the colour, shape and smell of an object is integrated from different sensory pathways.

Various mechanisms of binding have been proposed, ranging from convergence (the transmission of information from various more primary processing areas to be integrated in another region of the brain) and gamma synchrony (the temporally coordinated oscillation of certain neuronal populations)[95] to quantum coherence (oscillatory cohesion produced by quantum-level effects).[96] A focus of particular attention has been the 40-Hertz oscillations characteristic of thalamocortical circuits as a possible mechanism of binding and thus as the neural correlate of consciousness. In a similar line is the theory put forward by Giulio Tononi, who envisions consciousness as 'corresponding to the capacity of a system to integrate information',[97] possibly a necessary by-product of this ability to process information in an integrated manner. The integration and processing of information has even been seen as the *function* of consciousness, which is understood as permitting coordinated interactions among otherwise independent response systems or modules within the brain. Neuroscientist Ezequiel Morsella thus speculates that, in evolutionary terms, 'conscious processes evolved to mediate large-scale skeletomotor conflicts caused by structures in the brain with different agendas, behavioral tendencies, and phylogenetic origins'.[98]

It is perfectly plausible that this capacity to integrate information rather than relying merely on its spatial transmission should be associated with consciousness. The question, however, is the nature of this relationship: whether consciousness really is *constituted by* the integration of information or whether it is merely causally *dependent on* such integration. The underlying puzzle remains *why* the integration of information – whether by gamma synchrony, quantum coherence or the integrative capacity of a particular brain region – should give rise to experience or consciousness.[99] Equally, one might wonder *why* phenomenal states should be necessary to mediate information from distinct response systems so as to produce adaptive action.[100] The link is far from obvious.

What is notably absent from attempts to explain consciousness in terms of the processing of information is any element of intrinsic reflexivity. For an approach based on minimal selfhood, by contrast, the integration of information is better conceived as a mechanism of self-containment, ensuring that a multiplicity of diverse response systems – a manifold of component parts – are successfully coordinated and unified within an integrated whole (i.e. that no rogue subsystem behaves as though it were a self in its own right, waywardly pursuing its own interests). As an aspect of the functional unity of self-containment and thus of unitary selfhood, the integration of information furnishes a foundation for consciousness, but cannot simply be equated with it. For consciousness to arise, the integration of information by a system must be undertaken not only 'within' the system[101] but *for the sake of* the system in question, i.e. as a mechanism enabling it to pursue its own interests as the self-maintaining self that it is.[102] There is no more reason to ascribe consciousness to an 'integrative' region of the brain than to the sensory apparatus that provides the informational input in need of integration, however good this region or this apparatus may be at bringing together and combining information or at registering and representing changes in light or odour intensity. On the contrary, consciousness is meaningfully ascribed only to a self that is endowed with sensory and integrative faculties and that uses these faculties to guide its movement towards what is better for itself and away from what is worse for itself and so to perpetuate itself through time. Only in such a context does rudimentary consciousness make sense.

This is not to say that the binding problem does not exist as a computational issue. However, empirical solutions to it relate not to the unity of consciousness in the sense of a cohesive mental representation,[103] but to the question of how an organism is able to coordinate its behavioural responses to complex environmental inputs in such a way that they are coherent and, more basally, serve its own interests. The question of the unity of consciousness is at least partly 'resolved' by approaching it from the perspective of minimal selfhood, for a self – which we have already defined as a unit of self-interest – is in this sense definitionally unitary. To the extent that a failure to integrate information is bound to express itself in movements that are contradictory or mutually conflicting or that do not comply with the creature's self-interest, it makes no more sense than a cellular organism simultaneously activating two mutually interfering metabolic pathways. Predatory animals that fail to align their visual and auditory maps of the environment, for example,[104] will be less likely to find their prey and less likely to be successful in their striving to survive and reproduce.

Of course, neural pathways can malfunction; organisms and biological individuals may be multiple or fractured in their selfhood. Particularly striking is the alien hand syndrome, or 'Dr Strangelove syndrome', suffered by a number of epilepsy patients who have had the corpus callosum linking the two hemispheres of their brain surgically severed.[105] One might also cite the 'perspectival drift' and 'attentional disturbance' characteristic of schizophrenia, a 'failure to stay anchored within a single frame of reference, perspective, or orientation'.[106] Like auditory hallucinations and passivity experiences, such episodes are believed to have their origin in disorders of tacit selfhood affecting mechanisms of corollary discharge or proprioception that are normally taken for granted.[107] It is above all in such contexts that fragmented forms of consciousness are conceivable, i.e. as a consequence of fragmented forms of selfhood.

The question of cognitive binding is one of seven 'easy' problems famously identified by David Chalmers in an influential essay on consciousness. In designating these problems 'easy', Chalmers means that they are 'directly susceptible to the standard methods of cognitive science, whereby a phenomenon is explained in terms of computational or neural mechanisms'.[108] As well as the integration of information by a cognitive system, these 'easy' problems include the ability to discriminate, categorize, and react to environmental stimuli; the reportability of mental states; the ability of a system to access its own internal states; the focus of attention; the deliberate control of behaviour; and the difference between wakefulness and sleep. It is noteworthy that while one of these problems (the reportability of mental states) relies upon the possession of language, and another (internal access) falls back on a 'meta-mental' model of consciousness, the five other easy problems are all – as I hope will become clearer below – in some degree pertinent to single-celled organisms.

Chalmers contrasts the 'easy' problems of consciousness with what he calls the 'hard' problem, which he associates with the subjective or experiential nature of consciousness, the notion of it *being like something* to be a conscious organism. This hard problem is considered so intractable that it has led some thinkers to conclude that a theory of consciousness will be forever beyond our grasp. Chalmers' own response is to suggest that consciousness can only be understood in non-reductive terms as something fundamental, in other words as something that – like mass or space-time – cannot be explained in terms of anything simpler. It is the notion of 'information' that provides this explanatory bedrock. Chalmers' self-confessedly speculative proposal is what he calls the 'double-aspect' theory of information, which is based on the observation that information has both a physical and a phenomenal aspect.[109] Among a raft of other questions,[110] however, one is again left wondering who or what the information is *for*? Surely information only has a phenomenal aspect when it is being used *by* a self *for* that self in the pursuit of interests that matter *to* that self.

In fact, questions such as Nagel's[111] about what it is like to be a bat are not necessarily so intractable. For a start, they generally only make sense if a context is specified. The question thus needs rephrasing as: what is it like to be such-and-such an organism in such-and-such a context or performing such-and-such an activity? In more concrete terms, one might rephrase it as: what is it like to be such-and-such an organism in such-and-such a context having just eaten copiously, as opposed to undergoing a longer-than-usual period of food deprivation? The difference between the two scenarios can be empirically observed in the conduct (no words are needed) of a hungry as opposed to a satiated human, but also in the behaviour of other, non-human and arguably even microscopic predators. The ascription of hunger in one scenario (food deprivation) and not in the other (satiety) implies an empathetic bridge that may span the width separating us from the most phylogenetically remote of organisms. Question: what is it like to be a food-deprived bat or amoeba in the presence of, or within perceptual range of, a potential prey? Answer: it is like being hungry.[112] So how far are we prepared to go in attributing appetites and aversions to non-human organisms?

I shall argue below that a capacity to experience various degrees of appetite, aversion, motivation, pleasure and discomfort is not only something I have in common with other human beings and bats, but also perhaps the only thing – or one of only a very few things – that I have in common with amoebae, euglyphids and dinoflagellates. Concepts such as appetite, motivation and pleasure lay the groundwork for a potentially informative answer to the question of what it is like to be an organism other than a human.

III.

From Motionlessness to Directed Motility

Non-Movers and the Almost Immobile

Minimal selfhood is here grasped in terms of an intrinsically reflexive self-concern, a striving to perpetuate oneself through time that recalls the time-honoured notion of *conatus*. Given a ceaselessly fluctuating environment, moreover, the intrinsic reflexivity of self-maintenance or self-production in turn underpins and entails that of self-adaptation, insofar as a self-maintaining self must necessarily adapt itself to the ever-changing context in which it is embedded.[113] The argument of the present chapter is that consciousness is inextricably bound up with one particular strategy of self-adaptation, namely with directed self-movement.

The idea, therefore, is not that minimal selfhood is by its very nature endowed with consciousness, but that directional self-movement and the resulting possibility of consciousness constitute *just one strategy among many* available to minimal selves striving to perpetuate themselves through time. The present section will start by looking at various *other* strategies of self-adaptation that may make locomotion and consciousness unnecessary. It will then look at how far various selves – or self-like entities – may or may not exhibit a capacity for self-movement that makes them plausible candidates for the possession of consciousness. It should be stressed, once more, that the presence or absence of self-movement and consciousness cannot be equated with a higher or lower rank or rung on some sort of 'phylogenetic' scale or ladder. Endosymbionts such as *Buchnera aphidicola* – prokaryotic cells that have made a home for themselves ensconced *within* a certain set of greenfly cells – are almost entirely passive beings, yet they used to be free-living bacteria.[114] Collectively and as a lineage, they have made a lifestyle 'choice', finding a particularly stable niche that relieves them of the need to 'live freely' (i.e. move) or have much, if any, awareness of their surroundings. The various other strategies of unicellular or multicellular self-adaptation are neither more nor less 'sophisticated' than motility.

Such adaptability may take the form, for example, of what is known as phenotypic plasticity, which allows micro-organisms to grow and flourish in a wide variety of physiological conditions rather than necessarily having to go and find more favourable conditions if a key nutrient is missing. The most intensely studied example is the ability of *E. coli* to change to using lactose as a source of nutrition in the absence of the more habitual glucose. As soon as lactose is encountered in a glucose-free environment, a genetic switch is thrown and the appropriate lactose-digesting enzymes are produced, a process that occurs even if the bacteria have never previously come across lactose.[115] In such conditions, the genetically controlled fine-tuning of metabolism enables the bacteria to stay put and renders locomotion superfluous. Human beings benefit in particular from the phenotypic plasticity exhibited by symbiotic gut bacteria such as *Bacteroides thetaiotaomicron*, which are endowed with a remarkable capacity to vary the digestive enzymes they produce according to cues in the intestinal environment. This bacterial versatility redounds to *our* advantage in that it permits us to degrade otherwise indigestible plant polysaccharides and thus broaden the range of carbohydrates we can assimilate.[116]

Perhaps the most versatile of all micro-organisms is a rod-shaped bacterium called *Rhodopseudomonas palustris*, which belongs to the class of 'purple non-sulphur bacteria'.[117] The remarkable biochemical flexibility and nutritional adaptability of this single cell, endowed with a genome of just 5.5 Mb, enables it to swap between the four fundamental modes of metabolism,[118] getting by as required with or without oxygen, adopting an ancestral, anoxygenic form of photosynthesis or feeding on organic or inorganic compounds. By way of a rough comparison, it is as though we humans were able to switch, when necessary, from powering ourselves heterotrophically on organic compounds (as we do in our capacity as animals) to doing so autotrophically by means of photosynthesis (like plants), before in turn changing to inorganic energy sources such as hydrogen sulphide, elemental sulphur or molecular hydrogen, while still keeping another nutritional option ('photoheterotrophy') up our metabolic sleeves for the lean times to come. Biochemically and metabolically, *R. palustris* is the most complete jack of all trades, resisting the tendency to specialize to which other, possibly less ancient lineages have yielded. The *R. palustris* way is to leave its metabolic options completely open. Such biochemical versatility makes directional locomotion unnecessary insofar as the creature in question is likely to be able to extract energy from the environment *wherever* it happens to be. Exempt from the need to search for nutrition elsewhere (wherever 'elsewhere' may be), consciousness of any 'elsewhere' will thus be surplus to requirements. Yet in metabolic terms, writes microbiologist Harald Brüssow, 'we are dwarfs with respect to this bacterium'.[119]

Another form of self-adaptation available to bacteria occurs not at the level of the individual cell, but rather that of the collective or lineage. Specifically, the phenomenon of hypermutation or adaptive mutagenesis confers upon bacteria an increased chance of communally coming across a beneficial mutation that will help them to cope with variations in local environmental circumstances. Such bacterial group intelligence is augmented by the ability of bacteria to engage in the apparently purposive exchange of genetic information by means of non-genealogical horizontal gene transfer (HGT), possibly with phages (i.e. bacterial viruses) serving as a manner of 'genetic repository'[120] that can be used to optimize their efficiency in self-defence and self-maintenance.

Accomplishments of this sort have led bacterial geneticist James Shapiro to describe bacteria as 'sophisticated natural genetic engineers', concluding that 'even the smallest cells are sentient beings'.[121] Biological physicist Eshel Ben-Jacob referred to the bacterial genome as 'an adaptive cybernetic unit with self-awareness'.[122] Such claims raise not necessarily straightforward questions relating to whether self-adaptation that is essentially *communal* can be associated with any manner of 'agency' on the part either of the individual cells or the genome. Above all, a multicellular logic seems to be at work, and it perhaps makes more sense to interpret this genomic adaptability as the property of a collective self rather than of the individual bacteria. Nor does it seem necessary to propose the existence of consciousness in such a context. Although there is no doubt that the process of collective self-adaptation involves the cognitive processing of informational input, the scenario has more in common with the metabolic self-adaptation of a bacterium responding to a shortage of glucose. It does not entail directed self-movement so much as non-locomotive self-modification.

To reiterate: the basic idea underlying this approach to elementary consciousness is that a capacity for conscious experience of the world can be ascribed to an intrinsically reflexive being (a self) precisely to the extent that its motility or locomotion, where present, is considered to be caused by itself and implemented for the sake of itself (for its own sake). Such self-movement is purposive in that it consists in getting from here to there *in order to* achieve something, for example to reach or find what is good or better for self (say, the nutrients that it requires to fuel itself). It is directed towards[123] meaningful non-self, which is the 'object' of its consciousness,[124] and this consciousness of a valenced world is what makes appropriate, self-guided movement possible. Insofar as behaviour or action of this kind presupposes an investment of energy to produce the work required, it can be understood in terms of appetite or drive, for an appetite or drive is something an organism will perform work to satisfy. This is tantamount to saying that its successful consumption involves a reward.[125] This will become clearer below.

*

Like an intracellular symbiotic lifestyle, biochemical versatility may make directional locomotion and thus consciousness unnecessary from the outset. Yet there are other forms of selfhood, mobile or otherwise, that can also be presumed to get by perfectly well without consciousness. A brief review of such non-conscious forms will help pave the way for an analysis of the types of self-moving selfhood that may indeed entail consciousness.

Most obviously, perhaps, there is no need to posit the presence of consciousness in cases of 'latent life' or *cryptobiosis*, the state of ametabolism brought on by extreme desiccation or freezing.[126] With metabolic and locomotive activity reduced to barely discernible levels, such 'suspended' selfhood tends to go hand-in-hand with a state of sensory and motor closure. Often assuming the form of cysts or endospores, cryptobiotic micro-organisms are effectively 'dead' to the world – to a world too hostile or inimical to life for consciousness to be of much use anyway. Mind you, a certain residual sensory 'alertness' has to be maintained to allow for the possibility of resuscitation when conditions improve.[127]

Viruses and viroids can also be excluded from the realm of conscious beings, as can mobile DNA.[128] As sequences of DNA capable of 'jumping' to new locations on a genome, selfish retroelements such as LINE-1 may certainly *seem* to display a type of activity or animation, yet the self-movement in question not only throws up logical conundrums (in that the 'movement' is in fact the displacement of an identical replica) but fails to comply fully with the criterion of genuine self-causation. Although the retroelement encodes the enzymes needed for getting itself moved, it is crucially dependent on a highly specific cellular environment that provides the requisite chemistry and energy. In short, the 'jumping gene' does not *perform work* in hopping from A to B; its movement is made possible merely by its own largely invariant configurational features within the framework provided by the metabolic activity of a self-maintaining host cell. It can jump simply by virtue of remaining as it is rather than engaging in any form of activity.

Selfish though such genetic material may be, the lack of a self-maintaining metabolism of its own can be taken to debar mobile DNA from full minimal selfhood. The same applies to viruses. The reflexivity of a virus or phage is thus indirect rather than direct, manifesting itself as a capacity to *get itself* replicated, assembled, coated and above all *moved*. Although it is essential for a recently assembled virion to find, recognize and penetrate a new host in order to perpetuate the lineage, this movement is not a consequence of behaviour or action on the part of the virion in question, which relies instead on environmental contingency, with random encounters assisted by diffusion and convection currents, as well as possible additional help from self-encoded 'movement proteins'.[129] Most importantly, there is again no investment of energy or performance of work: no drive or reward. When the *E. coli* bacteriophage T4 is described as using its 'host cell recognition sensors' to 'recognize' a potential host and then attach to the cell surface,[130] this sensory activity – for all its complexity[131] – can be fully understood without any need to invoke consciousness: the phage 'recognizes' and 'senses' its host, but it is not conscious of it.[132] Here we may indeed speak of philosophical zombie-hood.

In some instances it is the viral factory – a protective structure inside the host cell within which viral replication and assembly take place – that is thought to provide a better expression of viral 'selfhood' than the infective virion.[133] On this view, the viral 'self' is confined to an intracellular existence, again ruling out genuine movement and dispensing with the possibility or need for consciousness. In this sense, such viral factories are reminiscent of bacterial endosymbionts such as *Buchnera aphidicola* and *'Candidatus* Tremblaya princeps*',[134] which enjoy a life of intracellular plenitude but forfeit (almost) all behavioural or locomotive versatility.[135] In the case of these cells-within-cells, moreover, it is not just that they do not have to *move* anywhere to find their nutrition; they do not even have to operate a *mouth*. Such cells acquire their nutrients by means of an ongoing process of predominantly passive exchange determined by chemical concentration gradients rather than any activity on their own part.

More generally, a distinction can thus be drawn between osmotrophy, which refers to the uptake and assimilation of dissolved organic compounds across the cell membrane by means of osmosis,[136] and phagotrophy, which involves the active engulfment of food in particulate form. Phagotrophy may take the form of phagocytosis by pseudopodia in the case of amoebae, in which case the amoeba as a whole *is* its mouth (and the amoeba is described as 'pantostomate'). Alternatively, ingestion may be restricted to a specific part of the cell, a mouth or groove known as a cytostome that is specialized to perform the task of engulfment, as in some ciliates. Further variants exist. Among dinoflagellates three categories of feeding mechanism are known, including not only direct engulfment of intact prey, but also the deployment of some form of tube (usually a cytoplasmic 'peduncle') to suck the contents out of prey, or a 'pallium' (a type of pseudopod formerly known as a 'feeding veil') to envelop the prey and digest it extracellularly.[137]

In all these cases, work is required, performed in the main by the cellular cytoskeleton, and there are clear parallels between the work involved in locomotion (a search or pursuit) and that required for the ingestion of prey (the self-contortions of engulfment). Nor is the extent of this work to be underestimated. Rapacious ciliates such as *Didinium* feast on prey (often *Paramecium*) that may be much bigger than the predator, requiring an expandable cytostome to engorge their quarry. Dinoflagellates too are renowned for devouring whole prey that may be up to five times their own size.[138] The operation of a mouth can thus be regarded as a significant form of self-movement. The work involved suggests appetite, motivation and the possibility of reward. To the extent that osmosis is purely passive, by contrast, effort is unnecessary and motivation is superfluous. No reward is needed.

The Sessility of Plants

Plants are generally viewed as archetypically immobile organisms. Defined by the sessility that keeps them rooted to the spot, they have traditionally been regarded as purely passive beings, bereft of sensory awareness. The contrast with animals corroborates this conception: whereas plants sustain themselves by converting a readily available supply of solar energy into food, animals convert solar energy into the neuronal signalling that makes vision possible, enabling them to identify, target and then eat these plants or pursue other animals that have already done so.[139] Unlike animals, it is argued, plants do not need to 'see' for they do not go anywhere. Their immobility also makes pain redundant. As moral philosopher Peter Singer puts it, 'it is difficult to imagine why species that are incapable of moving away from a source of pain or using the perception of pain to avoid death in any other way should have evolved the capacity to feel pain'.[140] A complementary argument is put forward by Leonardo da Vinci in his *Notebooks*, where he reasons that since plants are not motile they do not need pain to protect themselves from potentially damaging collisions[141] – motility here being seen as the possible *cause* of damage as opposed to the possible *escape route*. For Leonardo, movement brings the need for pain; for Singer, pain signals the need for movement. In both cases, the aim is to avoid harm or injury.

The idea that plants are passive and insentient has generally been traced back to Aristotle, who attributes to vegetation the nutritive but not the sensitive/locomotive or intellectual levels of soul and accordingly locates the plant kingdom at the bottom of his hierarchy of life.[142] Yet sessility is not to be associated with pure passivity. Aristotle in fact distinguishes four categories of movement – locomotion, alteration, decay and growth – all but the first of which are present in plants.[143] As living beings endowed with souls, moreover, plants are characterized by what Aristotle terms 'entelechy', an intrinsically reflexive term that implies the inherent possession of an 'end'. Plants are ends in themselves, in other words, existing for their own sake (i.e. as selves) rather than merely for the sake of humans.[144] Aristotle's pupil Theophrastus, widely known as the father of botany, goes further in his appreciation of plants as autonomous, intentional selves that actively strive to pursue their own interests.[145] This contrasts starkly with subsequent thinkers such as Hegel, who divests plants of selfhood and in the process justifies their instrumentalization for human purposes: by means of fruits, he writes, 'the silent essence of self-less (*selbstlos*) Nature ... offers itself to life that has a self-like (*selbstisch*) nature'.[146]

Yet plants *are* selves: they maintain themselves and reproduce themselves, and although the element of self-containment may be more indeterminate (resulting in uncertainty about the relevant unit of selfhood), it is not absent.[147] Moreover, plant growth may be considered a form of self-adaptation, i.e. a mechanism by which each organism modifies itself according to environmental circumstances in such a way as to maximize its wellbeing and fitness. Modern-day botanists refer to the 'phenotypic plasticity' of plants, meaning their capacity to exhibit flexibility not only in physiology – i.e. rates of photosynthesis and transpiration – but also in morphological development in a way that presupposes both an assessment of the external conditions and the selection of the best response. The question is whether such growth and plasticity imply the presence of plant *consciousness*.[148] The answer depends on whether self-adaptation of this sort can indeed be classified as a mode of self-movement. There are some good arguments to suggest that it can. As plant scientists Anthony Trewavas and František Baluška[149] and philosophical botanist Matthew Hall have argued, it is the roots that play a pivotal role in plant movement and cognition:

> *Rich soil patches are exploited by increased plastic root branching and root growth. In the presence of few nutrients, root growth has been found to accelerate in order to facilitate the detection of new, more nutritious patches of soil in other locations. There is clear and active perception of the resources available, which ... involves the construction of a 'three dimensional perspective' of the local space. Here plants display their behavioural intelligence with an ongoing assessment of the costs and benefits involved in exploiting the resources that exist in the soil. ... Root plasticity allows plants to make choices about the*

soil patches they feed in – to the extent that plants have been referred to in ecological studies as 'foragers'.[150]

If the notions of plant intelligence and even consciousness[151] tend nonetheless to be given short shrift, this is possibly because of the 'timescale chauvinism' described by Dennett, which leads us to assume that all minds must operate at the same velocity as ours.[152] It is perhaps also because so much plant behaviour goes on out of sight underground. While plant movement is liable to be dismissed as *mere* tropism (such as the negative phototropism and thigmotropism displayed by roots), moreover, this overlooks the extent to which one tropism may override another, thus requiring the integration of a considerable number of potentially conflicting signals.[153]

Even so, there is one consideration relating to the nature of plant self-movement that really does cast doubt upon whether the term 'consciousness' is apposite. For what seems to be lacking in the case of foraging plant roots is any sense of distance or deferral between the searching organism and the object of its search. Distinguishing how animals and plants fuel their ongoing self-maintenance, Hans Jonas thus highlights the 'interposition of *distance* between urge and attainment' and 'the possibility of a distant goal':

> *Its apprehension requires distant perception: thus development of sentience is involved. Its attainment requires controlled locomotion: thus development of motility is involved. But to experience the distantly perceived as a goal and to keep its goal quality alive, so as to carry the motion over the necessary span of effort and time, desire is required. Fulfillment not yet at hand is the essential condition of desire, and deferred fulfillment is what desire in turn makes possible.*[154]

If Jonas is right, the constant contiguity or adjacency of the root and its nutrition means that there is no space for the emergence of appetite, desire and thus the fulfilment of a goal. Whereas the plant is *immersed* in the immediate satisfaction of its organic needs, therefore, the 'great secret of animal life lies precisely in the gap which it is able to maintain between immediate concern and mediate satisfaction, i.e. in the loss of immediacy corresponding to the gain in scope'.[155] One might query whether it even makes sense to speak of a *search* for environmental nutrients – and thus the possible awareness of such nutrients – if there is no gap between the searcher and the sought-for. Expressed in epistemological terms, consciousness presupposes a degree of *separation* between subject and object.[156]

Plant-like and Animal-like Unicellulars

The question of motility and sessility can be misleading in attempts to distinguish animals from plants. Adult sponges, the basalmost metazoans, lack eyes, mouths, nervous systems and the power of movement, whereas certain carnivorous plants such as the Venus flytrap and the sundews use rapid movements to trap living prey and supplement their phototrophic lifestyle with a meaty side-plate. Attempts to differentiate plant-like from animal-like unicellulars are even more problematic. Micro-organisms were traditionally 'shoehorned'[157] into one kingdom or the other, the sessile green algae being classified among the plants and mobile predatory amoebae among the animals. In an article in the eighth edition of the *Encyclopaedia Britannica* (1859), the famously grumpy palaeontologist Richard Owen proposed 'protozoa' (a translation of the German *Urthiere* or 'first animals') as a third kingdom beside animals and plants, but this was conceptually flawed by the association of *zoa* with animals as opposed to plants. Ernst Haeckel coined the term 'Protista' for this 'third' kingdom, a category that he subsequently divided into subgroups such as 'Protozoa' (understood to be ancestral to the animals) and 'Protophyta' (ancestral to the plants).[158]

However, it has long been apparent that many protists *combine* the characteristics of plants and animals. For example, single-celled phototrophy – feeding on the sun – need not necessarily entail the passivity and immobility commonly associated with many-celled plants. The flagellate eukaryote *Euglena*, traditionally known as the 'eye animalcule', is a photosynthetic organism that is also active and fully motile, using its eyespot to detect the light and then swimming towards the best location for harvesting it.

One major classificatory distinction drawn at present in a marine context is between phytoplankton, which are autotrophic light-harvesters (*phyto* designating plants), and zooplankton, which are heterotrophic predators (*zoo* designating animals). However, the very term 'plankton' is misleading to the extent that it implies a drifter or wanderer (denoting an inability to swim against a current), whereas the opposite term 'nekton' is generally only used for macroscopic free-swimming animals.[159] The classificatory system thus fails to reflect the varying *degrees* to which the movements of micro-organisms may be active, directional and non-random, ranging from the merely passive drifting characteristic of many light-dependent algae to the vigorous phototaxis of the euglenids and from the sit-and-wait sessility of filter feeders to the active predation of microscopic hunters. The nature of the self-movement shown by such creatures is a decisive factor in considering the possible attribution of consciousness to them.

By contrast with the pursuit of moving prey, the often invariable and reflex-like nature of phototaxis – as noted by Fodor – tends to rule out an association with conscious behaviour. The merely mechanical character of much phototactic movement need no more imply an awareness of the surroundings than the most passive planktonic going-with-the-flow. Yet even here the possibility of a clear-cut distinction is undermined by the capacity of organisms such as *Euglena* to acquire their energy not only from the sun but also from the pursuit, capture and consumption of living prey in the form of bacteria: when light levels are low, the cell switches from autotrophy to heterotrophy and survives by eating as though it were an 'animal'. It is significant that *Euglena gracilis* can get by either with or without its chloroplast, and can even be 'cured' of its plastid by treatment with ultraviolet light.[160] Cells treated in this way become irreversibly dependent on a phagotrophic lifestyle, i.e. on ingesting food instead of harvesting light. The cryptomonads constitute another clade that spans the dichotomy between *phyto* and *zoo*, manifesting themselves either as brightly pigmented algae or as heterotrophs that feed on bacteria and other algae.[161] 'Phytoplankton' and 'zooplankton', observes botanist Nicholas Money, are 'categories of function rather than meaningful taxonomic arrangements'.[162]

Among phagotrophic protists, there are three main strategies of food acquisition. Varying degrees of locomotion and 'action' are required, suggesting a need for varying degrees of 'awareness' of the world: the more passive the strategy, the less important it is for the predator to be 'conscious' of its prey prior to ingestion. The strategy known as *filter feeding* involves the use of either existent or specially generated water currents from which food particles and suspended matter are strained; *diffusion feeding* involves the use of bodily extensions such as axopods with which approaching prey collide and to which they subsequently adhere; *raptorial feeding* involves the pursuit and active engulfment of prey.[163] Requiring hunt and capture, it is the latter that is most suggestive of a creature armed with an awareness of its surroundings, and we shall return to this strategy in subsequent sections.

Diffusion feeding is typified by radiolarians and heliozoans, etymologically known as ray animalcules and sun animalcules respectively,[164] whose delicate cytoplasmic axopods protrude radially from a central body to capture the prey that inadvertently gets stuck to them. It is also illustrated by the suctorians, sessile ciliates provided with sticky, extended tentacle-mouths to which passing protozoa adhere before having the cytoplasm sucked out of them.[165] Although the strategy is largely passive, some work is required, for the prey has to be incorporated or engulfed by the predator's body and then transported – by cytoplasmic flow – to the inner part of the cell for digestion; one might perhaps speak of internalized self-movement rather than the externalized self-movement of locomotion. Nevertheless, there seems little need to posit consciousness of a 'world' on the part of the predatory organism. An item of prey only becomes relevant to the organism once it is already physically adjacent and adhering to it and on its way to being materially assimilated. A similar strategy is employed by animals such as the Gorgon's Head basket star, a type of echinoderm that perches in a prominent position, extends its arms as though to create a Medusan bouffant, and ensnares small crustaceans that venture too close.

In itself, filter feeding also suggests a broadly sessile or passive lifestyle and a non-discriminatory process of ingestion that renders sensory awareness superfluous. Yet there are great variations in the amount of work performed by different sorts of filter feeder. Within the slightly broader category of 'suspension feeding',[166] a distinction has been drawn between active and passive forms according to whether ambient water currents are exploited to drive water across the filtering apparatus or whether the organism's own metabolic energy produces the flow.[167] Such currents may be generated by appendages such as cilia but also by the movement of the animal as a whole, rather in the manner of the filter-feeding baleen whales that swim through areas rich in zooplankton, gulping or gaping while their baleens sieve prey from the water. As in the case of animals, there are some unicellular filter feeders such as *Paramecium* that likewise pursue their prey in an actively motile manner (sweeping water with bacteria and algae into their oral groove as they move along), whereas others such as *Vorticella* tend rather to be sessile, relying on environmental currents to bring the suspended material to them. Among the flagellates, filter feeding is generally carried out by sessile organisms.

Even the lack of discrimination sometimes imputed to bacterivorous filter-feeding ciliates may not be as all-embracing as once thought. It was initially assumed that the feeding of such ciliates was predominantly 'automatized' and that they were unable to differentiate between different kinds of particles except in terms of their geometrical properties.[168] Although filter-feeding ciliates may indeed lack the 'discernment' of raptorial predators attacking individual prey items, and certainly the shape and size of potential prey are a 'first-order' determinant in particle selection,[169] there is evidence that biochemistry – the 'taste' or 'smell' – plays a role as well. Researchers have shown that prey items of similar morphology 'are not always ingested from mixtures with equal alacrity by filter-feeding ciliates', putting such selectivity down to 'biochemical differences perceived by the grazer'.[170] In addition to being able to differentiate among morphologically similar prey types in mixed assemblages, such ciliates can distinguish live from dead bacteria, discriminate between living cells and inert microspheres, and on occasion actively reject unattractive prey items in the course of processing them.[171]

The *aversive* behaviour exemplified in particular by the filter-feeding ciliate *Stentor*, the trumpet animalcule (illustration page 160), likewise suggests that the life of a filter feeder need not be a matter merely of meek and undiscriminating quiescence. In a famous experiment conducted by H. S. Jennings, a specimen belonging to the species *Stentor roeseli* was bombarded with a stream of potentially harmful carmine particles. In response to this noxious chemical stimulus, *Stentor* went through a whole sequence of adaptive measures, first ingesting the particles, then trying (several times) to bend away from the source, then reversing the motion of the cilia around its mouth so as to drive the particles away, then trying (several times) to contract its whole body towards its point of attachment to the substrate, before eventually – when harassed persistently enough – making a violent contraction of its whole body and swimming away. Once it had settled down again, *Stentor* proceeded to 'explore' the local terrain, or so it seemed, until it had come across a suitable site less bothersome to it, where it duly embarked upon a series of elaborate measures to establish and construct a new tube to live in.[172] The persistence of *Stentor*'s endeavours to avoid what was 'bad for self' – and the intricacy of its behavioural response – represent a marked contrast with more genuinely sessile or plant-like ways of life.

An underlying distinction among feeding strategies is thus between those that require no energy expenditure on the part of the organism (involving sessility or the random dispersal to which Brownian motion may subject small free-floating bacteria) and those that entail active locomotion. This in turn may take the form of either directional or non-directional movement. As a manner of indiscriminately 'aroused' behaviour, undirected locomotion does not in itself suggest consciousness, precisely because it does not presuppose discernment between one location and another, or between directions that are 'better' and 'worse' for self. Such behaviour was traditionally ascribed to the voracious hunter-ciliates of the genus *Didinium*, which were believed to move around at random eating whatever they bumped into and were physically capable of ingesting. Jennings described the 'process of food-getting' in *Didinium* as 'one of trial of all sorts of things'. Denying that it perceived its prey at a distance or took a decision to attack certain organisms, he posited that *Didinium* simply tried everything out and held fast to what was good.[173] More recent research has suggested that *Didinium* is not in fact a 'random contact hunter' but shows discrimination and chemotactic sensitivity.[174] As shown by the motile filter-feeding ciliates, however, the strategy undoubtedly makes sense to the extent that – given certain size requirements[175] – even haphazard movement increases the likelihood of encounters with potential prey.

A corresponding phenomenon in the plant world is nastic movement, such as the so-called thigmonasty of carnivorous plants, an unvarying and undirected reaction to touch or vibration. The non-directional movement characteristic of the Venus flytrap (the trap merely closes) makes it logically superfluous to posit any 'awareness' of the prey on the part of the plant, which does not need to perceive *where* the prey is located in order to be able to trap and consume it. The Venus flytrap simply produces an invariant mechanical response to what is in effect the pulling of a trigger.

Chemokinesis is another class of non-directional response to a stimulus. Like chemotaxis, this refers to chemically induced movement, but it is distinguished from chemotaxis by the random orientation of the locomotion, as when the presence of a particular substance causes an organism to speed up, slow down or engage in aleatory movements such as turning. If the organism finds itself in a favourable location (characterized, for example, by greater nutrition or humidity than elsewhere), a chemokinetic response thus entails it reducing its speed of locomotion or increasing the percentage of time that it remains stationary. This is known as *orthokinesis*. Provided that its fellow organisms generally do likewise, the statistical result will be that they tend to aggregate at the spot that is 'good for self', even though this effect has not been produced by the attraction or repulsion of any individual creature towards or away from a stimulus. Methodologically, the distinction between chemotaxis and chemokinesis may not be straightforward. In both cases accumulations are produced, in one instance as a result of organisms swimming at random until exposed to a sufficient concentration of a preferred chemical (and then slowing down), in the other as a result of actual attraction by the chemical in question.

A second category of chemokinesis is termed *klinokinesis*, where the intensity of some stimulus determines not the speed of movement, but the frequency of turning. The effect is similar: a statistical accumulation. If organisms increase their rate of turning in response to an 'unfavourable' gradient characterized (for example) by diminishing food, they will tend to spend more time in what for them are favourable locations, where there is nourishment in greater abundance. Klinokinesis is often taken to be exemplified by the 'biased random walk' – or 'run-and-tumble' – of bacteria such as *E. coli*, where episodes of straight swimming are interrupted by random changes in direction whose frequency depends on changes in the concentration of certain chemicals sensed by the individual bacterium. But more on this below.

Motile Bacteria: Escherichia coli *and Company*

In the context of unicellular consciousness there is a perhaps natural tendency to dismiss bacteria out of hand, yielding to the temptations of 'eukaryocentrism'. Eukaryotic cells include all human and non-human animal cells, all plant and fungus cells, as well as the multifarious pageant of free-living single-celled amoebae, radiolarians, dinoflagellates, diatoms, euglenids, euglyphids and ciliates that populate these pages. They are normally at least a thousand times larger than prokaryotes[176] and are characterized by exquisitely complex structures such as organelles, membranes, vesicles and the dynamically self-assembling cytoskeleton that not only provides support but also makes movement and manoeuvrability possible. The cytoskeleton has in itself been considered brain-like in its capacity to mediate sensory input and appropriately flexible motor responses. Eukaryocentrism is based on the sort of prejudice encountered above, namely the idea that – by contrast with eukaryotes – prokaryotes such as the model bacterium *E. coli* are simply too streamlined and lack the complexity to be able to give rise to anything as sophisticated as consciousness.

Indeed, size *is* relevant to the possibility of consciousness, and small size does in itself exclude some bacteria. However, this exclusion is grounded not in considerations of complexity or the lack of it, but in the limits to directional self-movement imposed by small-scale hydrodynamics. The question is whether the work required for self-propulsion is worth performing in metabolic or energetic terms. There are two main reasons for this. The first is that – owing to their diminutive size and low speeds – bacteria swim at a very low Reynolds number. This dimensionless quantity, which allows flow patterns to be predicted in different fluid contexts,[177] can be conceived as the ratio of the force of inertia to that of viscosity, two parameters whose relative magnitudes strongly influence the nature of flow. At low Reynolds numbers, viscosity predominates and the flow is laminar and sluggish, whereas at high Reynolds numbers inertial forces prevail and the flow is fast and often turbulent. What this means in practice is that bacteria – whose Reynolds number of 10^{-5} contrasts with the 10^5 of medium-sized fish and the 10^8 of the blue whale[178] – inhabit a realm of such extreme viscosity that the self-propulsion of micro-organisms has been likened to humans swimming in molasses.[179]

In these conditions, inertia and momentum are minimal and 'coasting' is ruled out. Unlike fish, some of which are able to glide for more than five body lengths between each propulsive stroke, bacteria must work their flagellar engines flat-out all the time. For a bacterium some two micrometres long such as *E. coli*, the distance it coasts after switching off its propulsive apparatus (its 'stopping distance') may be much less than the diameter of a single atom.[180] The effect of such 'viscous damping' is to thwart any attempt to move by imparting momentum to the surrounding fluid as in paddling, precluding the swimming strategies used by larger organisms such as fish or whales.[181] Bacteria of course have their own, different strategies, such as the highly inefficient rotating flagellum.[182] Corkscrewing their way through an ocean of treacle, bacterial self-propulsion is a constant struggle.

Yet not only is prokaryotic self-movement more likely to be a waste of energy. Another physical constraint on the possibility of successful chemotactic locomotion is exerted by Brownian motion, the random, thermal movement of water molecules that incessantly buffet any bacteria that may be trying to follow a chemical gradient. The upshot of this buffeting, as biophysicist David B. Dusenbery has demonstrated, is that bacteria unattached to a larger surface will be unable to keep up a steady orientation for more than a matter of seconds, undermining their capacity to find their way to nutrients or a mate.[183] Beneath a certain size, micro-organisms seeking to ascertain a gradient by means of successive measurements of a chemical concentration will be thwarted by the random jostling that disarranges the information from one measurement to the next: 'as the orientation of an organism changes in unknown directions', writes Dusenbery, 'past measurements become useless for determining gradient direction. Measurements made in an unknown direction are of no use'.[184]

Dusenbery's quantitative analysis of the size limit below which the signal-to-noise ratio will be insufficient for an organism to pursue its interests effectively by means of guided self-propulsion predicts a minimum diameter of 0.6 micrometres.[185] His prediction is corroborated by his earlier comparisons of the relative differences in the actual dimensions of motile and non-motile bacteria. These attribute a length of 0.8 micrometres to the bacteria of the smallest known motile genus, whereas 19 per cent of non-motile genera consist of bacteria that are smaller than this, unequivocally reflecting a more general tendency of bacteria endowed with motility to be larger than those that do without.[186] If we are right to conclude that there is a minimum size beneath which directional self-propulsion is simply ineffective, and if we are justified in grounding consciousness in directional self-propulsion, this implies a minimum size – at least given the hydrodynamics prevalent on our planet – beneath which consciousness itself is logically superfluous.

Though hamstrung by such limitations, many bacteria nonetheless show a remarkable capacity for adaptive self-movement. The combination of small size and the absence of membrane-bound organelles led to a traditional view of bacteria as static, homogeneous structures (little more than bags of freely diffusing enzymes), yet bacterial cells are now known to be endowed with homologues of the eukaryotic cytoskeletal proteins and likewise display an organized and dynamic subcellular 'architecture'.[187] It has been proposed, indeed, that despite the lack of a conventional cytoskeleton the bacterial cytoplasm is structured by an 'enzoskeleton',[188] a dynamic network of associations among cellular proteins generating 'enzyme superstructures' that play the *role* of a cytoskeleton. Irrespective of the details of their inner constitution, however, the point here is that bacterial cells – as 'selves' – exist in a world comprising entities that are 'meaningful' to them (good or bad for self; nutritious or deleterious) and the presence or absence of which is relevant to their continued well-being. They are able to detect features of the external environment and in many cases – provided they exceed a minimum size limit – generate self-movement that is appropriate to their interests. The question is whether these factors are sufficient to suggest the presence of consciousness.

Like prokaryotes in general, *E. coli* is a 'biocomputational' entity in the sense that the cognitive 'gap' between sensory input and motor output is not merely a matter of spatially relaying the sensory information (such that a particular stimulus produces a particular response) but involves the processing and integration of this information.[189] The chemotactic circuitry, for example, does not operate in isolation but must be interconnected with networks responsible for assessing environmental variables such as temperature as well as acidity and salt concentrations, for a self-maintaining self cannot allow its 'appetite' (its search for food) to take it to a location where the temperature, acidity or salinity is incompatible with its continued functionality. As it happens, writes Dennis Bray, each of the bacterium's myriad cellular processes, linked by their shared dependence on a limited pool of chemicals, can be presumed to be directly or indirectly interconnected with every other.[190]

The openness of *E. coli* to meaningful environmental non-self – the 50 chemoattractants and chemorepellents that make up its world – is mediated by its transmembrane receptor proteins, which 'recognize' the relevant molecules in the environment. This means that the molecules in question attach to the receptor's binding site, causing a conformational change in the receptor that duly activates the biochemical circuitry within the cell, a process that involves the addition or removal of phosphates to or from a sequence of proteins. As noted above, it is the degree of phosphorylation of a protein called CheY that regulates the activity of the rotary motors of the cell's flagella. High concentrations of the phosphate-bearing version of CheY cause a clockwise rotation of the motors (and a 'tumbling' or random change in direction of the cell), whereas low concentrations suppress the tumbling and prompt the cell to continue swimming in the same direction as hitherto. The logic behind this 'run-and-tumble' strategy is that if *E. coli* is moving in a direction that is 'good for self' it should keep more or less straight on; if not, it should try out a new direction.

In fact, what is at stake is not so much what is 'good for self' as what is 'better for self'. *E. coli* does not respond to the concentration of an attractant (say, glucose or the amino acid aspartate) *per se*, but to the rate of change in its concentration.[191] It is a sudden increase or decrease in concentration that results in a change in the frequency of tumbles, whereas a steady concentration has no effect. This assessment of a relative rather than an absolute value requires a type of short-term memory, which in turn calls for a second type of protein modification to the receptor. This involves the addition or removal of methyl groups rather than phosphate groups. Methylation tends to cancel out the original signal conveyed by the attractant, but it does so with a time lag, thus functioning as a measure of attractant *in the recent past*. This time lapse between phosphorylation and methylation enables the bacterium to gauge the rate of change in the concentration of attractant, in other words to discern the concentration gradient as it moves. If it is heading in a direction of increased concentration, the probability of tumbling is lowered and the bacterium will keep swimming in a straight line for a longer average time. The overall tendency will be to approach what is 'better for self' (a higher concentration of glucose or aspartate) and to tumble away from what is less favourable or is noxious.

This process is commonly designated 'chemotaxis' because the net effect, statistically speaking, is that the bacteria succeed in 'detecting' the gradient and targeting the area of maximum concentration. It may thus appear to be an exemplary case of microbial self-movement and an ideal candidate for the sort of locomotion that could imply consciousness. Yet two doubts present themselves regarding the nature of this self-movement. The first doubt is a reiteration of Hans Jonas's demand for distance as opposed to material proximity. Given that there is no real gap between the seeker and the sought-for, the question is whether *E. coli* can genuinely be claimed to be *seeking* the 'good' or the 'better'. *E. coli* seems to remain firmly immersed within the realm of what is directly present to it (the realm of 'taste', one might say), in other words the attractants or repellents that are immediately adjacent or contiguous. There is no perception at a distance.

One way to approach this question is to consider whether the mechanism of bacterial chemotaxis is based on nutritional input or informational input.[192] Is it the effects of nutrients such as aspartate *as nutrition* that drive chemotaxis (say, by increasing internal levels of the energy currency ATP), or is it their effects *as signals*? As a matter of fact, an aspartate gradient (for example) is now known to function as information. The nutritional absorption of the aspartate into the cell through a process called 'facilitated' diffusion – a variant mode of passive diffusion that uses transmembrane carrier proteins to help relatively large molecules across the membrane – is distinct from the action of aspartate as a signal molecule.[193] In the former case a transport protein termed a permease is involved; in the latter case receptor proteins designated 'chemoreceptors' are used, i.e. a specialized sensory system whose purpose is to capture the relevant information. The two processes, nutrition and signalling, are thus biochemically independent of one another.

Clearly, the idea is that the signal should *lead* the organism to locations where nutrition is favoured. Increased concentrations of aspartate signal 'this way for more aspartate'. Yet the element of information introduces the possibility of being *misled*; bacteria can be 'deceived'. They can be attracted to chemicals they cannot metabolize, and they can fail to be attracted to chemicals they do metabolize. Mutants lacking the 'aspartate receptor' may nonetheless assimilate and oxidize it.[194] This separation of nutritional and informational input – with the concomitant possibility of error and misinterpretation – thus opens up a new dimension of *metaphorical* distance in the 'chemotaxis' of *E. coli*, a figurative gap that distinguishes it from the immediacy of mere growth. Bacterial self-movement of this kind is mediated by information. Whether this distance is 'real' enough to satisfy Jonas's stipulation must remain an open question.

The second doubt relates to the nature of bacterial run-and-tumble, which is tellingly also known as a 'biased random walk'. Despite its efficiency as a form of chemically stimulated locomotion, the biased random walk is effectively the result of a (non-random) choice between two modes of (random) movement. In fact, neither the straight run nor the tumble in itself presupposes true directionality on the part of the bacterium; neither of them implies an 'intentional' aim at a sensory target. So even though run-and-tumble may be classified as 'chemotaxis' in the broad sense of a change in the organism's patterns of motility in response to chemical stimulation, it has been argued that it does not correspond to 'true' taxis[195] (where the direction of the organism's movement is correlated with the direction of the chemical gradient) but is non-directional and only merits the appellation 'chemokinesis'.

Of course, this randomness is far from being as absolute as it would be in the hypothesized case of a truly random hunter. It is 'biased' or 'weighted' by the cell's ongoing monitoring of the environment, with behavioural variability inhering in the time interval with which these two 'blind' and invariable movements succeed one another. Instead of providing orientation for targeted locomotion (an objective at a distance), assessment of the chemical gradient thus regulates the relative frequency of two random behaviours. Collectively (or statistically), this enables *E. coli* to produce an adaptive response to the differential chemical environment in which it is immersed, yet it remains questionable whether one can even begin to speak of self-movement guided or oriented by any sort of 'awareness' of a goal.

For a long time, temporal sensing of a gradient in conjunction with a biased random walk was deemed to be all that bacteria had up their sleeves in the way of chemotaxis, 'true' manifestations of which were the prerogative of eukaryotes.[196] To complicate the picture, however, one species of bacteria has now been shown to be capable of true taxis (suggesting at least the *possibility* of further such species). The species in question is a sulphur-oxidizing bacterium called *Thiovulum majus*, a spherical cell between five and ten micrometres in diameter and largely covered in flagella, which propel it to swimming velocities of up to 600 micrometres a second. This is the highest speed known for bacteria[197]: a hundred cell lengths per second (and through the equivalent of treacle at that). These cells display various strategies aimed at keeping their preferred position within a gradient of oxygen concentrations.[198] One strategy is to attach themselves to a solid surface by means of a mucous stalk. Alternatively, they may remain free-swimming and use chemical signals to form narrow bands at their preferred oxygen concentration. This they achieve on the one hand by a mechanism of 'steered turning', a phobic – and basically non-directional – response that consists in changing direction whenever they stray from their comfort zone. The other trick they use is known as helical klinotaxis, which exploits the natural tendency of cells to swim in a helical trajectory.[199] Sampling the chemical concentration at successive points in time as they follow a helical pathway along their preferred isopleth, *Thiovulum* cells are sensitive to periodic changes in concentration resulting from the helical geometry of their course. In response to undesirable deviations, they regulate the activity of their flagella, modulating the rotational and translational components of their helical motion – the parameters of the helix – in such a way as to maintain their pathway.[200]

The adherence of *Thiovulum* to an oxygen isopleth is notably lacking in the 'distance' presupposed by consciousness. It makes little sense to distinguish the informational from the energetic function of the oxygen, and the bacterium remains firmly ensconced within the immediacy of metabolic need fulfilment. Yet although we may be disinclined to see the truly chemotactic locomotion of *Thiovulum* as grounding anything like consciousness in itself, what it announces is that genuinely directional self-propulsion cannot be denied *on principle* to prokaryotes.

Motile Protozoa: Oxyrrhis marina *and Company*

There is certainly an overlap between prokaryotes and eukaryotes in the strategies deployed in the pursuit of nutrients or fuel: just as true taxis may be available to bacteria, protozoans may resort to random encounter and biased random walk. The similarities and differences can perhaps be more clearly gauged, however, by direct comparison of bacterial run-and-tumble with the self-movement of one of the model protozoans, the well-known heterotrophic protist *Oxyrrhis marina*. This will in turn shed additional light on the possible ascription of genuinely directional self-propulsion.

Along with stalwarts such as *Paramecium, Amoeba* and *Dictyostelium*, the naked dinoflagellate *O. marina* (illustration page 159) is one of the best-studied eukaryotic organisms on account of its near-global availability and ease of cultivation.[201] It is an aggressive and extremely versatile predator that is known to feed on bacteria, algal cells and small and medium-sized flagellates (such as *Pfiesteria piscicida*), as well as on other protists as large as itself.[202] Indeed, it has even been recorded 'attacking' multicellular amphipods – an order of crustaceans – that have recently moulted,[203] and when short of other prey it may turn to cannibalism.[204] It is highly selective in its choice of nutrition, discriminating between prey on the basis of size, motility, surface properties and chemical cues, where such properties and cues may be taken to serve as indicators of prey quality (as manifest in the ratio of carbon, nitrogen and phosphorus).

The opportunism and adaptability of this cosmopolitan protozoan[205] come to light in its capacity to cope with the 'feast and famine' cycles associated with unstable, heterogeneous environments, i.e. with sweeping fluctuations in food availability. This flexibility is reflected in its own physical pliancy. Though only 20 – 30 micrometres in size, it is able to fill its entire body with prey, taking advantage of a sudden pulse of food to gobble up its algal quarry at extremely brisk rates of up to 35 cells per hour, multiplying its own initial volume fourfold. Its slow digestion time and considerable ability to store food means that it is capable of dividing even when its food has run out.[206] The versatility of *O. marina* is further exemplified by the variety of feeding mechanisms it has at its disposal, adopting not only the *raptorial* method of active search plus engulfment for protist prey, but also using *filter feeding* for its ingestion of bacteria (employing one of its two flagella to generate feeding currents that sweep the bacteria towards the circular depression that is its mouth) and even engaging in *osmotrophy* – the assimilation of dissolved organic molecules – in certain environments where decaying organic matter is present.[207]

In addition to its behavioural versatility and complexity, three fundamental differences stand out with respect to *E. coli*. Firstly, whereas bacteria are restricted to osmotrophy as a mode of nutrient assimilation, the active phagocytosis of *O. marina* involves the *work* of a non-permanent cytostome or 'mouth', necessitating the opening and subsequent closing of an arrangement of microtubular bands – i.e. part of the cytoskeleton – near the ventral surface of the cell.[208] As with locomotion itself, such work calls for an investment of energy that in turn suggests the presence of an appetite or motivation, and the implicit anticipation of reward. Notably, the anticipation is *implicit* in that it does not involve an explicit 'visualization' of a pleasurable end-state, or what might be called 'foresight'. Implicit anticipation – if the term is deemed acceptable – nonetheless incorporates the twin elements of goal-directed work (i.e. metabolically powered self-movement) and a subsequent 'reward' or 'satisfaction'. To express it differently, it makes little sense for a self-maintaining self to go to the trouble of opening up a mouth unless it is *motivated* to do so by the implicit expectation of something nutritious or 'rewarding' being engulfed within it.

A second difference is that whereas for *E. coli* the chemical gradient is only 'metaphorically' distanced from the reward (in that the gradient from less to more glucose or aspartate simultaneously constitutes, as it were, both the information and the nutrition), for *O. marina* there is a more clear-cut distinction between nutrition and the 'infochemicals' that point to the nearby presence of nutrition,[209] i.e. cues such as specific prey exudates or certain amino acids signalling quarry *at a distance*. For the predatory dinoflagellate, in other words, the chemical gradient represents information concerning a source of nutrition that may yet be attainable if work is performed, but that is far from guaranteed.[210] There is a real temporal and spatial distance between the information and what it represents. Such distance and deferral are associated with the need for appetite, motivation and reward, returning us to Hans Jonas's distinction between the immediacy of plant life and the distance that co-emerges with the appetite and motility of animals.[211]

The third difference between *E. coli* and *O. marina* resides in the degree of control of the cell over its self-movements. Exceptions such as *Thiovulum* notwithstanding, bacterial flagella are generally restricted to generating straight runs interspersed with random tumbles, and *O. marina* likewise seems to have a version of relatively random run-and-tumble movement among its behavioural options.[212] By contrast with *E. coli*, however, the workings of the two eukaryotic flagella – the transversal flagellum and the trailing flagellum – can also be varied to fine-tune the course of the cell's helical swimming path.[213] Three degrees of freedom are at stake. While only the trailing flagellum produces the translation of the cell, the asymmetrical position of *both* of the flagella leads to two independent rotational components, which in turn determine the overall helical or corkscrew-like trajectory. By changing the beat frequency of one or both flagella or altering the direction of the trailing flagellum, dinoflagellates such as *O. marina* are thus able to control these three degrees of freedom – the translational velocity and the two rotational components – so as to modulate their helical swimming path and thus enhance the efficiency of their foraging or searching behaviour.[214] By following a helical trajectory as they swim approximately perpendicular to a chemical gradient, moreover, such cells can discern the changing chemical concentrations as their path moves closer to or further away from the source. This technique – the 'helical klinotaxis' likewise exhibited by *Thiovulum* – permits an organism lacking paired receptor organs to orient itself within a graded three-dimensional chemical environment. As with the klinokinesis of *E. coli*, therefore, the cell's response to a chemical gradient requires it to be able to move itself about and sample concentrations from diverse points within the three-dimensional space of the gradient in question. In the case of *O. marina*, however, the movement and the sampling are controlled rather than merely random.

Chemoreception of dissolved infochemicals brings the dinoflagellates to a nutrient-rich location, yet the prey still has to be recognized, captured and processed prior to ingestion. This is thought to involve proteins such as lectins on the surface of the predator cell that bind to specific prey-associated ligands such as the carbohydrate mannose.[215] In addition to the direct cell-cell contact of mannose-binding lectins, the flagella too are considered possible mediators of prey recognition.[216] An element of randomness seems to play an important part in the capture of prey; the absence of visual acuity makes the foraging process appear 'clumsier'. Accordingly, it might be asked whether the goal of the chemotactic search is an individual item or merely a productive prey patch (an area rich in nutrients). Having sniffed out a hunting ground, the predators might be imagined 'groping' about in a microscopic game of blind man's buff, where it is contact chemoreception (i.e. 'cell-surface recognition'[217] or 'taste') as opposed to distance chemoreception ('smell') that gets the results.

This in turn raises a further question, namely whether a nutrient-rich prey patch signalled by a 'gradient' of infochemicals really amounts to a 'target'. To the extent that the gradient is gradual (which, etymologically speaking, is exactly what a gradient is) and each minuscule 'step' (*gradus*) towards the prey patch constitutes a statistical improvement in the chance of bumping into an item of prey, the movement might be interpreted not as motion towards an objective, but simply as an immediate chase from 'good' to 'better' to 'even better' in probabilistic terms. Whether this represents a gradual progression up a gradient of what is 'better for self' or the intentional pursuit of a target at a distance is perhaps best deemed undecidable. Indeed, this ambiguity may well have been the logical legerdemain by which intentionality itself was first made possible, i.e. as a product of the seamless transformation of an incremental sequence of micro-steps (towards or away from what was directly contiguous according to whether it was statistically more likely to be better or worse for self) into the all-or-nothing targeting of a goal. One might speculate that this was the mechanism by which minimal selfhood was first 'manipulated' into moving itself directionally for a reward yet to come.

Even though directional chemotaxis towards a prey patch followed by random hunting at close quarters is doubtless a perfectly viable strategy for snatching a meal, chemotaxis can in fact be used to target *individual* items even at a unicellular scale. A striking example of this occurs in the realm of mate attraction rather than nutrition acquisition and features the small (10-μm-long) flagellate *Chlamydomonas allensworthii*,[218] the females of which release a pheromone while the males pursue the resulting gradient to find the individual female with which to fuse. Perhaps unsurprisingly, the mating involves specialized cells akin to gametes. Sperm chemotaxis occurs in ferns and is common throughout the animal kingdom, including human spermatozoa, a small fraction of which show both chemotaxis and chemokinesis toward a factor or factors within follicular fluid.[219]

Within the domain of food acquisition, the stereotypical pre-capture circling behaviour of predatory dinoflagellates has also been taken to hint at the chemotactic targeting of individual prey items. Such behaviour is shown by *O. marina*, which swims in tight circles around its prey prior to ingestion. It has also been studied in *Protoperidinium pellucidum*, a small to medium-sized dinoflagellate that catches its planktonic prey – preferentially diatoms but also other dinoflagellates – on an individual basis and uses a pallium to digest each cell externally.[220] When *Protoperidinium* passes in the vicinity of a potential food item, it goes through a characteristic routine of zigzagging around its meal, usually without contacting it, before eventually attaching its pallium and sucking the living daylights out of it. Such stereotypical movements have been interpreted by some as a way of recognizing and locating a potential quarry. They have even been understood as a way of 'sizing up' the prey.[221] Others have interpreted this apparently 'intentional' activity as a merely chemokinetic strategy designed to minimize the risk of the predator swimming away.[222] Once the dinoflagellate has come within a certain distance of its prey, the idea is to keep it there and rely on random encounter for the actual capture. The appearance of intentionality, on this view, is an illusion.

Whether or not *O. marina* and other protozoan predators target their prey individually or collectively may indeed be considered irrelevant in assessing the possible ascription of consciousness to such organisms. It may be felt, perhaps, that terms such as 'target' and 'goal' are themselves inappropriate to the extent that the organism does not set out on its trajectory with an objective 'in view', but 'blindly' follows wherever the gradient leads it: there is no explicit perception of where the pursuit will end. Even here, in other words, the organism remains mired in immediacy, lacking the distance that Jonas deems essential to consciousness. It is the faculty of vision, one might argue, that generates the spatial context allowing a goal to be 'visualized' as the endpoint of a trajectory, the summit of a gradient.[223]

Yet a consequence of the demand for organisms to be able to visualize their goals prior to pursuing them is that consciousness is restricted to those endowed with an optical or some other image-forming system. Though natural given the human paradigm, this insistence on image-formation as a prerequisite for consciousness need not be applicable to the phenomenon of consciousness *per se* or in its deepest roots. If sightless organisms simply 'follow their nose' (i.e. their powers of olfaction) in pursuing a gradient, they will admittedly not 'know' when they can expect to arrive at the coveted source of a chemical attractant, or whether their target will be single or multiple. Rather obviously, they will lack a (visual) image of their objective, i.e. of its consistency, structure or geometrical form. Yet some sort of goal can nonetheless be assumed to be implicitly present to them, for otherwise it makes no sense to claim – as will be claimed in greater detail below – that they are *motivated* to perform the work of locomotion for a reward yet to be attained. Provided the direction is mediated by information rather than determined by an immediate nutritional reward, the very concept of self-caused, directional self-movement implies the pursuit of a goal, though possibly one that is not explicitly envisioned by the organism in question. The nature of this goal, i.e. of the 'object' of microbial consciousness, will be further discussed below.[224]

On preliminary consideration, therefore, it seems reasonable to suggest that *O. marina* may in some sense be conscious of the nearby presence of its potential quarry, whether severally or as a group. It may be aware of the 'smell' its prey exudes from a certain distance, and perhaps even the 'taste' of mannose on finally grasping it. Insofar as these cues interact with the predator's receptors, they serve as signals of the prey in question *as the type of prey that it is*, in the way that for a hungry human the shape, smell and taste of an apple reveal the apple *as an apple*. Equally, it seems tenable to propose that protozoans such as *Oxyrrhis* may on occasion experience a sensation of *hunger* that spurs them to pursue this trail of cues and procure themselves the pleasure of satisfying their appetite. The following section will look at these proposals in greater detail.

IV.

Appetite and Tacit Selfhood

Hunger, Satiety and Siesta

So far I have attempted to convince the sceptical reader that there is no *a priori* reason *not* to apply the same criterion in attributing consciousness to certain single-celled organisms as to multicellular organisms. This criterion is their capacity to exhibit behaviour, i.e. to move themselves. In the face of the lingering suspicion that unicellular behaviour is not *really* self-caused 'action' but a mere 'response' imposed by extraneous forces (taxis), the previous chapter showed that single cells vary greatly in the ways in which and the extent to which they depend upon and are capable of self-guided locomotion. However, it remains to be demonstrated that some eukaryotic self-movement is *more* than a fixed response to an external stimulus and can thus meaningfully be described as self-caused. The example of the rapacious dinoflagellate *Oxyrrhis marina* betrayed that appetite in particular may be considered a plausible candidate for the sort of internal state that might induce an organism to invest metabolic resources in the work of non-random, self-generated movement (pursuit of prey), at the same time calling for elementary consciousness in the form of an awareness of the prey that is the object of its pursuit (i.e. of the direction that needs to be followed in order to secure its meal). To shed further light on the role of appetite in the generation of basal consciousness, the present chapter will shift the focus from *O. marina* to another notorious eukaryotic predator, *Amoeba proteus* (illustration page 161), arguably the most widely studied amoebozoan.

Like *O. marina*, *A. proteus* uses the technique of phagocytosis to engulf its prey. A fascinating early paper on 'The Daily Life of Amœba Proteus' (1908), by David Gibbs and O. P. Dellinger, provides a series of detailed observations on its predatory habits. The authors note that 'the intensely interesting sight of an amoeba after numerous trials gradually sliding its pseudopods around a feeding paramecium, throwing a cover over it, closing the pseudopods, and gradually squeezing the struggling victim down to a rounded mass can hardly be described without using anthropomorphic terms'.[225] Nicholas Money has more recently described how the cell 'embraces its microbial quarry in a pseudopodial hug, casts the morsel into a vacuole, and showers the terrified bacterium with digestive enzymes. ... Later, any waste materials are voided by the reverse of the feeding process at the posterior end of the amoeba. No mouth, no anus, but the essence of all animal life is there'.[226] Collectively, in fact, amoebozoans are not restricted to phagocytosis of this classic sort. In a phenomenon known as trogocytosis, the parasitic protozoan *Entamoeba histolytica* has been found to take bite-size chunks out of intestinal cells as it grazes through the human gut.[227] More than 100,000 people are killed each year by the amoebic dysentery to which it gives rise.

Also like *O. marina*, *A. proteus* is selective in what it consumes. As Gibbs and Dellinger comment, the amoeba 'shows distinct food preferences: with diatoms and unicellular algae, it takes algae, but when feeding on algae it will leave them to "pursue" ciliates. In the presence of large paramecia, some amoebas leave algae and ciliates to catch these larger forms. Amoeba eats nothing dead'.[228] As a rule, it also avoids eating members of its own species, although it is observed to eat amoebae belonging to other species. Indeed, *A. proteus* is known to emit an identity marker – a peptide called A-factor – that reveals its presence not only to its clone mates (thus preventing clonal cannibalism), but also to various species of potential prey, allowing certain ciliates of the genus *Euplotes* to beat a hasty retreat and avoid amoeba's pseudopodial hug. While reducing prey uptake by letting more ciliates escape than otherwise, this form of collective 'self-recognition'[229] presumably pays its way in preventing collective self-consumption.

Whereas the locomotion of *O. marina* involves the coordinated use of its two flagella, *A. proteus* and amoebozoans in general use their cytoskeleton to move themselves. In spite of the connotations of the term 'skeleton', the cytoskeleton is far from being a fixed framework, but is a self-assembling structure that dynamically and adaptively responds to cues from the environment mediated by scores of interacting regulatory proteins.[230] The protein actin, which constitutes up to a tenth of the total protein complement of mobile cells, plays a pivotal role in the dynamic functioning of the cytoskeleton. Regulatory actin-binding proteins modify the rates of polymerisation and depolymerisation – assembly and disassembly – of actin filaments, generating coordinated forces that drive movement and changes in cell shape. Locomotion occurs when self-assembling networks of highly branched filaments push the plasma membrane forward at the leading edge of the cell, for example, but these branched filaments are in turn terminated before they grow too long to be able to push effectively. The network is disassembled, allowing the components to be recycled for subsequent rounds of polymerisation. Powered by ATP, this controlled assembly and disassembly of protein structures underlies the work of locomotion and phagocytosis required for amoebae to pursue and then ingest their prey.[231]

While the designation *Amoeba proteus* thus implies formlessness and disorder (an impression seemingly corroborated by the cell's constant shape-shifting when foraging), its success as a highly active predator tells a different tale. As Franklin Harold points out, 'what looks like a drunken stagger becomes better directed when the amoeba senses prey and achieves a speed of several hundred micrometers per minute'.[232] Nonetheless, amoebae can hardly be described as fleet of pseudopod.[233] 'Several hundred micrometres a minute' amounts to little more than five micrometres a second (or 18 mm an hour), whereas ciliates – some of them powered by tight clusters of fused cilia called 'cirri' – may be two orders of magnitude faster (500 – 1000 µm/s), and even flagellates attain speeds a good order of magnitude greater (100 – 200 µm/s).[234] Perhaps the secret of the amoeba's predatory prowess is the coordinated flexibility of its form.

This predatory efficacy emerges in the paper by Gibbs and Dellinger, which brings to light an alternation of periods of work or chase with periods of rest: in other words, the amoeba's pursuit of prey is successful enough not to be its *only* pastime. Prior to the work of Gibbs and Dellinger, it had been doubted whether this rhythm of work and rest – long regarded as necessary for 'higher' animals – was equally essential to the lifestyle of the protozoa. As the authors ascertain 'very definitely', however, *A. proteus* does indeed 'have periods of activity and of rest as reactions connected with search for, and attainment of food. These periods apparently have nothing to do with light or darkness, day or night. The amoeba moves actively feeding until well filled with food when it remains quiescent for a time'.[235] The contrast drawn by the authors is with previously studied protozoa such as the ciliate *Vorticella*, the bell animalcule, which seemed unceasing in the work it performed with its cilia (sweeping food towards its mouth and driving away waste particles) and whose tireless activity had led some investigators to believe that protozoa 'never rest'. The rhythm of work and rest, it was thought, 'was only gradually evolved with the more complex forms of life'.[236] Unicellular *A. proteus* proves otherwise, for the work of the chase and the feed is followed by what might best be described as a post-prandial nap. As Gibbs and Dellinger construe the phenomenon, 'the period of rest appears to be simply the result of organic satisfaction, or a period of recuperation. It suggests the lowest form of sleep; for this tendency to rest, to sleep, as a food reaction is illustrated by the higher animals'.[237]

We shall return below to consider the question of 'sleep'. Another interpretation might be to dismiss this period of non-movement as a purely 'biomechanical' phenomenon determined by changes in body structure. Indeed, the explanation for an amoeba's 'satiety' could simply be that the contents of its food vacuoles, when full, are too 'massive' or 'bulky' for the creature to be energetically or metabolically capable of dragging itself around in pursuit of further nutrition. A possible analogy from the metazoan world is the female mosquito, whose weight increases fourfold after it has drunk its fill of (usually vertebrate) blood and for whom rest and digestion thus become an urgent priority.[238] Motion proves to be an energetic extravagance if one's weight has quadrupled, and a newly sated mosquito is unlikely to go far. Whether an organism's post-prandial immobility is biomechanically or biochemically 'enforced', however, is perhaps secondary to the present argument. The point here is simply that – unlike the indefatigably[239] feeding ciliate *Vorticella* – the amoeba is sometimes disposed to perform the work required to capture and ingest an item of prey, and sometimes not. Its disposition to move depends not exclusively on external circumstances (say, the presence of prey), but also on the internal state of the amoeba in question (how many it has already eaten).

This clearly contravenes an understanding of unicellular self-movement as mere taxis or tropism. To provide a full explanation of the causes of such locomotion it is not enough to cite the stimulus or chemical cue emanating from the prey; we also need to know the internal state of the amoeba. Manifest as a disposition to behave or move itself to such-and-such an end *or not*, an internal state of this sort is indistinguishable from what is commonly referred to as a 'mental' or 'psychological' state or, more commonly still, how an organism 'feels'. To the extent that mental states can only be differentiated in terms of the behaviour that they cause or as which they express themselves (depending on our theory of mind), differential behaviours in otherwise equivalent circumstances make it meaningful to ascribe a particular internal or mental state to an organism.

Essential to the ascription of such states is the possibility of discriminating them. More specifically, it is only in the context of the possible absence of appetite – visible to an observer as an amoeba's disinclination to pursue prey that it otherwise *would* pursue – that it genuinely makes sense to speak of 'hunger'.[240] So while hunger cannot be ascribed to *Vorticella* insofar as there is no distinction between it being hungry and it *not* being hungry (although it too can in fact lose its appetite in certain, exceptional circumstances[241]), *A. proteus* can non-vacuously be described as 'hungry', because sometimes it is and sometimes it is not.

Confronted with Jennings' whale-sized amoeba, therefore, the question 'is it hungry?' would be anything but an idle one, the answer determining the speed with which we took to our heels. By contrast, the question would be a waste of breath if we were in danger of being swept into the mouth of a tree-sized *Vorticella* by its unstinting cilia: *Vorticella*'s behaviour remains the same whatever (broadly speaking), so the ascription of hunger or otherwise is empty. Substantial light is shed on the relative nature of 'hunger' by the human 'hunger for air', which – despite our absolute dependence on the oxygen we need to burn our food – is not a state of which we are normally aware. In general, the impossibility, or the unknowability, of air-satiety makes air-hunger equally unknowable, and we only become conscious of the incessant work performed by our lungs if there is a malfunction or a serious problem. As Charles Darwin put it, breathing with ease 'is a blessing of every moment; yet, of all others, it is that which we possess with the least consciousness'.[242]

Recognizing Hunger: Some Doubts

There is something charming and quaint about the paper by Gibbs and Dellinger, dating back as it does to 1908. But presumably there are other, more recent studies that might cast light on the phenomenon just in case Gibbs and Dellinger cooked the whole thing up (which of course they did not). The search for such corroboration proves fruitful but raises a number of doubts. The underlying question is how to *recognize* hunger in a free-living eukaryotic cell. I have been suggesting that to do this requires us to be able to distinguish between different behaviours (different degrees or forms of self-movement) in otherwise similar external circumstances.

A rather fundamental doubt relates to how far the proposed distinction between hunger (as manifest in the pursuit of prey) and satiety (as manifest in non-pursuit) overlaps in practice not only with a distinction between behaviour and non-behaviour but by extension with that between wakefulness and sleep. A variation on this theme comes to light in the behavioural patterns of the haptorid ciliate *Pseudomonilicaryon anser*, formerly known as *Dileptus anser*.[243] Measuring as much as a millimetre in length, this voracious predator is armed with a trunk-like proboscis that sweeps through the surrounding waters to increase its chances of hitting upon prey organisms, which it then disables by firing toxic trichocysts.[244] Groups of this protozoan have been observed to start feeding shortly before dawn and to terminate abruptly, four hours later.[245] This cut-off varies in time from one day to the next but always takes place more or less in unison. A group engaged in finding and ingesting prey switches to a state of complete quiescence within a matter of minutes, with little or no more feeding occurring throughout the rest of the 24-hour cycle (during which time cell division takes place and broken proboscises are regenerated). The precise nature of this biological 'clock' remains uncertain,[246] as does the extent to which it provides the foundation for a possible distinction between wakefulness (used for hunting and ingesting prey) and a sleep-like state (used for bodily renovation). During their limited period of feeding activity, can the dileptids meaningfully be described not only as 'hungry', but also as 'awake'?[247] Are the two terms synonymous?

Similar concerns are raised by *O. marina*, which has been shown to exhibit periodic rhythms in its feeding behaviour, manifest as higher rates of ingestion during the day than at night.[248] These rhythmic activities of *O. marina* seem very likely to be circadian in nature, for they are not determined solely by diel light cycles but persist when the cells are subjected to 24 hours of darkness. This suggests that, although the cycle may be entrained by environmental cues, it is governed by endogenous biochemical processes.[249] Given such 24-hour periodicity, it is tempting indeed to extrapolate from human experience to propose that *O. marina* feels both 'hungrier' and more 'awake' during the daytime. However, other flagellates are nocturnal in their habits. Diel variations in feeding rates are also exhibited by bacterivorous nanoflagellates, yet some of these tiny protists graze primarily in the day whereas others graze primarily at night.[250] Perhaps the deeper question unearthed by these differences among protozoans is whether their periodic reduction in activity is itself *caused* by the organism having fed to satiety or merely *coincident* with a cessation of feeding brought on by exogenous (light-related) and/or endogenous (biochemical) rhythms. The diversity in behaviour seems both to substantiate the existence of some sort of parallelism between satiation and a sleep-like state while also calling into question any over-tidy correlation.

The possible equivalence of satiety with a condition akin to sleep may also be felt to have other logical ramifications for the question of consciousness. To the extent that it is not 'like anything' to be in a state of sated sleep (there is no reason for it to be like anything in that no directional self-movement is undertaken), the converse state of 'wakefulness' or 'hunger' lacks a foil, or point of contrast. If my experiential world consists solely of either feeling hungry or not feeling anything at all, i.e. of alternating between 'hunger' and 'nothing', then 'hunger' is my only experience, and in the absence of any counterpoint, it becomes as empty an experience as it is in the case of *Vorticella*.

This perhaps becomes clearer if the putative distinction involves not merely daily or relatively short-lived and above all reversible changes of internal state, but longer-term transformations, as exemplified by the stages of a life cycle. Many sessile ciliates, including the suctorians encountered above,[251] produce motile ciliated larvae called swarmers upon division. Such swarmers do not engage in any feeding, but swim around in search of a suitable location to settle down, and only once this has successfully been completed do they become 'trophic' or food-eating organisms. Any temptation to invoke consciousness in this case is countered by the sessile nature of the feeding stage, a 'suitable location' implying the availability of plentiful nutrition. But what about the swarmers? It is surely an anthropomorphic projection to envision them as 'driven' by hunger.

Or what about when the trophic stage is motile, as in the case of the ciliate pathogen *Ichthyophthirius*,[252] well known for burrowing into the epithelium of freshwater fish and gorging themselves on the cell fragments and blood cells they find there? In this instance, not only is there a clear separation between the infective stage as a free-swimming, host-seeking swarmer (or theront) and the feeding stage as a trophont; there is also a reproductive stage (as a tomont), which is initiated once the voracious trophonts have ballooned from 30–40 micrometres to as much as 1000 micrometres in size[253] and 'satiety' is reached. Again, there is something like a division of labour among the distinct life stages: the theront does nothing but seek a host; the trophont does nothing but eat. It is difficult to imagine it being 'like' anything to be a trophont because eating is the only thing it ever does, 'hunger' the only condition it ever knows. For the duration of the trophont's life *as a trophont*, it is an 'eating machine'. Or is it legitimate to speak of a 'hungry' stage and a 'non-hungry' stage of what is, after all, the same self?

A further point of comparison is provided by a naked amoeba known as *Flabellula baltica*, which is able to adopt a variety of morphotypes according to its nutritional circumstances.[254] By contrast with other organisms, *Flabellula* can switch between its six morphs in a relatively flexible way that in many cases need not be irreversible.[255] The most characteristic type is the fan-morph, which has a single broad pseudopod at the front and can be considered the food-seeking form, appearing when nutrition becomes scarce and lending itself to dispersal. The fan-morph can transform itself into any other morphotype and back. If food continues to be in short supply for more than a few hours, fan-morphs change into 'resting' stages, either as pseudocysts, 'pancake' morphs or the flamboyantly named 'Salvador Dali' morphs, all characterized by minimal motility. Trophozoites are the 'feeding' cells. Compared to the fan-morphs, these too are relatively slow-moving, because it pays for them not to stray too far from where food has been found. At the same time, they have a substantially higher metabolic rate than resting cells, as reflected in the fraction of their volume taken up by mitochondria.[256] Again, various questions present themselves, such as whether one might envision the condition of a pseudocyst, for example, as akin to 'sleep', or describe a fan-morph as hungry, or a well-fed trophozoite as satiated. Does it in any sense *feel different* to be a Salvador Dali morph from a trophozoite? Or is a trophozoite rather to be considered on its own terms: as a mere 'eating machine', endowed with no more consciousness than *Vorticella*?

There is certainly something to the objection that the parallelism between the hunger-satiety dichotomy and the wakefulness-sleep dichotomy – or even longer-term distinctions based on life stages – deprives 'hunger' of an experiential counterpoint, thus leaving it empty of content and, logically speaking, postponing the appearance of rudimentary consciousness for the time being. Yet two possible responses spring to mind. The first response is that the above line of argument misinterprets the hunger in question as an object of explicit reflection, whereas it is in fact a *pre-reflective* form of self-awareness, i.e. an expression of the underlying tacit selfhood that necessarily shapes or structures our perception. This being so, what distinguishes experiential state A from experiential state B – and thus provides a logical foundation for the emergence of consciousness – may inhere in what is perceived rather than in the tacit selfhood of the perceiver. The relevant difference might therefore be between hungrily perceiving a paramecium and hungrily perceiving a diatom or perhaps hungrily perceiving nothing palatable at all. We have already encountered the 'preferences' of *A. proteus*. The existence of such preferences implies that hungrily perceiving a favourite prey item is *not the same as* hungrily perceiving a lower-ranked snack, differing behaviourally in the likelihood with which it motivates directional self-movement (for example, when a choice is available).

The second, associated response is that, like wakefulness, hunger need not inevitably be an all-or-nothing phenomenon, a binary state that can be switched on and off with no gradations in between. In some cases, we may be able to speak of 'degrees' of hunger, a series of rungs on a ladder of increasing appetite ranging from 'satiated' to 'famishing'. Hungrily perceiving a paramecium can be taken to be different from doing so in a *very* hungry or a ravenous state.[257] In practice, different levels of appetite may manifest themselves through variations in clearance rates. The time taken by a given culture of bacterivorous protozoans to clear a population of bacteria will thus depend on whether the protozoans have been starved or recently fed. The ingestion rate of *O. marina* may drop from exceedingly high levels of 35 algal cells per individual per hour at the beginning of a meal to stabilize at four cells per hour after 100 minutes of feeding.[258] As mentioned above, moreover, *Oxyrrhis* shows relative but not absolute discrepancies between night and day.[259]

Differences in appetite also come to light in the *selectivity* of predators, bringing us back to the notion of preferences. Such behavioural flexibility has been demonstrated, for example, in two species of small bacterivorous flagellates, which were offered particles of similar size but divergent nutritional quality (bacteria on the one hand, latex beads on the other) in conditions of changing food abundance.[260] The flagellates became markedly more 'choosy' when food was more abundant and they were (presumably) less hungry;[261] the poorly rated food was chosen relatively less, and the more 'desirable' food was chosen more. As hunger increased, the flagellates were more likely to take whatever they could get.[262] Such behaviour is considered to conform to 'optimal diet models', which prove to be adaptive in the context of natural variations in the quality and quantity of food: 'weaker selection under starvation', note Klaus Jürgens and William R. DeMott, 'increases the chance to acquire nutritive particles even when they are not bacteria (detritus and perhaps viruses and macromolecules). Under high food concentrations, more selective feeding should increase net energy uptake by excluding poor-quality particles from food vacuoles that might be occupied by high-quality particles'.[263] The strange thing is that such behavioural patterns are not universal. Populations of marine ciliates have been found to become *more* choosy when food is short.[264]

Statistical analyses of this sort receive further corroboration from observations of variations in the conduct of individual organisms. One might cite the example of dileptids setting upon potential prey organisms, where the occurrence of subsequent ingestion is seen to depend on the amount of feeding that has already taken place.[265] Or the cannibalistic attacks witnessed among populations of the dinoflagellate *Polykrikos kofoidii* only in circumstances where other prey are scarce – and at the end of which the mutually antagonistic predators end up pulling free from one another instead of proceeding with the engulfment.[266] Two per cent of *O. marina* individuals actually proceed to engulf their conspecifics, but again only when food is short.[267] Despite possible doubts and reservations, therefore, it does seem legitimate to speak of protozoan hunger, manifest in the behavioural variability not only of our trusty *Amoeba proteus* but a wealth of other species whose activities have been both observed individually and recorded statistically.

Appetite, Motivation and Pleasure

Hunger and appetite have at times been described as emotions. The neurophysiologist Derek Denton, for example, uses the term 'primal' or 'primordial' emotion to refer to what he calls the 'subjective element of instinctive behaviour', which 'subserves control of the vegetative systems of the body'.[268] Also referred to as 'homeostatic' emotions,[269] primal emotions such as thirst and hunger monitor and regulate the constancy of the body's internal conditions, prompting *behaviour* whenever this is necessary to counter an inner imbalance. According to Denton, such primordial emotions represent the origins of consciousness.[270] The neuroscientist E. T. Rolls, by contrast, opts to use the word 'emotion' to denote 'states elicited by rewards and punishers', where a reward is 'anything for which an animal will work' and a punisher is 'anything that an animal will work to escape or avoid'.[271] In these terms, 'emotion' corresponds more to the state that arises from the *satisfaction* of an appetite, or to that associated with a failure to avert harm or homeostatic disequilibrium.

Yet the use of the term 'emotion' in the context of appetites and their satisfaction is not uncontroversial. To be sure, both emotions and appetites are *feelings* in the sense that it 'feels like something' to be angry or hungry. Subtler light is thrown on the matter, however, by the dissection of the concept of a 'feeling' – in all its bewildering breadth – undertaken by Bennett and Hacker.[272] This includes not only affections such as emotions (feeling love or hatred, fear or jealousy) and moods (feeling happy or gloomy), but also feelings in the sense of bodily sensations (feeling pain or pleasure, feeling ill or well, feeling warm or cold), feelings in the sense of tactile perceptions (feeling a cold object or a rough surface), as well as feelings in the sense of appetites (feeling hungry, thirsty or lustful). Although both emotions and appetites are something we are said to 'feel', they do not belong in the same category of 'feeling'. The word is being employed in a different way.

It is misleading, therefore, to refer either to the appetite displayed by a hungry amoeba or the state arising from its satisfaction as an 'emotion' (even though in humans both appetites and appetitive satisfactions may well be *accompanied by* or *associated with* emotions). The attribution of an appetite to a single-celled organism is not in itself tantamount to the attribution of an emotion. Given the contentious nature of claims ascribing even minimal psychological states to protozoans, the aim in the present subchapter is to clarify the terminology in order to leave no doubt as to what those claims are. This will involve specifying the precise implications of – and possible objections to – the use of terms such as 'hunger', 'pleasure' and 'motivation' in a unicellular context.

At least part of the reason for the confusion between appetites and emotions is the component of value they have in common. Just as emotions are aroused by things that mean something to us, i.e. by circumstances or people about which we care and to which we are not indifferent, appetites and their possible gratification likewise presuppose a world that *matters* to us. The foundation of an organism's drive to perform the requisite work to get from here (no food) to there (food) is the elementary self-concern that spurs the organism to stay alive and that divides the world into what is good or better (for self) and what is bad or worse (for self). At bottom, it is by virtue of this relative goodness or badness – or perhaps by virtue of the relative pleasure or discomfort to which this goodness or badness gives rise – that the world is infused with valence or value to a self-interested self.

In this valenced world tasty prey are perceived *as* tasty, and menacing predators are perceived *as* menacing. These are properties that are not intrinsic to the entities in themselves but that arise through their relationship to the self-concerned self. At this rudimentary level, all consciousness of the world is structured and charged with life-sustaining or life-threatening value or significance. What is irrelevant or neutral is not perceived: the less appetizing diatom or the unappetizing detritus can be assumed simply not to be present to the amoeba when the hungry predator is focusing on a coveted paramecium. Our human notion of a world of 'indifferent' phenomena – a world perceived as though through a lens of unconcerned or carefree objectivity – is very much a derived form of experience.

To reiterate: a world infused with value to a self-concerned self is what makes emotion possible, yet the word 'emotion' is not usually employed in such a broad, basal sense. Appetites such as hunger are not normally categorized as emotions. The terms 'emotion' and 'motivation' have lent themselves to analogous confusion, both of them etymologically rooted in the idea of movement, or rather the *cause of movement*. The greater logical proximity is in fact between motivation and appetite, which are two sides of the same coin: if we have an appetite such as hunger, then we are *ceteris paribus* motivated to search for food. The feeling of hunger incorporates the unease that disposes us to make the necessary self-movement to satisfy the appetite. To make a claim about unicellular appetite is thus also to make a claim about unicellular motivation, but not a claim about emotion.

Three archetypal appetites are commonly cited: hunger as a desire for (i.e. a motivation to search for) food, thirst as a desire for drink, and lust as a desire for sexual intercourse.[273] In the context of amoebae, however, it is the first that can be pinpointed as fundamental, to the extent that thirst only induces a search for water once animals have moved onto dry land, and reproduction only calls for a search for a mate if it is sexual in nature or involves conjugation (as sometimes in bacteria and ciliates). For an aquatic organism that divides by mitosis and passes its genome from generation to generation without partnering its conspecifics, the primordial search is the quest for food. An appetite for prey, not drink or sex, is the motivation that spurs the solitary amoeba to move itself from here to there.

Motivation or appetite can be defined in terms of reward and in terms of the work that an organism is willing to perform in order to attain the reward.[274] The ethologist Wallace Craig wrote one of the most lucid papers on the nature of appetite (in a multicellular context), specifying it as 'a state of agitation which continues so long as a certain stimulus, which may be called the appeted stimulus, is absent. When the appeted stimulus is at length received it stimulates a consummatory reaction, after which the appetitive behavior ceases and is succeeded by a state of relative rest'. Such a state of agitation, which may also be associated with aversion, is 'exhibited externally by increased muscular tension; by static and phasic contractions of many skeletal and dermal muscles, giving rise to bodily attitudes and gestures which are easily recognized signs or "expressions" of appetite or of aversion; by restlessness; by activity, in extreme cases violent activity; and by "varied effort"'. Once the consummatory action has taken place, adds Craig, the organism is said to be 'satisfied'.[275] Appetite is thus logically linked with the possibility of reward or satisfaction, or – to use a more loaded but also more expressive term – with the possibility of *pleasure*.

A key implication of Craig's analysis is that in such cases the immediate aim or purpose of the organism's activity inheres not in its survival value (say, the restoration of an internal chemical balance), but in the gratification or satisfaction of an appetite by a consummatory act. A dehydrated organism thus drinks copiously not in order to rectify a lower-than-optimal plasma volume or reduce an excessive salt concentration, but to slake its thirst; a starved organism eats not in order to redress a shortage of glucose, but to quell its hunger. The case of thirst is vividly illustrated by Derek Denton, who describes the life-saving ability of many herbivorous animals to find a water hole, quench their thirst as rapidly as possible, and leave the area immediately to avoid the threat of lurking predators. Whereas thirst is produced by *gradual* changes in blood chemistry, notes Denton, it is gratified within three to five minutes, followed by an abrupt decline in the desire to drink. This is long before the water imbibed could have been absorbed from the gut or used to rectify the chemical imbalance in bodily fluids that gave rise to the thirst in the first place. Such rapid satiation is achieved by a conjunction of sensory data, including the taste of water in the mouth and nerve impulses 'metering the passage of water through the pharynx and upper oesophagus' and 'signalling distension from [the] filling of the stomach with water': input from these sources, he writes, 'is jointly sufficient and severally necessary to contrive satiation and a precipitate decline in interest'.[276]

In other words, it is the pleasure of the 'reward' (that for which it has performed the work of pursuit and ingestion) that mediates the subsequent benefits for the organism. A distinction is sometimes drawn between proximate and ultimate causes. In this instance, the immediate pleasure of satisfying one's hunger, quenching one's thirst or finding sexual gratification is the *proximate* cause that motivates behaviour of a certain sort (i.e. the work invested in the search or the chase); the fact that such behaviour is in the interests of the organism in terms of its well-being, fitness and chances of reproductive success is the *ultimate* cause that justifies it as a viable existential strategy. Accordingly, the implicit anticipation and the attainment of pleasure function as a signal, albeit not a wholly reliable one, of what is *good for self*.[277] To return to our eukaryotes: if we conceive of an amoeba as 'hungry' in its pursuit of prey, the logical correlate of this is that the satisfaction of its appetite is in some sense 'rewarding' or 'pleasurable' to it. To describe the amoeba as driven by its appetite is to claim that it is motivated by the implicit prospect of a reward, in that an appetite is definitionally bound up with the possible pleasure of its satisfaction. The 'preferences' noted by Gibbs and Dellinger, moreover, suggest that the consumption of big, juicy, nutritious paramecia produces greater pleasure than that of smaller ciliates, which in turn is more pleasurable than that of diatoms and lesser morsels.

The distinction between proximate and ultimate causation – between the motivational mechanism that produces self-movement and the evolutionary function of this self-movement in terms of efficient self-maintenance and successful self-reproduction – implies that when an organism engages in an activity such as eating its 'favourite' food this is on the one hand because it is in its interests to do so (the ultimate cause) and on the other hand because it feels good (the proximate cause). In these terms, pleasure can be understood as a reward for adaptive behaviour, motivating a self to pursue what is *good for self*. It is a vehicle, writes ethologist Jonathan Balcombe, 'by which nature promotes evolutionary success'. It can be considered 'one of the blessings of adaptation'.[278]

The fundamental nature of this dual impulse to do what is good for oneself and eschew what is bad for oneself has led many to believe that the mediatory role of pleasure and pain must reside at the very roots of consciousness. One of Darwin's best-known followers, the evolutionary biologist George Romanes, placed the distinction between pleasure and pain, or between more and less pleasure, at the origins of the evolution of mind and subjectivity:

> *[In] whatever way the inconceivable connection between Body and Mind came to be established, the primary cause of its establishment, or of the dawn of subjectivity, may have been this very need of inducing organisms to avoid the deleterious, and to seek the beneficial; the raison d'être of Consciousness may have been that of supplying the condition to the feeling of Pleasure and Pain. ... Indeed, if we contemplate the subject, we shall find it difficult or impossible to imagine a form of consciousness, however dim, which does not present, in a correspondingly undeveloped condition, the capacity of preferring some of its states to others.*[279]

Pleasure, pain and the concomitant consciousness of a (pleasure- and pain-producing) world are adaptive measures that indicate what it is in our interests to do and not to do.

More recently, this notion of the adaptive utility of pleasure has been taken up by the physiologist Michel Cabanac, who has highlighted the homeostatic nature of pleasure: when we feel cold, we are motivated to seek warmth, and this warmth feels good; when the warmth becomes too much for us, we look for a cooler place. When we are hungry, we search for food, and once we have found it, eating it is acutely enjoyable. Once we have sated our appetite, our enjoyment rapidly declines, and before long we stop.[280] Cabanac indeed describes pleasure as the 'common currency' by which the relative strengths of motivational drives can be compared and appropriate action undertaken.[281] In other words, when there are competing or clashing motivations (such as food intake versus thermoregulation; pursuit of prey versus inactivity), pleasure is the yardstick by which an organism ranks its priorities and optimizes its behaviour. In Cabanac's view, the 'algebraic summation' of pleasure and displeasure occurs 'not only within one sensory modality such as taste, but across different modalities of perception and experience'.[282] An example of such cross-sensory assessment might relate to how much cold an organism is willing to tolerate, or how much work it is willing to perform, in order to attain a nutritious treat, the resultant behaviour thus representing a disposition to maximize the sum of pleasure.

In the field of behavioural ecology, the actions of organisms are often regarded as corresponding to what is optimal on a cost-benefit curve: the 'common currency' enables the animal to weigh up rewards and costs and then choose the behaviour with the maximal net reward or minimal aversive outcome. Although pleasure thus serves as the common currency of decision-making, there is no implication that the ensuing decision need be a product of conscious reasoning or deliberation. What such decision-making does presuppose is a creature that is conscious *of the world* and can choose rationally among its behavioural options on the basis of expected outcomes.[283] 'Rationality' here refers not to logical argument, therefore, but simply to behaviour that promotes the well-being of the organism itself[284]; it is the rationality of a 'selfish' or 'self-interested' self that (by definition) *has reason* to pursue its own interests.[285] Once endowed with the gift of motivated, directional self-movement, a self thus becomes an entity that has not only interests but also the capacity to behave or take action *in accordance with* those interests. It is with motivated locomotion that 'interests' in a genuinely intrinsically reflexive sense – interests as gauged and pursued by a self rather than ascribed by an 'other' (i.e. an observer) – come into being. Defined in terms of appetites and pleasures, true self-interest co-emerges with the motivated self-movement or behaviour that permits its pursuit.

Such an understanding of pleasure as a sensation that may be attributed not only to humans and dogs but also to nematodes and amoebae will be anathema to many. It is argued, understandably, that most animals have their work cut out simply ensuring their immediate survival; there can hardly be time for an animal to indulge in 'happiness'.[286] However, the claim here is not about 'happiness', a notoriously slippery concept at the best of times. Nor is the aim to analyse specifically *human* pleasure, but rather to confront its deepest logical (and phylogenetic) origins. The present claim thus relates to basalmost pleasure, which can be reduced to little more than a preference for certain sorts of physiological states over others, but which nonetheless infuses the world with a valence and significance specific to any particular individual at any particular moment of his, her or its life. After a while without refuelling, it *matters* to me as it does to an amoeba to get my paws or my pseudopods on something to eat.

Further factors have fostered time-worn dismissals of pleasure. The very term 'pleasure' has traditionally been weighed down by ideological connotations suggesting the sensual abandon or moral self-indulgence of hedonism, while the doctrine of utilitarianism – which raises the pleasure of others to a principle of moral guidance – has tended to be spurned as too calculating and rational. The deeper point here, however, is the morally neutral one that pleasure and displeasure provide the ultimate foundation from which the motivations for the actions of selves, human and non-human alike, can be properly understood. This point is 'morally neutral' because it is not a matter of celebrating or lamenting how good or bad people or animals are, but of unpacking the non-obvious implications of the word 'self'. To the extent that a self is conceived as the unit of selfishness or self-interest, and to the extent that pleasure is conceived as the common currency that serves as a basic (though far from infallible) yardstick for what actually *is* in one's interests, a self-moving self is a *pursuer of pleasure*. Within this analytical or conceptual framework, it makes perfectly good sense at a human level to speak of the pleasures of the ascetic life, self-sacrifice and renunciation, and more generally of the deferral of pleasure. The pursuit of pleasure may well follow a circuitous route.

Yet the proposed conceptual association between self-movement and the pursuit of pleasure may be doubted for other reasons too. In addition to the traditional moral misgivings about pleasure, there is the self-evident disjunction between pleasure and utility, i.e. the failure of what is pleasurable to coincide with what is 'good'. This is typified by the delights associated with the consumption of *intoxicants*, which are said to hijack the reward pathways designed to motivate us to eat and to mate.[287] Intoxication is dangerous and maladaptive,[288] and animals with a predilection for the pleasures conferred by psychoactive plants tend to be more accident-prone, vulnerable to predators, and neglectful of their offspring. Another, more debatable illustration of the apparent non-coincidence of pleasure and utility is the archetypically 'non-functional' pleasure of *play*, which is often defined as activity that is *autotelic* or an 'end in itself'. In the case of play, however, longer-term benefits are generally considered likely to compensate for the hazards it may occasion and the energetic extravagance it represents.[289]

The connection between what is pleasurable and what is in one's interests is perhaps most graphically undermined by the timelessly well-attested fact that most children need to be force-fed what is 'good' for them. In the popular imagination 'healthy' and 'fun' tend to be regarded as more or less antonymous. Again, however, a widespread proclivity to stuff our face with sugary treats of dubious nutritional value should probably be understood as harking back in evolutionary terms to a time where our sugar intake took the form not of milk chocolate and caramel goo but of ripe fruit loaded with energy, minerals and vitamins, and a sugar-rich fruit-based diet was of unquestionable benefit.

Although the link between pleasure and what is *good for self* is certainly flawed, therefore, such flaws are derived or secondary effects in complex systems where sub-optimal 'viability' will in most cases do the trick. Importantly, an amoeba's sense of what is good for itself can be presumed to be reliable enough, statistically speaking, to ensure that it passes on its genes to the next generation. Jennings hits the nail on the head, once again, in discussing the concept of 'choice': in its regulatory sense, he notes, choice 'is not perfect ... in either lower or higher organisms. Paramecium at times accepts things that are useless or harmful to it, but perhaps on the whole less often than does man'.[290]

Persistent sceptics will question whether the satisfaction of an appetite really is a sufficient condition to speak of 'pleasure'. A distinction has been drawn in psychology between 'liking' and 'wanting',[291] where the key feature of 'liking' is that it is reflected in positive behavioural reactions to the 'immediate hedonic impact of pleasurable events', whereas 'wanting' is not considered a sensory pleasure or an inherently 'hedonic' state and does not 'potentiate positive affective reactions to pleasure'.[292] Pleasure-less, compulsive drives and addictions are spotlighted as cases of wanting rather than liking. Surely, one might suppose, the 'hunger' of an amoeba is a case of pleasure-less wanting rather than hedonic liking. This impression is reinforced by the failure of amoebae to exhibit any 'positive affective reactions' when they engulf paramecia. After all, they have no lips to lick, no eyes to roll, no vocal cords with which to emit hyperbolic groans of delight; they are not even equipped with the taste buds that would enable them to *enjoy* their meal. Can there be gastronomic pleasure without taste buds?

Two related points need to be made. The reason an amoeba neither has nor needs taste buds is that – amongst many other things – it *is* its taste buds. The amoeba's 'tasting' or 'smelling' of the chemical cues that emanate from potential prey organisms is precisely what alerts it to the nearby presence of something desirable. Moreover, the nature of the relationship between pleasure and the expression of pleasure is itself a matter of contention. Many mammals exhibit positive and negative 'affective reactions' to taste in the form of facial and gestural expressions. These resemble human reactions and lend themselves to hedonic interpretation. Monkeys and apes repeatedly stick out their tongue if offered something sweet; rats likewise show rhythmic tongue protrusions. Bitter tastes elicit a triangular gape, head shakes and arm shakes.[293] The 'yuck!' displays shown by mammals or birds on interacting with distasteful food items have been found to put observing conspecifics off similar items, signalling unpalatability and fostering the social acquisition of avoidance behaviours.[294] Yet if a non-social animal, in consuming its preferred prey, *failed* to produce a hedonic response but simply gobbled up its meal with no public expression of delectation, would we withhold the ascription of pleasure on these grounds? The absence of an overt expression of pleasure should not be confused with the absence of pleasure. 'Watch someone eating' suggests Jonathan Balcombe.[295] 'Especially if they are alone, you won't find facial expressions or other conclusive signs that the food is pleasurable'.

The social component in the expression of pleasure is likely, therefore, to rule out any such expression on the part of the solitary amoeba. Imagine the hypothetical case of an amoeba endowed with a flagellum-like appendage which it wagged vigorously on perceiving, capturing or ingesting a paramecium.[296] What could such a signal possibly be *for*? Would we be any more justified in attributing pleasure to the creature merely on the basis of this wagging? The basalmost behavioural sign of pleasure is not lip-licking or tail-wagging, but the fact that a self-interested self will *perform work in order to reach the target or attain the gratification in question* (not always, but sometimes: i.e. until it is sated or has had enough, or until the pleasure has turned stale).[297]

Yet this still fails to rule out the possibility that zombie-like 'wanting' may be the only form of appetite available to expression-less amoebae, or any other expression-less creatures. Proponents of this view would insist that less mentalistic terms such as 'utility' or 'reward' are perfectly adequate to describe what is going on when an organism makes the requisite behavioural adjustments to optimize its performance.[298] It is superfluous, they would say, to posit any explicit awareness of pleasure. But this is just the point. Explicit self-awareness *is not implied* by the above account of appetite and the concomitant possibility of pleasure, which are conceived not as objects of attention (so-called 'intentional' objects) but as part of the tacit or pre-reflective selfhood of a self-concerned self. The claim, in short, is not that the organisms in question have a capacity to reflect on their pleasure. What they experience is not reflectively conscious pleasure.[299] They do not think: 'boy, this is pleasurable!' or 'life just doesn't get any better than ingesting juicy paramecia!' Pleasure in this elementary sense is merely the pre-reflective experiential corollary of a successfully pursued reward. It is the pleasure-giving world – not the mental state – that is the object of the predator's attention.

Further Aspects of Tacit Selfhood: Pain and Emotion

Consciousness of the world – even of a world that consists of little more than paramecia, diatoms and lesser morsels – is always structured and shaped by the tacit selfhood of the self-interested self that is conscious. In this respect, consciousness is necessarily *tendentious*, involving a perspective[300]: namely, from me, here, now, hungry or otherwise, perhaps also anxious or angry, drowsy or distressed. Incorporating appetites, motivations and possibly emotions, this tacit selfhood is the precondition and foundation for the possibility of our consciousness of the world, enabling an organism to focus its attention on meaningful non-self and to perceive prey *as* prey, and predators *as* predators. In answer to the question whether the organism 'knows' that it is hungry or is 'aware' of its pleasure in satisfying its hunger, an appeal might be made to a time-honoured distinction between dispositional and propositional knowledge. Though not propositionally explicit, its appetite is what tacitly guides its disposition to move itself appropriately to where food is. The organism *embodies* and thus *is* its appetite, together with the attendant implicit anticipation of reward. This is what structures both its (tendentious) awareness of the world and its choice of action.

The conception of tacit or pre-reflective self-awareness is a crucial feature of phenomenological thought, going back to Husserl's insight that 'to be a subject is to be in the mode of being aware of oneself'.[301] For Heidegger too, experience of the world from a subjective perspective is indissolubly bound up with co-disclosure of the self. On this view, self-awareness is not something derived, secondary or 'higher-level' that may be optionally 'added on' to supplement a more basal form of consciousness; rather, it accompanies and shapes consciousness from the outset, albeit in a tacit or implicit form. This is not to deny that – in humans at least – these tacitly present appetites, pleasures, pains, moods or emotions may on occasion *become* the objects of explicit awareness. Although we do not need to be expressly conscious of our interoceptive signals (of hunger or satiety) for these to organize our perception of the world, we *may* become conscious of them, for example if a problem is encountered, if an obstacle needs to be overcome, or if our stomach rumbles obtrusively. While they may contribute to the phenomenology of hunger, however, our stomach contractions and the accompanying cacophony are no more the cause of hunger than a dry throat is the cause of thirst.[302] In both cases, it is a homeostatic imbalance that generates the appetite, the generalized feeling of which may be augmented by specific bodily sensations that subsequently enter our consciousness.

Appetites such as hunger, thirst or sexual drive are just one aspect of tacit selfhood among many others that shape our consciousness of the world. In the case of human and non-human animals, further crucial factors include pain and an array of emotions and moods. The present subchapter will look briefly at these aspects of pre-reflective self-awareness and their possible presence in protists, while leaving out of account other, more complex aspects such as corollary discharge and proprioception[303] which seem less likely – if only for anatomical reasons – to have analogues in the unicellular realm. In particular, it will focus on pain as a basalmost response to the world (or to what is harmful in the world) that is commonly thought to underlie and structure consciousness in a manner akin to an appetite, albeit resulting in movement *away* rather than *towards*.

The parallels between pain and hunger are striking. Philosopher Sydney S. Shoemaker famously argued[304] that one's awareness that one is in pain does not involve a kind of perception of oneself, conceived on the model of one's sensory perception of the external world. Nor does my sense of being in pain involve an act of identification (I do not have to recognize myself as the person of whom pain is predicated); pain is thus immune from the possibility of mis-identification. By contrast with the ascription of pain to other people, the self-ascription of pain is not based on criteria and does not require evidence. As Bennett and Hacker put it, no more grounds – whether behavioural or introspective – are required to say that one has a headache when one has a migraine 'than a groan of pain needs grounds'.[305] Philosophers of mind have traditionally mused on the existence of a sort of privileged 'inner access' or a logically private 'inner sense' that a person has to his or her own pain,[306] but this leaves unanswered the question how I recognize my inner sense as *my* inner sense unless I already have some prior sense of myself as myself. This is where our tacit selfhood steps in. As with hunger and other, similar psychological attributes, self-recognition is superfluous to the extent that a pain is something I not only have but *am*: the reason I cannot misidentify myself as the bearer of a particular pain is that *I am that pain*. There is no logical separation between the knower and what is known.[307] When I have a toothache my discomfort and my desire for it to stop structure and shape my entire perception of the world.

We have seen that Romanes and other thinkers locate pleasure and pain at the very origins of consciousness, regarding them as the most rudimentary manifestation of mind or subjectivity. As neurologist Antonio Damasio points out, however, pleasure and pain are not mirror images of one another, but 'asymmetric physiological states', belonging to 'two different genealogies of life regulation'.[308] Indeed, there is a sense in which the opposite of 'pleasure' is not 'pain' but 'less pleasure' or 'discomfort', and it is by no means obvious in what sense, if at all, the lower rungs of this scale of pleasure coincide with pain. This in turn raises the question of whether pain really is linked to consciousness in the same primordial way as pleasure, i.e. whether pain and pleasure are *equally basal* components of consciousness.[309]

For a start, a distinction is frequently drawn between suffering and nociception, where the latter refers to a reflex to withdraw from something harmful or damaging. Inflexible and to a certain extent *non-directional* withdrawal responses to stimuli such as heat, electrical currents, noxious chemicals and mechanical interference occur across the spectrum of motile organisms from bacteria and protozoa to insects and vertebrates. When poked with a fine needle, for example, paramecia modulate the rate at which their cilia beat – by means of changes in the electrical properties of the cell membrane – so as to take evasive action and avoid the mechanical insult.[310] If 'irritated' by water turbulence or sudden changes in acidity, cryptomonads may be seen to zigzag rapidly away, performing a non-directional, random escape movement or 'jump' triggered by the rapid expulsion of a pent-up protein ribbon known as an 'ejectisome'.[311] As an invariable reflex, nociception implies not that an organism is *conscious* of an unpleasant experience or its cause, but simply that its body registers a harmful stimulus and is immediately prompted to recoil from it. By contrast with appetite, indeed, a painful stimulus is one that is already present.[312] Accordingly, there is no call for anything like a self-guided search or pursuit involving perception at a distance. The resulting 'escape' movement is relatively indiscriminate: more or less anywhere will do, provided that it is AWAY! If the cause of pain is at *a*, it is simply a matter of getting to *not-a* as quickly as possible (where *not-a* is circumscribed solely by the bounds of physical feasibility). To the extent that pain is deemed no more than a nociceptive reflex, therefore, it seems that there is no need to invoke *consciousness* of the cause of harm, whether in protozoans or metazoans.

To be sure, pain may fulfil other functions, inducing creatures to protect injured body parts while they heal ('pain guarding') and above all keeping them away from what has harmed them in the past – although it can only serve this latter purpose in conjunction with a capacity for associative learning. The question, therefore, is how extensively these other functions are found among living organisms. There has been a pervasive reluctance to attribute anything more than nociception to invertebrates. Yet whereas insects, for example, are generally considered not to show limping behaviour or 'guard' injured bodily parts,[313] there is abundant evidence of learning in invertebrates such as fruit flies, snails, leeches, locusts, bees and molluscs, all of which learn to withdraw from a conditioned stimulus that has previously been paired with an electric shock.[314] In particular, highly intelligent cephalopods such as octopuses – some of which are also known to tend and guard their injuries[315] – suggest that across-the-board dismissals of invertebrate pain are overhasty.

Unlike invertebrates, unicellular organisms are generally assumed to have at most a minimal capacity to learn from experience, although the matter is far from cut and dried.[316] The morphological flexibility and the absence of limbs characteristic of amoeboid protozoans seem likely to render pain guarding superfluous, and the idea of flagellates or ciliates 'tending' their wounded flagella or cilia is bordering on the frivolous. To the extent that these premises are justified, the 'pain' of protists can indeed be reduced to a matter of nociceptive withdrawal (i.e. an invariant and relatively non-directional reflex) and need not be associated with conscious awareness of whatever is causing them harm. As yet, however, these assumptions should remain provisional. A relevant finding would be some form of (preferably directional)[317] learned avoidance behaviour in protozoans.

By contrast with invertebrates and protists, it is generally accepted that the response of most vertebrate animals to painful stimuli goes beyond a mere reflex withdrawal, including not only learning, general immobility and guarding, but also a persisting loss of appetite and reduced sexual activity. Whereas insects and arachnids do not seem to 'mind' their pain (if such they have), vertebrates certainly give the impression of doing so. Analogy with humans suggests that vertebrates in general have a capacity to feel bad or even 'miserable'.[318] What is awful about pain, it often seems, is *an associated emotional state*. The notion of 'not minding' a pain may seem counterintuitive or even contradictory to the extent that a pain is something that we by definition do mind having. Nonetheless, the distinction between 'having' and 'minding' a pain is known to exist in certain cases of excruciating human pain, as shown by the emotional transformation that occurs when specific parts of the frontal lobes are operated on in people with the condition trigeminal neuralgia, or *tic douloureux*.[319] Damasio thus draws a distinction between 'pain sensation' and 'pain affect', pointing out how certain drugs (analgesics) can block the sensory awareness of pain, while others such as Valium or beta-blockers do not affect the signal transmission of tissue damage but blunt the emotion and thus do away with the *suffering* that would have otherwise accompanied the pain.[320] Human pain is a multidimensional phenomenon, involving a whole nexus of affective and cognitive factors that may include stress, anxiety and depression.

There is a sense, therefore, in which the attendant emotions may represent a large part of what is *bad* about pain, or what turns pain into *suffering*. Insofar as the pain undergone by non-human animals is dissociated from emotion (less burdened, perhaps, by time-dependent factors such as anticipation and the anxiety to which this gives rise), it may be felt that their suffering is in some sense *less severe* than human suffering. However, there are clear indications that mammals such as rats scarcely differ from humans in this regard, displaying a number of bodily corollaries of fear in anticipation of pain.[321] Moreover, animal suffering seems to be connected with other affections and states of mind instead of or as well as pain. Animal scientist Temple Grandin accordingly claims that for animals fear is 'worse' than pain,[322] while Hans Jonas associates animal suffering not directly with pain, but with the exigencies of unsated appetite: 'the suffering intrinsic in animal existence', he writes, 'is thus primarily not that of pain (which is occasional and a concomitant) but that of want and fear, i.e., an aspect of appetitive nature as such'.[323]

*

There is no doubt that – along with appetites – *affections* constitute an integral part of the tacit selfhood of mammals and especially humans.[324] Affections in this sense include not only emotions such as fear, anger or love, but also shorter-term affective disturbances, or 'agitations', such as excitement, amazement or disgust, as well as longer-term dispositional states, or 'moods', such as depression, joy, boredom, irritability or cheerfulness.[325] Within the context of tacit selfhood, the point is that although the individual emotions, moods and agitations may be transient, consciousness itself cannot be conceived except as structured by *some sort of* affection or appetite. Although the range of affections may be much smaller, the same principle applies equally to non-human consciousness.

In *Consciousness Explained*, Dennett notes that wherever there is a conscious mind there is a *point of view*, highlighting this as 'one of the most fundamental ideas we have about minds – or about consciousness'. As a general rule, he adds, 'we can consider the point of view of a particular conscious subject to be just that: a point moving through space-time'.[326] This is quite right, but it is much too weak a conception of perspectivity. As a conscious self (human or unicellular), I am not merely the constant occupant of my own spatio-temporal whereabouts (namely here, now), but an intrinsically reflexive being to whom it intrinsically *matters* when I am where. Possessed of an appetite, I thus move myself from here to there in order to reach, for example, wherever I perceive my food to be or anticipate it being. To recapitulate a formulation proposed in the Introduction: to the extent that it is self-contained, a self is always here, now; to the extent that it concurrently transcends itself, a self goes beyond the here and now, opening out towards the there and then. Given my nature as a self-interested and self-moving self, I perceive the world through the tendentious prism of my own selfishness, a prism necessarily shaped or structured by the appetites and affections that I am and embody. In this sense, my 'attunement' to the world – Heidegger uses the word *Stimmung*, which suggests not only 'mood' but a musical tuning – is not something intermittent or transient, but a fundamental mode of being in the world. It is the underlying precondition for the *specific* emotions, moods, appetites or agitations that come and go with varying degrees of awareness.[327]

Yet although the tacit selfhood of humans may be coloured (as we know from our own experience) by a multitude of emotions and moods, the question is just how far basalmost or unicellular consciousness is susceptible to such affections – indeed to anything more than mere appetite, desire, and states of greater or lesser pleasure. Can we attribute even the most primitive of emotions, such as fear, to a retreating amoeba that has one of its more sizeable conspecifics hot on its pseudopodial heels? In the case of fear the answer will depend, at least in part, on whether the escape response is considered a mere reflex. If a chemical cue emitted by a predator *invariably* produces the same non-directional reflex withdrawal, there is presumably no need to posit any further 'awareness' of the predator, any 'emotional' response to its presence, or any subjective sense of it 'being like anything' to react in this way. The explosive 'jump' of a cryptomonad in reply to a chemical or mechanical disturbance should not be taken to imply an affective correlate. The same goes for the insect-like, wingless hexapods known as springtails, which are equipped with a specialized jumping organ, or furcula, that catapults them out of the clutches of potential predators and into the air in a spectacular but uncontrolled leap.[328] Insofar as escape strategies need to be modulated (escape is not always just AWAY!), however, a merely invariable reflex may not be enough. Some capacity to discriminate relevant features of the environment may be required. In animals there is frequently a rather sophisticated mixture of directional and non-directional factors in operation.[329]

The question of unicellular fear was indeed a matter of 19th-century controversy. Whereas Romanes declined to attribute emotions to protists, considering the most ancestral emotions such as fear to have first found expression in worms,[330] Binet countered forcefully that 'there is not a single ciliate Infusory that cannot be frightened, and that does not manifest its fear by a rapid flight through the liquid of the preparation'. If a drop of acetic acid is added to a preparation containing plentiful Infusoria, he pointed out, these will flee in all directions 'like a flock of frightened sheep'.[331] Binet may appear to have succumbed hook, line and sinker to the temptations of anthropomorphism,[332] yet he remained agnostic on the question of consciousness, thus implying the possibility of unconscious fear.

To the extent that Romanes is right to deny unicellulars even the most ancestral of emotions, and to the extent that Binet's sheep-like ciliates are in fact displaying a merely invariant, non-directional aversive response, it would seem that protozoans lead a life animated only by appetite and the possibility of its pleasurable satisfaction or less pleasurable non-satisfaction. However, there is one category of affection that may yet be of relevance to the tacit selfhood of a unicellular predator: namely agitation in the form of varying degrees of arousal, wakefulness, alertness or attention.

Attention, Arousal and Their Absence: Sleep and Anaesthesia

A capacity for *attention* implies the selective spotlighting that makes specifically appropriate action possible. What this means is that a particular signal or set of signals stands out from a manifold of other signals, acquiring meaningfulness through its salience. The importance of being able to focus in this way again comes to light in the paper by Gibbs and Dellinger:

> *An amoeba suddenly placed in the midst of a large number of paramecia, which bump it and knock it about, usually makes no response to the separate stimuli, but seems 'confused'. Later, some amoebas in these circumstances put out pseudopods and may 'pursue' a single paramecium without much regard to touches from the others; while some appear never to get their equilibrium, but move off or take the spherical form.*[333]

Attention is in this respect bound up with the directed targeting of an object implied by intentionality; it suggests the focus required by pursuit. A failure to 'pay attention' results in indecisiveness and inaction, and ultimately in a meal missed. More recently, Dennis Bray has reported the same capacity for attention not only in amoebae but also in the trumpet animalcule *Stentor*, when it embarks on its 'search' for a new site for attachment after being harassed by noxious particles: 'while engaged in this search it ignores other stimuli such as changes in temperature or chemical signals that produce an immediate reaction in a free-living individual'. Attention appears to be necessary, Bray suggests, in that it is 'usually impossible for a cell to react simultaneously to two or more kinds of stimuli'.[334]

Yet caution is due. Jennings[335] describes other circumstances in which the distinct pseudopodia of an amoeba seem to have a mind – in the sense of an intentional focus – of their own. This may occur, for example, when two pseudopodia on opposite sides of the amoeba's body both come into contact with an appetizing encysted *Euglena* cell. Each of them 'stretches out, pulling a portion of the body with it, and follows its cyst, until the body forms two lobes, connected only by a narrow isthmus. Finally, one half succeeds in pulling the other away from the attachment to the substratum, and the entire Amoeba follows the victorious pseudopodium'.[336] It is as though the pseudopods are competing with one another; one might say competing for attention. This attentional split clearly reflects a potential split in selfhood and suggests an episodic lack of integration between transiently existing 'subselves'. But such disharmony is not unique to amoebae. It recalls the alien hand syndrome experienced by people who have undergone commissurotomy, the operation severing the major neural pathways between the two hemispheres of the brain.

In his discussion of *Stentor*, Bray adds that he is using 'attention' here in a 'colloquial' sense to avoid its 'psychological ramifications'. It is not, he reiterates, the same as human attention.[337] Such circumspection seems slightly excessive: *Stentor* attention is certainly not the same as human attention, but it shows undeniable logical and structural similarities. It involves a focus on what *matters* to a self to the exclusion of what does *not* matter, or what matters less. In the modern human world, of course, attention is not normally associated with the pursuit of prey. Other phenomena now concentrate the mind. Pain seems to enjoy privileged status in this respect. More generally, attention is required when cognitive problems arise, i.e. when the automaticity or predictability of routine existence is fractured and new or unexpected challenges have to be confronted. As with *Stentor*, however, this entails a suppression of distractions and the relegation of what is less important to an undefined realm of marginal, deferred or merely potential awareness.

A common question in the philosophy of mind is how far consciousness is to be viewed as synonymous with attention: are we really only conscious of that to which we pay attention? There has been a tendency to dismiss any facile equation of consciousness with attention, arguing that the phenomenal content of experience is not exhausted by what we explicitly notice – think of the hum of the computer or the ticking of the clock – and distinguishing focal from peripheral consciousness. Much experience, it is claimed, goes unnoticed.[338] Yet perhaps this so-called 'phenomenal background' is best understood not as a supplementary kind of object-consciousness, but as akin to, or part of, the pre-reflective awareness of tacit selfhood, a form of structural framework which only comes to the foreground if a problem crops up.[339]

By contrast with human consciousness in all its multisensory and reflective complexity, it seems reasonable to conjecture that elementary consciousness can be reduced to attention with little or no remainder. In ascribing consciousness to amoebae, there are no other criteria to go on than the focused action of pursuit, which is more or less 'insulated' against potential distractions (input that in other circumstances might have itself been salient). With the limited behavioural evidence available, it makes no sense to speculate on whether a paramecium-chasing amoeba might be peripherally aware of the lucky diatom that has (temporarily at least) escaped its attentions. In practical terms, the observation that during a given pursuit the amoeba fails to respond to a stimulus that is usually sufficient to elicit a response can be interpreted *equally* as the amoeba not paying 'attention' to it and not being 'conscious' of it. By the same token, a failure to respond to anything *at all* can be identified with a state of more generalized non-attention, which is tantamount to not being 'conscious' at all (i.e. to being asleep, unconscious or dead).

In fact, the possibility of both transitive and intransitive consciousness – a distinction outlined by Bennett and Hacker[340] – is only meaningful against the background of their possible absence, in other words the possible non-occurrence of a behavioural response to a specific stimulus or the possible non-occurrence of a behavioural response to any stimulus at all. Whereas an amoeba's *transitive* consciousness of a particular diatom has its negative counterpart in a failure to pay attention to it (as when the amoeba is satiated or when something tastier is present), the negative counterpart of *intransitive* consciousness is sleep or anaesthesia, both of which appear to occur in certain protozoa. Unlike transitive consciousness, which is assessed in terms of whether an amoeba pursues a particular item or not, intransitive consciousness may wax and wane in level, manifesting itself as a fluctuating *propensity* to pursue potential prey.

We have already broached the question of how far the distinction between the hunger and satiety of protozoans may correspond to that between wakefulness and sleep. The question is implicitly raised in the Gibbs and Dellinger paper on the daily life of *A. proteus*, where the authors describe how the amoeba alternates between *varying degrees of* activity (searching and feeding) and *varying degrees of* inactivity, observing 'that the greatest activity was immediately following a period of rest, that the degree and length of rest were in proportion to the degree and length of activity, [and] that the rhythm of activity and rest was most pronounced during the twenty-four hours before division'.[341] The amount of activity was also seen to depend upon the amount and type of food present: when feeding on prey distributed more sparsely over an area, the amoeba was more active than in the vicinity of an abundance of ciliates, where it would reduce its movements to a minimum but send out its pseudopods in the form of 'pockets' ready to pick up unwary prey.[342] As evidenced by the post-prandial 'drowsiness' of satiated amoebae, therefore, consciousness and its opposite are not all-or-nothing phenomena, but shade into one another as a spectrum of gradations of arousal or animation.[343] They should not be conceived on the model of a switch that is flipped on or off, but rather a dimmer switch[344] covering a scale of intensities – more like drunkenness.

The amoeba's feed-and-sleep strategy is far from being a rarity. The female mosquito, as noted above, may balloon its weight by a factor of four in sating itself on the blood of its host, after which it will generally rest on a nearby wall to digest the nutrients so they are available for the development of its eggs. The strategy occurs particularly among animals such as giant pythons and other predators endowed with what is known as a 'compliant' stomach, an anatomical 'larder'[345] designed to store voluminous meals that will sustain the creature for the coming days or weeks, but the very size of which may condemn it to long stretches of immobility. The energy provided by the prey tends to be required to perform the work of digestion (the metabolism of a recently fed python may be running flat out) rather than being channelled into activity and locomotion. Movement itself becomes mechanically burdensome and metabolically wasteful, given the additional mass and bulk that has to be lugged around.

However, the example of the predatory ciliate *Pseudomonilicaryon anser* – which is only 'hungry' at certain times of the day – suggests that the correlation between satiety and sleep may not be quite as straightforward as *A. proteus* would have us believe. More generally, the digestive quiescence that alternates with periods of searching and feeding in amoebae and certain metazoans contrasts with the 24-hour cycle of activity and rest determined by the body's 'circadian rhythms'. This we already encountered in *Oxyrrhis*.[346] Such an internal molecular clock – based on rhythms that are in large measure endogenous but also entrained by external cues such as daylight – pervades the living world. It is found not only in plants and animals, but also in fungi, protozoa and cyanobacteria. Evolutionarily ancient, highly conserved light-sensing molecules such as cryptochrome regulate the day-night cycle in plants and fruit flies alike, determining the opening and closing of a plant's leaves and the daily patterns of activity and inactivity, responsiveness and unresponsiveness, studied in *Drosophila*.[347] DNA sequence comparisons yield an age of over 3,500 million years for the primordial rhythm gene of cyanobacteria.[348] This suggests that biological clocks had evolved long before multicellularity entered the scene and long before plants and animals branched into two distinct kingdoms, presumably permitting early micro-organisms to shield light-sensitive processes such as DNA replication from the deleterious effects of UV radiation or perhaps serving to partition mutually incompatible metabolic functions (such as oxygenic photosynthesis and nitrogen fixation) between daytime and night.[349]

The circadian rhythms of cyanobacteria regulate the diurnal patterns of expression for most of their genes, giving rise to daily fluctuations in metabolic rates, nitrogen fixation and reproduction.[350] In autotrophic dinoflagellates, such rhythms govern crucial physiological functions such as cell division, photosynthesis, phototaxis and bioluminescence, with mitosis usually taking place in the dark phase.[351] In plants the effects of the circadian clock are witnessed not only in leaf movements, but also in rhythms of growth, germination, enzymatic activity, gas exchange, photosynthesis and the opening and closing of flowers.[352] Yet the presence of circadian rhythms in such photosynthetic organisms raises the question of how far these rhythms can be identified with cycles of wakefulness and sleep and how far this distinction between wakefulness and sleep can in turn be equated with that between consciousness and its absence. Although circadian rhythms are certainly responsible for regulating an organism's levels of metabolic and physiological activity, not all such activity necessarily coincides with the specific, directional forms of self-movement associated with consciousness. The activity of an organism need not be 'action' in the sense outlined above.

A circadian 'sleep-like' state has thus recently been attributed to the upside-down jellyfish *Cassiopea*, a cnidarian and as such one of the most ancestral metazoans.[353] Not only does *Cassiopea* exhibit periods of rapidly reversible night-time quiescence marked by delayed responses to stimulation, but the day after being deprived of this quiescent period it is less active and less responsive to sensory stimuli. Such homeostatic regulation of the condition of quiescence is commonly considered one of the key features of sleep.[354] To the extent that the pulsing movements of the active jellyfish are not genuinely directional in nature, however, it must be doubted whether consciousness and by extension 'wakefulness' can justifiably be inferred. And if *Cassiopea* is never truly conscious and thus never truly 'awake', it must be doubted whether its daily periods of quiescence really correspond to *true* sleep. In spite of the behavioural and even biochemical similarities with sleep, therefore, the discoverers of the phenomenon wisely describe the state as sleep-*like*.

There is a natural temptation to equate circadian rhythmicity with a cycle of wakefulness and sleep. Charles Darwin and his son Francis referred to the 'sleep' of plants on the basis of their diurnal cycles of leaf motion.[355] Yet insofar as it lacks the counterpoint of a waking state characterized by guided locomotion, such plant 'sleep' is just as metaphorical as that of the upside-down jellyfish. Understood in these terms, circadian rhythms are not in themselves sufficient to generate the distinction between consciousness and its absence. Even so, they provide the mechanisms and lay the foundations for daily oscillations in alertness and responsiveness to stimuli that may come to form part of this distinction in self-moving organisms.

*

Like sleep, anaesthesia is generally associated with the immobility – in this case the induced immobilization – of an organism, where the absence of behaviour is interpreted as betokening an absence of consciousness. Like sleep, anaesthesia is a phenomenon that can occur not only in vertebrates and invertebrates but also in protozoa such as ciliates and amoebae. Motor responses are even suppressed in sensitive plants (such as *Mimosa* and the Venus flytrap), and both Gram-negative and Gram-positive bacteria alter the composition of their cell membrane on exposure to volatile anaesthetics, prompting the proposal that the biochemical response to such substances is of an ancestral prokaryotic origin.[356] Like sleep, moreover, anaesthesia in unicellular as in multicellular organisms is of relevance in the present context precisely to the extent that the absence of consciousness may shed light on the nature of its possible presence. Of course, the immobilization of an otherwise motile organism does not in itself provide proof of a shift from consciousness to unconsciousness. As we shall see, consciousness might not be truly abolished by immobilization (it might persist in an immobile body).[357] In an organism whose locomotion is restricted to taxis, it might not have been present in the first place. Yet these conundrums are not in principle different at a unicellular from a multicellular level.

The whole issue of anaesthesia is beset with controversy. One of its most remarkable features is that chemically highly diverse gases can induce it, ranging from nitrous oxide, ether, chloroform and isoflurane to the inert element xenon.[358] This has traditionally fostered the notion of a unitary molecular mechanism common to the various chemical agents in spite of their structural and pharmacological diversity. The focus has generally been on either of two main features of cells that are known to be affected by volatile anaesthetics, namely the membrane and the cytoskeleton.

The original unified theory of general anaesthesia was the 'lipid hypothesis', which propounded that anaesthetics act by non-specific interference with the lipid plasma membranes of neurons, thus preventing conduction of electrical impulses, or action potentials. More recently, the emphasis has been on ion channels and neurotransmitter receptors, but here too the effect resides in the capacity of anaesthetics to inhibit the transmission of signals among neurons. In particular, the breakdown in communication among neurons has been associated with a disruption of the 'functional connectivity' deemed necessary for consciousness, i.e. a failure to integrate information among various cognitive networks that are thus left uncoupled and uncoordinated.[359] Indeed, circuits involved with the integration of information are thought to be among those most directly linked with anaesthesia, which has been attributed, for example, to a loss of connectivity within the corticothalamic network. As argued above,[360] however, connectivity and the integration of information are best regarded as constitutive not of consciousness itself, but of the unitary selfhood or self-containment that *grounds* consciousness. This line of investigation may thus be taken to imply that it is by undermining minimal selfhood that anaesthesia extinguishes consciousness.

To the extent that they have highlighted the disruption of signal transmission and connectivity within nervous systems, membrane-centred interpretations have tended to limit themselves to the multicellular anaesthesia of animals and disregard the case of single-celled organisms.[361] This is less so in the instance of the other main centre of attention in studies of anaesthesia: the cytoskeleton. As early as the mid-19th century, physiologist Claude Bernard exposed amoebae to chloroform and noted that this arrested the 'protoplasmic streaming' (the organized flow of cytoplasm) within the cell interior, in the process immobilizing the cell. In the light of his observations, Bernard suggested that anaesthesia was produced by the reversible 'coagulation' of cellular proteins.[362] The mobility of amoebae is now known to depend on the assembly and disassembly of the cytoskeletal protein actin, and it seems plausible that volatile anaesthetics work by blocking such actin-based activity. This has also been shown to occur in non-neuronal animal cells called fibroblasts,[363] motile cells that synthesize collagen and extracellular matrix and play a major role in the healing of wounds. At the same time, actin dynamics – the morphological plasticity made possible by actin polymerization – is crucial to synaptic signals between neurons, and volatile anaesthetics have been found to inhibit such dynamics at brain synapses during general anaesthesia.[364] On such an interpretation, actin would thus furnish a potential bridge between unicellular and multicellular anaesthesia. The former would involve curbing actin-based motility in free-living cells (as also occurs in motile animal cells such as fibroblasts), whereas the latter would work by interfering with actin-based signalling mechanisms, thereby impeding neural communication and indirectly inhibiting motility at a multicellular level.

For both single-celled protozoans and multicellular metazoans, sleep and anaesthesia alike are states that can be defined in large measure by a temporary or reversible incapacity for self-movement, whether as a consequence of diurnal rhythms, digestive requirements or the immobilizing effect of specific chemical substances. Physiological self-maintenance is not interrupted, but locomotion ceases to be possible. As we have seen, however, the correlations between the mobility/immobility dichotomy and those of wakefulness/sleep and consciousness/unconsciousness are not to be trusted blindly. The effect on humans of curare – a poison traditionally used in blow-pipes by indigenous tribes in South America – is a case in point, producing widespread paralysis of the muscles under voluntary control yet without resulting in general anaesthesia.[365] Mistakenly believed to be a general anaesthetic or analgesic, it was administered on a number of occasions in the 1940s to patients undergoing major surgery. The patients in question, who were effectively paralysed, were 'quiet under the knife, and made not the slightest frown, twitch or moan', but subsequently complained bitterly of having been in excruciating pain and fully aware of each stroke of the scalpel.[366] The behaviourist quandary is beautifully illustrated by the hypothetical case, proposed by Dennett, in which such surgery is performed using curare in combination with an imagined drug that produces complete amnesia.[367]

At the unicellular level, too, curare produces a less-than-complete form of anaesthesia. In practice, this means that some kinds of activity or responsiveness are suppressed, whereas others are not. Under the effects of tubocurarine, the ciliate *Spirostomum* has been described as 'relaxing' and failing to contract (as it usually does) to a mechanical stimulus or direct touch, but still contracting to direct electrical stimulation.[368] Yet although in humans there may evidently be immobilization in conjunction with persisting consciousness, such a scenario makes little sense in micro-organisms for the simple reason that movement is all we have to go on in our ascriptions of protozoan consciousness: chemically induced immobility deprives us of our only yardstick for any such ascription. So while we can perfectly well *conceive* of an immobilized amoeba still yearningly 'conscious' of a nearby paramecium, or a curarized ciliate bearing the discomfort of a mechanical insult in long-suffering motionlessness, we have no *criteria for inferring* such yearning or such pain.

V.

Where Consciousness is Superfluous

Taxis and Reflexes

The claim of the present tract is neither that all selfhood displays consciousness nor even that all self-moving selfhood entails consciousness. An indispensable part of any attempt to demonstrate that some micro-organisms may in certain respects be endowed with consciousness is to show other, related respects in which they are almost certainly *not*. The underlying idea is that consciousness, in its logical origins, enables a self-concerned self to guide itself successfully towards what is 'better' or away from what is 'worse' for itself. In these terms, a self's consciousness of what is relatively 'good for self' in the world around it (say, potential nutrients) is logically inextricable from the capacity and disposition to *behave* or *take action*, i.e. to move itself to wherever this relative 'goodness' may be.

This has already been seen to render consciousness logically superfluous where the organism is *not big enough* to resist the disorganizing effects of Brownian motion, the random jostling that prevents it from maintaining a steady orientation and thus pursuing its interests by means of guided self-propulsion.[369] Consciousness is also pointless where the acquisition of nutrition is by osmotrophy – the passive assimilation of dissolved organic compounds – or by other forms of passive capture such as the diffusion feeding of radiolarians, heliozoans and suctorians. Little or no locomotive work is presupposed by such feeding strategies[370]; nor is appetite required to motivate the performance of work for a reward yet to come; nor, again, is consciousness of a world required to guide the organism appropriately to where the nutritional reward may be found. Similar considerations suggest that fish have no reason to be conscious of water: unlike terrestrial reptiles and mammals, they can be assumed neither to experience thirst nor to possess water-seeking activity within their behavioural repertoire.[371] Awareness of the location of nutrition within the environment is equally redundant for modes of non-specific restlessness or non-directional movement such as chemokinesis – presumably including the biased random walk of *E. coli* – and the thigmonastic behaviour of carnivorous plants.

At the same time, consciousness is only required if the locomotion of the self-concerned self is genuinely *self*-caused. This means, for a start, that the movement of the hungry predator should come from 'within' rather than having its causal roots in a purely physical force exerted by the prey. Hans Jonas thus visualizes the case of a target-seeking torpedo that is impelled by direct magnetic attraction between itself and its target, comparing this with a missile that uses magnetism merely as a signal to guide it:

> *What constitutes the difference in the two cases, assuming that magnetic principles operate in both, is that in the self-steering torpedo the magnetic factor does not itself provide the* power *for the acceleration of the entity whose steering arrangement it affects, and the effect on the latter is not a function of the* quantity *of the magnetic force acting on it. Given sufficient sensitivity, this force may be as small as you please, and given efficient coupling and sufficient motor resources, the effect in terms of power may be as large as you please. The torpedo is not attracted but is steered toward the target – in response, to be sure, to an influence emanating from it, but this influence is of the order of 'message' and not of acceleration.*[372]

On a human level, Jonas adds, this amounts to the claim that purposive behaviour involves perception. Yet while the conscious pursuit of prey may require an influence from the prey in the form of information (a cue or set of cues that is registered by the predator), the *force* comes from the predator. It is the predator's energy that drives the pursuit rather than a force exerted by prey on predator. The predator has to *work* for its meal; without work it is not truly *self*-movement.

In fact, magnetotaxis has itself been described as 'dumb'.[373] Magnetotactic bacteria such as *Magnetospirillum magnetotacticum* contain within themselves an organelle known as a magnetosome, enclosing magnetite crystals upon which the Earth's magnetic field exerts a torque.[374] In this way, the bacterium's body is oriented according to the local magnetic field lines, and the cell swims in the direction it happens to be pointing. This is self-movement, admittedly, to the extent that the locomotive work is performed by the bacterium. It can even be considered self-guided to the extent that it is guided by crystals that form part of the organism's own body. Yet the process of alignment is purely passive and takes place even in dead cells.[375] As a general strategy, this will presumably, on balance, take bacteria to where there is food, an optimal oxygen concentration, or conditions that are in some way *good for self*. It has even been suggested that magnetic orientation might serve to overcome the randomizing tendencies associated with Brownian motion, making it easier for bacteria to follow chemical gradients more efficiently.[376] In itself, however, it presupposes no *consciousness* of what is good (or bad), since the bacteria will unvaryingly pursue the strategy of swimming straight ahead (i.e. in the direction the magnetic field points them), irrespective of whether or not this actually does take them towards the good. Of course, magnetotaxis can be taken to have worked successfully enough for the species not to have died out *so far*. Yet such 'dumb' taxis has been distinguished from a 'smart' variety, which uses sensory apparatus to take in information about environmental variables and direct the cell more selectively towards what is good for self or away from what is bad.[377]

A broader consensus would probably view taxis as generically 'dumb'. To the extent that phototaxis (for example) constitutes an invariant response to an external stimulus, it is activity that is determined by extraneous factors – the presence or absence of light – rather than being genuinely *self*-caused. Given the presence of the living organism in conjunction with the presence of the external stimulus, the response can reliably be predicted to occur.[378] Though wrong to take it for granted that all microbial locomotion is mere taxis, therefore, Jerry Fodor was justified in arguing that phototactic behaviour *in itself* does not imply the presence of consciousness, let alone what he referred to as 'mental representations'. Equipped with a photoreceptor protein akin to rhodopsin, phototactic paramecia 'blindly' follow the light regardless of their own 'inner' state.[379]

In principle, all that is required for phototaxis of this order is a spatial relay of information from photoreceptors to flagella. In the case of green algae such as *Volvox*, spherical colonies of sun-tracking algae, the flagella are known to be directly integrated into the sensory apparatus used for detecting light.[380] One might imagine a simple, free-swimming, bilaterally symmetrical organism endowed with two paddles, one on either side, each of which is connected by a simple mechanism of information transmission to one of a pair of rudimentary eyespots that are stimulated by light to a degree proportional to its intensity.[381]

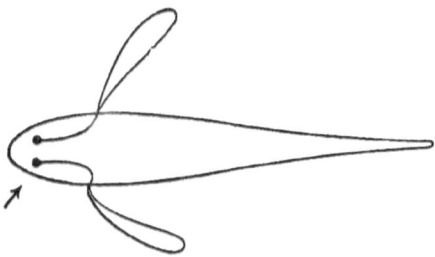

Figure 1: From: William McDougall, *An Outline of Psychology* (1923), page 60

If the degree of activity of each paddle is in proportion to the intensity of the light absorbed by the eyespot of the same side, a ray of light approaching from the left (as shown by the arrow in the diagram) will stimulate the left eye more strongly than the right, causing the left paddle to move more vigorously than the right and the organism to turn towards the right and away from the source of light. It will thus exhibit negative phototaxis. By the same token, an otherwise identical organism – different only in that each eyespot is no longer linked to the paddle of the same side but to that of the opposite side – will turn *towards* the light and thus be positively phototactic.

In practice, a somewhat more complex mechanism is required to detect the *direction* of light. Three-dimensional eukaryotic phototaxis thus commonly involves a light sensor with a view angle restricted by some form of asymmetrical shading body; this photosensor scans the environment as it rotates with the organism's helical swimming trajectory, periodically signalling to the flagella or cilia to modulate their beating.[382] Here too, however, there is a direct sensorimotor coupling between receptor and effector. In fact, a mechanism analogous to that described above is conjectured to occur in a species of marine bacterium that inhabits sediments within a rather narrowly specified range of oxygen concentrations. '*Candidatus* Thioturbo danicus' is a sideways-swimming rod that measures two by six micrometres and is endowed with sensory receptors and flagellar bundles at each lateral tip. The rotation speed of the flagellar bundles varies with fluctuations in the concentration of oxygen sensed; in turn the difference in rotation speed between the two bundles guides the bacterium's swimming path away from regions where the oxygen concentration is outside its comfort zone.[383] Here we have a vivid illustration of how a particular stimulus may give rise to a fixed locomotive response without any need to invoke either informational integration[384] or indeed any form of 'awareness' on the part of the organism.

To the extent that the 'hunger for light' of phototactic organisms such as *Volvox* or the 'hunger for oxygen' of a microaerophilic bacterium such as '*Ca. Thioturbo danicus*' is constant or unconditional, it differs from the hunger for food shown by an amoeba, which comes and goes as a variable appetite dependent on the creature's inner state. As a simple mechanism for relaying information from photoreceptors to flagella or cilia, the sensorimotor subsystem required for phototaxis need not be integrated into the organism as a whole: photoreceptor, 'nerve' and locomotor organ could in principle be excised from the creature without depriving it of anything except its capacity for phototaxis. In *The Minimal Self* this lack of informational integration – the fact that the information channels could be uncoupled from the rest of the self-propelling self in question without affecting anything *other* than its self-propulsion – was considered to be among the factors that excluded 'Cugnot's car', even in its more sophisticated, self-steering, self-fuelling guise, from the realm of conscious entities.[385] We shall touch upon this point again in the Epilogue.

Such a deficiency of integration is exemplified by the behavioural fixity (i.e. the notorious 'dumbness') of certain phototactic caterpillars, dismissed by Michael Tye as nothing more than 'stimulus-response devices':

> *Consider, for example, their sensitivity to light. Caterpillars have two eyes, one on each side of the head. Given equal light on both eyes, they move straight ahead. But given more light on one of the eyes, that side of the body locomotes more slowly. So, when caterpillars move, they tend to move towards the direction of most intense light. This is why caterpillars climb trees all the way to the top. The light there is strongest. Shift the light to the bottom of the tree, and the caterpillar will go down, not up, as it usually does, even if it means starving to death. Remove one of its eyes, and it will travel in a circle without ever changing its route.*[386]

Tye concludes that there is no more reason 'to attribute phenomenal consciousness to a caterpillar on the basis of how it moves than to an automatic door'.[387] Just as a door responds in a purely mechanical way to the application of pressure to a plate in the ground in front of it, the lowly caterpillar responds in a purely mechanical way to the presence of light.

Tye may or may not be right in his denial of 'phenomenal consciousness' to caterpillars, but his analysis seems to miss the point. The imagery he uses reduces caterpillars to mere machines or devices, leaving out of account that, conscious or otherwise, they are first and foremost *selves* and as such concerned for themselves in a way that an automatic door is not. So while it may be true, as Tye maintains, that consciousness cannot be inferred from phototaxis alone, it is equally true that a caterpillar is not simply a dumb light-sensor but also a voracious herbivore that is habitually successful in pursuing its nutritional interests. Although the environment may be manipulated by crafty experimenters (and hypothetical bioluminescent predators might resort to similar trickery), a strategy of following the light will *generally* take the caterpillar to a place that is *good for self*, i.e. to the plentiful food at the top of trees.

For Tye's reasoning about caterpillar consciousness to work, moreover, *all* caterpillar self-movement must be reducible to invariable, inflexible, purely automated responses to stimuli. As it happens, the legendary insatiability of caterpillars has indeed led to their common portrayal as 'eating machines', substantiating the comparison with the merely mechanical. Yet if the caterpillar, when presented with food, sometimes eats and sometimes does not, then its behaviour cannot be reduced in this way.[388] To the extent that its disposition to eat fluctuates, its conduct depends not only on extrinsic factors but on its own appetites, which may wax and wane. In view of the inner variability manifest as degrees of hunger or satiation, a given behaviour (pursuit or rest) can thus be viewed as being a consequence of *how* the organism is/feels and in this sense as genuinely self-caused. Once again, the point is that 'hunger' – as an inner state – can only meaningfully be ascribed to an organism that is also capable of 'satiety'. The action it undertakes is no longer a mere reflex, but is now associated with a specific bodily state. It can be taken to be *different* for a caterpillar to perceive a leaf when it is hungry from when, if ever, it is satiated.

Comprising no more than a spatial relay of information from sensory receptors to motor effectors, tropisms and taxes *per se* patently fail to account for consciousness. Yet even rather more complex modes of cognitive activity may not in themselves suffice for consciousness to emerge. As noted above,[389] a multiplicity of signals may be integrated and may override one another. The importance of this point was recognized by Jennings, who observed that paramecia as a rule show negative gravitaxis (i.e. they swim upwards), but that this can be outweighed by other factors such as heat, cold, mechanical shock or chemicals, all of which may cause them to swim downwards.[390] Such versatility implies that information is being *processed* rather than merely transmitted, a procedure equally possible in nervous systems or in the phosphoprotein circuits of single-celled organisms, where neural or protein 'switches' are capable of performing logical operations and thus generating a diversity of behaviours that may vary according to circumstance. Yet despite the cognitive sophistication engendered by processing of this kind, it still implies unidirectional causality insofar as it is the environment – albeit a multi-modal environment – that wholly determines the behaviour of the organism. The genuinely *self*-caused movement of a conscious self presupposes that endogenous signals, i.e. signals generated *within* the organism itself, can also be integrated into the informational circuits, which thus accommodate interoceptive cues relating to the body's own chemical state (its need for food or water, its temperature, etc.).[391]

In vertebrates, such integrative processes tend to be centralized in the brain, whereas the control of movement in itself – and rhythmic motion in particular – need not be. Aspects of the motor activity of the frog such as its stereotypical reflex reaction to remove irritants from the skin are known not to require any part of the brain, and this sort of brain-independent reflex can be assumed to be no more related to consciousness than the taxis of microbes.[392] In arthropods such as insects and crustaceans, the presence of other relatively autonomous concentrations of neurons (ganglia) in addition to the brain allows for even more spectacular feats of brainless, and presumably unconscious, movement. Headless cockroaches have been shown to be capable of learning how to avoid an electric shock. Brainless fruit flies can stand up if knocked over and perform a grooming reflex if prodded. As Greenspan drily points out, however, flying 'requires a head'.[393] Indeed, most (if not all) of the flexibly directional locomotion performed by animals endowed with a brain involves *the use of* that brain, an organ that evolved as the intermediary between sensory input and motor output meticulously attuned to the particular needs of the respective self. The question of whether *all* animal consciousness demands an anatomical brain will re-emerge in the Epilogue.

The analogy with metazoans has suggested to some that a similar, 'brain-like' centralization of the information-integrating function might be present in unicellular organisms. On a speculative note, Dennis Bray thus posits the presence in amoebae of a 'single executive complex' – an integrative protein, perhaps – that would 'receive relevant signals about the cell's internal state (metabolic level, position in the cell cycle, level of activity of organelles), as well as signals filtering from the outside (via membrane receptors relaying mechanical and chemical stimuli)'.[394] The strengths and timings of the relevant signals would be processed and compared, and on the basis of these computations executive decisions would regulate and guide the movements of the various regions of the cell.[395] Yet in fact there is no *a priori* need for centralization. Integration (i.e. communication among parts and between inside and outside) is what is required, and the fundamental unit of integration is the organismal self as a whole. Paradigmatic in this respect is the amoeba, an organism pervaded and structured by a cytoskeleton that, as mathematical physicist Roger Penrose puts it, functions 'rather like a combination of skeleton, muscle system, legs, blood circulatory system, and nervous system all rolled into one'.[396] The amoeba in its capacity as a self-moving brain and self-moving taste bud cannot be separated from the motile mouth or locomotive anus that it also *is*.

Metazoan Cells

The argument so far has been that rudimentary consciousness is intimately associated with (only) certain forms of self-moving selfhood. This provides a foundation for the possible ascription of consciousness to free-living protozoans, but rules out most of the individual cells that make up multicellular bodies such as animals, which are decidedly immobile. Indeed, the enforcement of such immobility is one of the recurrent features of multicellularity.

Anchored firmly in place by cell-to-cell and cell-matrix adhesion molecules known respectively as cadherins and integrins, the cells of metazoan bodies are kept alive, no less, by the constant emission of so-called 'survival signals' from the surrounding cells that confine them to their position. The cessation of the signal elicits immediate apoptosis or cell suicide in the individual cell,[397] a strategy designed to counter undesirable autonomy at the cellular level and thus ward off the threat of cancer.[398] This implies a collective logic in that it fosters cohesion, the unit of selfhood shifting from the individual cell to the community of cells. The transition from individual to communal selfhood is reinforced, in particular, by the individual cell's latent predisposition to suicide, which – for the benefit of the collective self – contravenes the intrinsically reflexive nature of the cell's own selfhood as a self-perpetuating or self-maintaining entity. In most eumetazoans at least, multicellularity thus involves not only the immobilization of the organism's constituent cells, but the subsumption of their selfhood within a collective or higher-order unit of selfhood where each individual cell 'knows' its place and keeps to it. Strictly speaking, such cells are neither self-moving nor even selves.

Whereas free-living protozoans are characterized by the versatility that permits them to move from place to place, find and capture food, avoid predators, respond to perturbations of the environment, and in the appropriate circumstances divide and reproduce,[399] the multicellularity of most metazoans except the most ancestral forms such as sponges is grounded upon a rigid division of labour among the animal's cells. A specialist liver cell or a neuron is defined and delimited by its narrow functional role and by its place within the totality of the organism. Such a cell is a compound of subservience to and dependence on the multicellular whole, lacking the all-round autonomy of its free-living counterpart.[400] Given the immobility and 'selflessness' of metazoan cells, therefore, it is hard to imagine that cell-level consciousness could fulfil a function or serve a purpose either for the cell or the organism. To the extent that they are programmed to *stay put*, there is simply no need for the body's cells to be aware of their surroundings.

This has not proved self-evident. Recognizing the importance of the cytoskeleton, Roger Penrose has raised what he describes as the 'significant' question of 'whether a paramecium – or, indeed, an individual human liver cell – might actually possess some rudimentary form of consciousness'. The theory of consciousness he proposes, which attributes a major role to quantum effects in cellular microtubules, does not provide for a satisfactory distinction between the two cases.[401] Rodolfo Llinás takes the idea even further in that he grounds the consciousness of animals on the proto-consciousness (or 'irritability') of the cells of which we are composed: 'if a single cell is not capable of having a modicum of qualia', he asks, 'how then can a group of cells generate something that does not belong to a given individual?'[402] Llinás is here succumbing to what is known as a fallacy of division, inferring something to be true of a part – or all of the parts – of an entity from the fact that it is true of the entity as a whole and thus overlooking the possibility that consciousness may be an emergent property.[403] More to the point in the present context, such views fail to take account of the deep association of consciousness with self-moving selfhood, whether the self-moving self in question be dinosaur or dinoflagellate.

As always, however, caveats are called for. The possible consciousness of multicellular cells cannot be dismissed quite so conveniently. While the case of a liver cell or a neuron seems relatively straightforward, what about *mobile* somatic cells such as the amoeboid macrophages ('big-eaters') of the immune system and the equally shape-shifting microglial cells that perform a similar range of immunological and general caretaking functions in the brain?[404] Again, one reason for refusing to ascribe consciousness to macrophages and microglia might be that they are not 'proper' selves, the organism as a whole constituting a superordinate self. In other words, it is the macroscopic animal that has interests and appetites, and that strives to behave in accordance with these interests and satisfy these appetites, whereas the macrophages and microglia are merely functional ciphers that serve – and ultimately sacrifice themselves to – the higher-order well-being. This may indeed be the case. However, the immunological function of these self-moving phagocytes itself involves them freely pursuing and ingesting bacterial non-self. Can they not therefore be said to be 'hungry' or have an 'appetite'? Can they not be characterized as 'motivated' to consume opsonised foreign bodies as they become 'aware' of them?[405]

One possibly decisive question is whether they ever reach a state of satiety like the amoebae portrayed by Gibbs and Dellinger. Or are they merely 'eating machines'? It has been argued above that it is superfluous to ascribe hunger or appetite to such automatic feeders, citing the example of the seemingly insatiable ciliate *Vorticella*.[406] There is no reason to suppose that it is 'like anything' to be such an organism. Consciousness need not be hypothesized, for its self-movement is a 'blind', invariant response to environmental cues. But what if macrophages and microglia *do* have an appetite that can be described as variable or satiable? This seems plausible at least.[407] In this case, one of two conclusions can be drawn: *either* I am mistaken in contending that appetite, motivation and by extension rudimentary consciousness depend on selfhood, *or* the unicellular selfhood of immunological phagocytes is not fully subsumed within the superordinate selfhood of the multicellular animal. The second conclusion again suggests that selfhood is not an all-or-nothing phenomenon but a matter of gradations that shade into one another. It may be that these unicellular big-eaters retain a residual selfhood that manifests itself precisely in their appetite to ingest bacterial non-self.[408]

VI.

Limits to Claims about
Rudimentary Consciousness

A World of Objects

It has emerged so far that consciousness is the attribute of selves capable of engaging in a certain sort of self-movement and that it is necessarily structured and shaped by the tacit selfhood of such selves. Minimally, this tacit selfhood may take the form of degrees of appetite and motivation and of degrees of attention and arousal relating to these movements. In less minimal cases (say, in certain animals), it may incorporate varieties of emotion such as fear and of implicit sensorimotor self-familiarity such as corollary discharge and proprioception.[409]

The rudimentary consciousness of protozoa can be assumed to be unfathomably different from what is experienced by human beings. To the extent that its logical origins involve guiding a self-moving self from here (no food) to there (food), it is much more limited in range and refinement than human awareness. In the present, rather more speculative chapter I shall briefly ask whether this elementary form of consciousness really has all the features expected of 'true' consciousness and, if not, how far this undermines our use of the term. Is it, for example, consciousness of a 'world' of independently existing 'objects'? Is it associated with, or does it even provide the foundation for, the possibility of freedom? Does it incorporate a sense of future or an ability to learn from the past? Although my suggested answers to these questions are tentative, the underlying premise is that the questions are *answerable*. I shall end the chapter by clarifying some of the features I am not inclined to ascribe to unicellular consciousness.

Questions such as whether 'consciousness' necessarily has to be 'consciousness of a world of objects' are liable to generate untold confusion. We have no reason to believe that non-human organisms theorize about the nature of their consciousness or possess highly abstract concepts such as 'world' or 'object'. Our question, therefore, is not to be confounded with the question of whether non-human creatures *know* that they are conscious of objects; one can perfectly well be conscious of an object without possessing the propositional knowledge that an object is what one is conscious of. The human notion of an objective world composed of persisting particulars of which properties and relations may truthfully or non-truthfully be predicated – i.e. re-identifiable and independent entities such as physical things or persons that exist in a unified spatiotemporal system – is a metaphysic that is deeply intertwined with the propositional nature of human thought.[410] There is no more reason to associate rudimentary consciousness with explicit awareness of such a world than with propositional thought.

A related question is whether consciousness of a world of objects presupposes intersubjectivity, i.e. my awareness of the existence of, and my interaction with, other selves beside myself (or, more strictly, my recognition of other selves *as selves*). The idea here is that for me to perceive an object in the world as a three-dimensional item within a spatiotemporal framework, the object in question must be implicitly understood to be perceivable by other selves. When I perceive an object, in other words, the fact that I am not only aware of the side facing me, but also of the hidden profiles of the object that are not currently in view, depends upon my implicit awareness of the possible presence of other selves to whom the concealed aspects of the object *would* be perceptually accessible. As Evan Thompson expresses it, the very meaning of 'object' inherent within the intentionality of the perceptual act 'implies being simultaneously perceivable by a plurality of subjects'.[411] More generally, one might argue, it is only through recognition of the existence of other selves – other perspectives on the world – that one can come to conceive of an 'objectively existing' world that is independent of one's own first-person perspective on it. Again, such intersubjective awareness presupposes a degree of cognitive sophistication that can presumably be denied to single-celled organisms.

This is certainly a deep point about our understanding of belief and truth, which hinges upon our capacity to disengage from our own first-person perspective and acknowledge the possibility of a third-person or 'objective' perspective. Such a capacity enables us to appreciate that other selves may have perceptual access to, and knowledge of, 'hidden' parts of objects or 'hidden' aspects of states of affairs that we ourselves cannot perceive. Yet neither intersubjectivity nor linguistic thought is necessary for an awareness of the three-dimensionality of objects. Three-dimensional consciousness does not presuppose an explicit understanding that objects or states of affairs may appear in different ways to different 'selfish' perspectives or that 'subjective' appearance may not coincide with 'objective' reality, but in itself assumes no more than a dispositional grasp of *how* to move so as to perceive an object from a different angle. The prerequisite for this is our familiarity with the functional interdependence of visual sensation and the movements of our own body: in other words, how our perception of the world is liable to change as a function of and in concert with our self-movements, as mediated by the proprioceptive sensibility that forms part of our tacit self. We know, unthinkingly, that certain movements of the eye or head, or of the whole body, will provide us with access to features of our environment that are currently inaccessible to us. In the words of philosopher Alva Noë, 'perceivers' have an 'implicit practical understanding that they are coupled to the world in such a way that movements produce sensory change'. The hidden parts of objects, he suggests, are present to perception 'virtually'[412] in that they are made available to us through our unspoken sensorimotor skills.

In these terms, consciousness of a three-dimensional world depends neither upon propositional knowledge and linguistic thought nor upon an intersubjective recognition of other selves. Rather, it springs from our own tacit grasp of the interdependence of self-movement and sensation, and in particular the remote sensing facilitated by vision. As the archetypal mode of what is sometimes called *teleception*, vision plays a special role in our apprehension of three-dimensional depth. It grounds the possible awareness of a goal *as a goal* – as the endpoint of an intended trajectory – in a way that is not feasible for other senses (imagine smelling one's way towards the source of an odour).[413] Hans Jonas points out that, by contrast with the olfactory and auditory senses, which construct their unitary perceptual manifold 'out of a temporal sequence of sensations which are in themselves time-bound and nonspatial', sight is 'the sense of the simultaneous or the coordinated, and thereby of the extensive'. A view 'comprehends many things juxtaposed, as co-existent parts of one field of vision'.[414] Again, this 'field' is by no means a passive construct, but one to which we have been indissolubly coupled ever since our first clumsy head and hand movements as infants.

The actual generation of depth awareness may be through various mechanisms. Many animals including humans are equipped with stereopsis, or binocular vision, which in itself can and does provide a certain amount of explicit depth information (particularly at relatively short distances), gleaned from tiny discrepancies between the images in the two eyes.[415] If vision is monocular, or greater distances are involved, the inference of depth may be based either on 'static' or 'dynamic' cues. Static cues include the relative sizes of objects and the relative occlusion of one object by another, and themselves presuppose prior experience of the three-dimensionality of the environment. Dynamic cues are furnished by what has been called the 'velocity flow field', i.e. the patterns of retinal motion resulting from one's own change of position relative to the surroundings.[416] One of the most relevant such cues is 'looming', which occurs when a small part of the flow field suddenly expands, indicating the rapid approach of an object (or predator). The 'looming' stimulus is a warning signal found across the animal kingdom, causing insects to fly off and humans to duck.[417]

To what extent, then, can unicellulars or simple metazoans be said to be endowed with the vision that might yield access to a three-dimensional world? Photoreception in itself cannot be equated with vision: a phototactic organism such as *Euglena* cannot be said to 'see' the light that induces it to move itself to where photosynthesis can take place. This is not to belittle its usefulness. Even without any optics, simple photoreception serves to distinguish day and night and determine depth at sea. The 'shadow reflex' we encountered in the Introduction prompts the sedentary barnacle to close its shell to protect its internal organs whenever a sudden decrease in illumination announces the proximity of a potential predator.[418] Yet the barnacle 'sees' neither the shadow nor the attendant predator. Its action is the purest of reflexes; not even elementary consciousness is called for. *Oxyrrhis marina* is thought to employ photoreception in locating of some of its prey, using rhodopsin to detect algae on the basis of their autofluorescence,[419] a natural emission of light from molecules such as chlorophyll in certain living organisms. Even though the role of rhodopsin might be taken to suggest some kind of vision, however, there is no reason why prey detection based on photosensation alone should differ in principle from that based on chemosensation. A change in the conformation of a transmembrane molecule signals the nearby presence of a particular category of prey, but only in the way that a smell betrays the proximity of the source.

The more sophisticated photoreceptive apparatus of the single-celled warnowiids possibly brings us closer to the realm of vision. Equipped with a lens and a cornea, the singular ocelloid of these predatory dinoflagellates is structurally similar to a metazoan eye and can be conjectured to allow greater resolution than an individual photoreceptor, not merely registering presence or absence but picking out a shadow or a figure against a background. It has been suggested that the warnowiid ocelloid might discern 'shadow effects' generated by the movements of potential prey or serve as a 'range finder' allowing the predator to fire its barbed nematocysts to immobilize its prey only when a clear image on the retina indicates that the distance is right.[420] It might be more specific in its sensitivity, enabling warnowiids to detect the bioluminescence generated by certain other dinoflagellates or the circularly polarized light more generally characteristic of their dinoflagellate prey.[421] As the only type of unicellular organism known to have such an 'eye', the warnowiids may well be unique in the visual nature of their experience. Yet bearing in mind the unusual, endosymbiotic origin of the ocelloid (with its bricolage of assimilated plastids and mitochondria doing the job of the retinal body and the cornea respectively),[422] the decisive point is the principle it embodies: namely that a single-celled organism may indeed be possessed of something approximating to vision.

Even so, a more general and less conjectural appreciation of the spatial nature of unicellular consciousness is perhaps afforded by the concept of klinotaxis, which was already introduced in the discussion of how *O. marina* swims towards prey under the guidance of chemoattraction. Again, the same principle may also be applied in the context of photoreception, which only requires a simple receptor to be waved from side to side, assessing the differences in luminous intensity, in order to be able to guide an organism towards or away from a source of light: 'this is what fly larvae do', notes neurobiologist Michael F. Land, and it is 'rather like the way we would use our nose to track down the source of a bad smell'.[423] As with such photoreception, the use of helical klinotaxis for chemo-orientation is grounded in a conjunction of sensory reception with guided self-movement. The depth in this case is not the three-dimensional depth of an object but of a *gradient pointing to an implicitly anticipated goal*. So even though the concept of an 'object' still seems wide of the mark, elementary consciousness is nonetheless founded upon a relationship between self-movement and some sort of inherent *objective*. *O. marina* may not be conscious of a 'world' of 'objects', but its consciousness presupposes a three-dimensional space structured by differential desirability.

*

Developmental psychologists study the phenomenon of 'object permanence', which denotes our implicit understanding that objects continue to exist even when they cannot be perceived in any way. Human infants are judged to acquire this ability at eight months, retrieving objects that they see being hidden. A sense of object permanence is also shown by primates and certain other mammals, and by some birds. Two-day-old chicks manifest it by being able to remember which of two opaque screens a familiar object is concealed behind and subsequently retrieving the object.[424] For a creature to possess this skill it must have a capacity to 'represent' an object without the stimulation of direct sensory cues. In this context the metaphor of 'representation' is appropriate in that it implies the evocation of something in its absence, for example when it is not present at the same location as we are, or when it is hidden from view.[425] In the presence of the object, by contrast, there is no need for representation, to the extent that the world can be taken to represent itself.[426] But is there any sense in which an amoeba can be said to 'represent' the absent or fugitive paramecium for which it has an appetite?

One factor that might be taken to suggest that it does is the *persistence* of its pursuit, described by Jennings in the episode of an amoeba chasing after an encysted *Euglena* cell that keeps rolling away from it:

> *The latter was perfectly spherical and very easily moved, so that when the anterior edge of the Amoeba came in contact with it the cyst merely moved forward a little and slipped to one side (the left). The Amoeba thereupon altered its course so as to follow the cyst. ... The cyst was shoved forward again and again, a little to the left; the Amoeba continued to follow. This continued until the two had traversed about one-fourth the circumference of a circle; then ... the cyst, when pushed forward, rolled to the left quite out of contact with the Amoeba. The latter then continued forward with its broad anterior edge in a direction which would have taken it past the cyst. But a small pseudopodium on its left side came in contact with the cyst. The Amoeba thereupon turned again and followed the rolling cyst. At times it sent out two pseudopodia, one on each side of the cyst ... , as if trying to enclose the latter, but the ball-like cyst rolled so easily that this did not succeed. At other times a single very long, slender pseudopodium was sent out, only the tip of which remained in contact with the cyst. Then the body of the Amoeba was brought up from the rear and the cyst pushed further.*[427]

Eventually the *Euglena* cyst was whisked away by the ciliary current of a passing infusorian, 'one of those troublesome disturbers of the peace in microscopic work'.[428] The amoeba continued its pursuit for a short time, before reversing its course and heading in a new direction.

Jennings is struck by the resemblance between the amoeba and 'immensely higher organisms': one 'seems to see', he writes, that 'the Amoeba is *trying* to obtain this cyst for food, that it puts forth *efforts* to accomplish this in various ways, and that it shows remarkable *pertinacity* in continuing its *attempts* to ingest the food when it meets with difficulty'.[429] Elsewhere, in describing the pursuit of one amoeba by another, he notes that 'it is difficult to conceive each phase of action of the pursuer to be completely determined by a simple present stimulus'.[430] What Jennings is almost bashfully[431] insinuating here is the influence of some form of – admittedly very short-term – memory trace (or 'representation') that keeps the predator focused on its prey even when the latter temporarily slips from its clutches.[432] The question is whether the predator ever really does leave the sphere of chemoattraction exerted by its prey, be it the 'smell' of something distant or the 'taste' of what is contiguous. Given the presumed limitations of unicellular learning (to be discussed below), an explanation based on the prey's ongoing 'presence' is perhaps more parsimonious than one involving an amoeba 'remembering' or 'representing' its prey as it fleets into and out of its presence. But the jury is still out.

Choice and Freedom

Amoeba proteus seems not to inhabit a world of lasting objects, which for some people may exclude it from membership of the exclusive club of truly conscious entities. Yet the space in which it lives is structured by the differential desirability that motivates it not only to move towards what it likes (to eat) and avoid what is harmful, but also to distinguish between things on the basis of *how much* it likes (eating) them: in other words, it has preferences and makes choices.[433] This has already come to light in its predilection for paramecia over other ciliates, and for ciliates over diatoms and other algae. A great deal of work has also been done to establish the impressive prey selectivity of *O. marina*, both between species and within species.[434] As we have seen, moreover, selectivity may depend on the physiological state of the predator, whose relative hunger or satiety conditions how 'choosy' it is.[435] Nor are a protozoan's preferences immune to modification over the course of its own life-history. The effects of 'dietary imprinting' have been demonstrated in the predator *Didinium nasutum*, which will preferentially ingest the stock of *Paramecium bursaria* on which it has been reared. It can even be 'trained' to feed on specimens containing mutualistic algae (called zoochlorellae) that are otherwise 'distasteful' to it, although this training is quickly overcome if it is subsequently presented with 'bleached' cells.[436]

Preferences also come to light in the *amount of work* a predator is willing to undertake in order to obtain an item of prey. The basic principle is that the more motivated an organism is to procure an item, the harder it will work to do so, just as a hungry organism is expected to work harder to get food than one that is satiated. The field of 'consumer demand' studies has focused on measuring the strength of this motivation both in vertebrates and invertebrates, requiring the animals under analysis to perform a specified task – such as opening a weighted doorway or pressing a lever repeatedly – in order to gain access to a more or less desirable item. In the case of many animals (e.g. mice or rats), it is not just food that is worked for, but also the 'pleasure' of a cage with nesting material, extra space, shelter or novel objects.[437]

An even more graphic measure of animal preferences than the mere performance of work[438] is the degree of discomfort an animal is willing to undergo, the obstacles it is disposed to overcome, or the risks it is prepared to take, with a view to gaining a reward. Such discomfort and risk-taking may take the form of subjecting oneself to an electric shock, for example by crossing a grid, in order to reach a goal. Jonathan Balcombe describes some of the lengths to which rats are prepared to go to get their preferred nutritional treat, repeatedly navigating a maze and entering a 'deadly cold room' to retrieve their favourite comestibles but subsequently staying at home in their cosy nests when they only find common-or-garden commercial rat food. Nor is this type of behaviour restricted to mammals:

> *variations on the same setup further revealed pleasure-based decision-making by ... lizards. They made forays to the gourmet banquet only if the temperature in the cold corner was above a certain level. When it got too cold, they stayed in the warm and ate the nearby food. By varying the food offerings, it was discovered that the better the food in the cold corner, the lower the temperature the lizards were willing to tolerate.*[439]

The willingness of macroscopic animals to overcome obstacles or put up with discomfort in order to obtain a net reward is easily observable. As Cabanac has argued, it is in such contexts that pleasure can be conceived as the 'common currency' by which the relative strengths of motivational drives can be weighed up against one another. It is the subjective dimension by which preferences are gauged and assessed.

The difficulties of designing such experiments at a microbial level make unicellular 'preferences' a more enigmatic phenomenon. If amoebae could be shown not only to engage in persistent locomotion to find and capture prey but also to overcome physical obstacles, material resistance or potential discomfort in acquiring some (but perhaps not all) nutrition, this would represent an even greater testimony to their powers of discrimination. Yet although there is clearly a distinction between the mere performance of work (with the implicit anticipation of ensuing gratification that this presupposes) and the overcoming of a concrete obstruction or inconvenience, there is not necessarily a divergence of principle involved. The difference resides primarily in the level of cognitive skill rather than the nature of the motivation required. It can be surmised that even an amoeba or dinoflagellate must (tacitly) decide whether to *continue* pursuing its most coveted microbial prey if this should stray, for example, outside the predator's range of thermal comfort. Nor is choice just a matter of choosing between two alternatives (pleasurable paramecium versus much less appetizing algal fodder). To the extent that appetite and the implicit possibility of pleasure are what instigate action in the first place, the ultimate choice is whether to do something or nothing, whether to move or stay put.[440] The *ur*-choice is fundamentally whether or not to invest energy in gratification that is yet to come, and thus not guaranteed. This too is a choice that self-moving microbes must face.

Discussion of choice and preference implies that the concept of freedom can be meaningfully ascribed not only to animals, but even to predatory protozoa such as amoebae. Such a liberal use of the term, doubtless disconcerting to some, is adumbrated by Hans Jonas, who goes further in attributing freedom to *all* living entities: 'one expects to encounter the term in the area of mind and will, and not before', he writes, 'but if mind is prefigured in the organic from the beginning, then freedom is. And indeed our contention is that even metabolism, the basic level of all organic existence, exhibits it: that it is itself the first form of freedom'.[441] Jonas's claim is rather more sweeping than can be vindicated by the present argument, for which freedom presupposes – and can only manifest itself in the form of – certain modes of *self-moving* selfhood. It makes little sense to ascribe freedom to the symbiotic bacterium *Buchnera aphidicola* as it sits tucked away in obligate motionlessness within the nutritive plenitude of aphid cells,[442] or in general to bacteria so diminutive that any possibility of directional self-propulsion is precluded by the randomizing effects of Brownian motion. Nor is taxis *in itself* truly an expression of freedom. For although such movement is powered by an organismal self, there may be no input from this self in 'deciding' whether or not the movement is actually performed or in determining the direction it takes; the occurrence and direction of the locomotion may be conditioned entirely by external contingency (i.e. by the appropriate environmental signals), irrespective of the internal state of the organism in question. To the extent that it is invariant with respect to a particular property of a given stimulus,[443] the swimming of a phototactic ciliate is no more an expression of freedom than the reflex kick I give the local doctor when she taps the quadriceps tendon at the front of my knee.

The intrinsic reflexivity of selfhood may provide the *foundation* for the possibility of freedom (as Jonas perhaps intuited), yet it is specifically consciousness that brings it into being, permitting appropriately directed action to be taken on the basis of how the world appears to a self, mediated by factors such as appetite, motivation and alertness, and – at a less elementary level – by emotions such as fear, anger and love. Freedom in this sense means that I am, at least in part, the *origin* of my action, the causal determinant of a specific, directional self-movement. Unfreedom, by contrast, means that these powers of self-movement are fettered, as when I am confined or restrained within a literal or metaphorical cage (i.e. '*allo*-contained' rather than *auto*- or self-contained). There is no contradiction or conflict with determinism. As Matt Ridley has put it, 'freedom lies in expressing your own determinism, not somebody else's. It is not the determinism that makes a difference, but the ownership'.[444] In the present context, Ridley might well have said 'selfhood' instead of 'ownership'.[445] To the extent that freedom can be conceived of as a determinism of one's own, or as 'self-determinism', or perhaps rather as self-determination (a notion rendered by the venerable German concept of *Selbstbestimmung*), it is above all an expression of selfhood. In the form of self-determination, freedom embodies a deep aspect of the intrinsic reflexivity proper to self-moving selves. A free self is one that determines whether and whither it moves.

It may be objected that such a viewpoint – elevating the ingestion of a paramecium by an amoeba to an act of freedom – remains too basal, failing to rise above the exigencies of material need. 'True' freedom, it might be argued, can only emerge once our fundamental needs have been met: once we have eaten and drunk enough to cover our bodily requirements, secured ourselves living conditions free from the risk of predation, and are left with surplus energy and time for play, i.e. for activities that are non-functional or are ends in themselves. People in conditions of extreme poverty, as well as animals in conditions of nutritional stress, are 'shackled' by their circumstances. In this respect protists cannot be free either, for they too are necessarily shackled by the requirements of their bodily constitution.

Alternatively, it might be felt, 'true' freedom encompasses the possible *subjugation* of these basic needs, for example by deferring or postponing their gratification in ways we shall encounter in the following section. At a deeper level, it might take the form of a capacity to overcome *conatus* and the instinct of self-preservation, and thus a capacity to overcome selfhood itself. Conceived in such terms, freedom may be understood to manifest itself in the Jainist *sallekhanā* or 'fast unto death' by which the devout embrace their own imminent demise,[446] or in the sacrifice of one's own selfhood for a higher-order collective good, a behavioural option available (at the very least) to humans, hymenopterans and the social amoebae. To the extent that freedom is understood as an expression of selfhood, of course, the renunciation of selfhood – though it may be a final act of freedom or even its consummation – is also, paradoxically, a renunciation of freedom.[447]

At a most elementary level, perhaps, freedom may best be seen to inhere in *how* one meets one's needs, 'basic' or otherwise. If there are no alternatives (as in conditions of stress or poverty), there is indeed no freedom. It can thus be characterized as an ability to choose and pursue *one's own* way of maximizing pleasure,[448] i.e. of seeking what is *good for self*, be it in the form of a paramecium or a pizza, the titillations of a life of luxury or the delights of an ascetic, altruistic or selfless lifestyle.

Future and Past

Consciousness of the present should not be envisioned as akin to a static or timeless image or snapshot of the world that resides 'inside' our brain or mind. Rather, the present moment is always experienced as incorporating the immediate past and future as part of an ongoing process. The conscious present is structured by the intrinsic relationship in which it stands to what has just gone and what is just about to come.[449] This is manifest even in the responsiveness of the bacterium *E. coli* to its environment, which incorporates a short-term memory (based on the time lapse between the phosphorylation and methylation of receptor molecules) that gauges the *rate of change* in the concentration of attractants or repellents. Rudimentary forms of openness to one's surroundings involve a comparison between earlier and later in terms of 'better' and 'worse'.

To the extent that what is registered is not nutrition in itself but information signalling the presence of nutrition, a *spatial distance* is prized open between the perceiving self and the 'object' of perception.[450] The fact that work, primarily in the guise of locomotion, is required to overcome this distance in turn implies a deferral of gratification that likewise suggests a sense of *temporal distance*. The appetite and motivation of a predatory protozoan – and the search or pursuit in which it engages – are by nature bound up with the implicit anticipation of satisfaction to come. Work is performed, and energy expended, for a reward that is not immediate. A similar deferral of gratification is in evidence when *Amoeba verrucosa* undertakes an elaborate sequence of folding movements in order to be able to gorge on filamentous green algae many times its own length.[451] This is commonly known as 'prey handling' and is also seen in certain dinoflagellates that have to 'reshape' their prey in order to engulf organisms that are bigger than they are. *Gyrodinium spirale* is able to devour whole chains of diatoms by breaking them up and transforming them into a round food package suitable for subsequent ingestion.[452]

Sensory openness to the environment is what makes appropriate, future-oriented behaviour possible. At the most basic level (prior even to learning), the clues garnered by dinoflagellates and amoebae ground the tacit prediction: if you follow this direction or strategy, you will (soon) find dinner/a pleasant taste/satisfaction/the 'good'. Where present, a faculty such as vision may beget a new experiential dimension by facilitating the explicit localization of a goal *at a distance*, allowing the meaningful world to become rather easier to control and predict. In itself, however, 'pursuit' – like the escape behaviour to which it may give rise – need entail neither deliberate planning nor any explicit awareness of the future. This throws up the question of whether elementary consciousness involves anything more than a purely *tacit* awareness of time.

Cognitive neuroscientist Michael Gazzaniga has argued that what makes us human has a lot to do with our ability to curb automatic responses in favour of ones that are calculated, reasoned or purposeful. Gazzaniga ventures that *Homo sapiens* is 'the only animal that can delay gratification by inhibiting our impulses over time'.[453] This is gratification 'deferred' in the more usual sense not just of work performed for a reward yet to come, but the postponement of one reward for the sake of another, presumably bigger and better. Notably, this ability to *control oneself* and postpone pleasure has been given the designation 'self' – in the sense of an executive control centre – and described as a 'limited resource' to the extent that it is not easy to make such choices.[454] Like more immediate and less circuitous strategies for pursuing pleasure, in fact, self-control may also be viewed as a class of work and as such dependent on the consumption of fuel. It has been shown that this 'limited resource' can be replenished by ingesting glucose.[455]

In support of his claim about human uniqueness, Gazzaniga invokes the so-called Bischof-Kohler hypothesis. The idea is that non-human animals are incapable of 'mental time travel' and therefore irredeemably 'stuck' in the present.[456] Without conventional language and thus unable to engage in propositional logic, non-human animals are presumed to lack an explicit concept of 'time' or 'future' or a conscious capacity to weigh up and compare two or more prospective scenarios. Contrary to customary belief, however, the self-discipline that manifests itself as a deferral of gratification is far from being a uniquely human attribute. It is exemplified by birds such as western scrub jays, which show self-control and a sense of future when they store their food resources in a cache (out of the sight of conspecifics) for subsequent retrieval, even re-caching their 'provisions' if they are aware of being observed when hiding them the first time around.[457]

Other corvids such as ravens, as well as great apes, also undertake the flexible hoarding of food, and experiments have shown that this is not merely a specialized adaptation confined to the sphere of food-caching but reflects a more general facility to plan and envision the future, which may cover areas of behaviour where they are not normally predisposed to act in this way.[458] Even hens have been found to exercise self-restraint in anticipation of the future, refusing an immediate reward in the expectation of receiving a 'jackpot' as recompense for holding back.[459] But where does this relatively explicit sense of time-to-come spring from? How is it possible in animals allegedly without a concept of 'future'? Perhaps it may be understood as a non-conceptual extrapolation from the *pre-reflective sense of time* that underlies the motivation of even the most primitive self-moving self to perform work for a gratification yet to come. As such, it too is grounded in the implicit anticipation of reward. The work may be different (holding oneself back rather than letting oneself go), but the reward is still gauged by the common currency of pleasure. Such an interpretation may indeed be sufficient for hens, where it is a *present* motivation that achieves greater satisfaction via the roundabout route of restraint. But is it enough for ravens and scrub jays, which seem to anticipate not only the reward, but their own *future* motivations?

Such an express sense of time-to-come is unlikely to feature in elementary consciousness. All the more remarkable, therefore, is the 'restraint' in evidence among populations of the social amoeba *Dictyostelium discoideum*, some of which have been found to engage in husbandry activities.[460] Instead of consuming all the bacteria present in their patch, these apparently forward-looking unicellular 'farmers' incorporate some of the available bacteria into the fruiting bodies they form for dispersal, thus seeding a new food crop at their future location. The easiest interpretation would perhaps be that such hoarding, though of undoubted usefulness in the future, is regulated simply by the farmers' present motivational state, i.e. the decline in their current level of hunger. Yet only some of the amoebae show this restraint. The fact that the farmers do more work for a diminished reward

– and thus seem to act against their own interests as individuals – may be explained by a collective logic dictating that the multigenerational benefits of their husbandry are reaped by existing kin groups.[461] Individual awareness of the future is perhaps made unnecessary by this multicellular logic. Whatever the explanation, the consequence of the 'selflessness' shown by the amoeban farmers is that they either 'lose' their appetite or are somehow able to 'overcome' it. Their motivation to eat transforms itself into a motivation to hoard, and not just into a *lack* of motivation to eat, as in satiety. The precise molecular mechanisms that produce this subsumption of short-term individual appetite within long-term collective well-being are not currently known.

*

A sense of time may manifest itself not only in the deferral of gratification, but also in a willingness to initiate an action (directed self-movement) *in the absence of* the anticipated reward. A striking example of an animal satisfying an appetite by a strategy that seems to involve planning and temporal awareness is the behaviour observed in African elephants, which trek vast distances to specific salt 'mines' such as Mount Elgon on the Kenya-Uganda border in order to meet their need for salt. After a lengthy expedition, herds of salt-hungry animals descend 100 metres into the pitch-black depths of the extinct volcano, where they use their tusks to gouge lumps of sodium sulphate rock from the cave walls. Ian Redmond, who has studied the elephants, believes that their knowledge of the caves and the salt they contain has been passed down from mother to calf over generations for perhaps hundreds of thousands of years.[462] The salt-appetite of the elephants, in conjunction with individual and possibly cultural memory, thus allows the animals to undertake a targeted 'pursuit' of the food they need – as opposed to a merely random search – in spite of the lack of any direct sensory stimulation from the target in question. The elephants set out on their journey far from the mountain, following established trails through the Kenyan forest long before any outward cue could betray the proximity of the salt on which they depend to restore their homeostatic equilibrium. Motivation and memories are what get the elephants to where they want and need to be.

This ability to initiate and perpetuate an activity in the absence of a sensory stimulus emanating from its target has been taken as essential to consciousness: 'Take your favorite sensory motor routine in some species and enforce a waiting period of a few seconds between the sensory input and the execution of an action', suggests neuroscientist Christof Koch. 'If the subject can't perform the task with the delay, it was probably mediated by a zombie agent'.[463] There is a good deal that is appealing about the idea that memory is indispensable to consciousness. A complete lack of memory conjures up the image of a zombie-like automaton in thrall to the sensory stimuli that are immediately present to it. Koch's criterion would almost certainly demote amoebae and unicellulars in general (though not, for example, fruit flies)[464] to abject zombie-hood, and I suspect he would want it that way.[465] It should be borne in mind, however, that zombies – whether philosophical or non-philosophical[466] – are not supposed even to feel hungry, and there is no reason to insist that an amoeba cannot be hungry just because it cannot think about, or remember, a particular paramecium in its absence. Memory is intrinsic to everything we value about human consciousness. Yet it is not self-evident that it is essential to elementary consciousness itself; the deepest nature of consciousness is not a function of what we value about consciousness. What Koch interprets as a zombie agent may actually be conscious but absolutely bereft of memory. Indeed, an *absolute* absence of memory is itself an idealization given that any sensory input into a living system may have physiological consequences that decay over time rather than instantaneously.

To the extent that the salt-seeking elephants are relying on memory handed down from past generations instead of on external cues, they are taking a certain risk. What if a malevolent, mountain-moving experimenter has shifted the environment around? As it happens, it is a negligible risk, and the elephants are justified in their sense of object permanence. Cross-generational 'memory' may also take the form of the hard-wired or fixed behavioural patterns bequeathed by genetic rather than cultural mechanisms. Here there is a greater risk of behavioural inflexibility. To be optimally adaptive, the inheritance from the past – whether genetic, neural or cultural – must be capable of modification by ongoing *learning*. A failure to modify memories can be as machine-like as the absence of memories in the first place. In other words, to engage in an activity on the basis *merely* of memory (e.g. genetic hard-wiring) may prove as inflexible as doing so on the basis *merely* of external cues in the manner of Koch's mnemonically challenged 'zombie'.

A much-commented example is the behaviour of the digger wasp *Sphex*, which is 'programmed' to bring a paralysed cricket to its burrow to serve as food for the grubs that will hatch from its eggs. The wasp's genetically inherited routine is to drag the cricket to the threshold of the burrow, enter the burrow to check that there are no intruders, and then drag the cricket in. If a human experimenter interferes by moving the cricket a few inches away while the wasp is inspecting the burrow, however, the routine is disrupted: on re-emerging from the burrow, the wasp drags the cricket back to the threshold and again checks for intruders, failing to take into account that it has already done so. If the cricket is again moved a few inches away while the wasp is inside the burrow, the procedure is repeated, and so on (until the experimenter loses interest). The wasp never remembers that it has already carried out its inspection and thus never deposits the cricket straight inside the burrow.[467] The lack of learning results in a dearth of flexibility that makes the behaviour seem *stupid* to the omniscient experimenter. Nonetheless, intelligence is not the same as consciousness.[468] Although being smart may permit behaviour to become more versatile and consciousness more sophisticated, at root consciousness does not depend on a capacity to learn.

Two sorts of behavioural flexibility may in fact be distinguished, one more fundamental than the other.[469] On the one hand, an environmental stimulus may elicit a flexible response that varies as a function of the organism's inner state: e.g. hunger or satiety, greater or lesser alertness. On the other hand, a flexible response may result from an organism's ability and disposition to try out new behaviours and repeat what works.[470] Learning of this kind is founded on the ability to associate previously unrelated percepts or experiences, for example by operant conditioning, i.e. learning that a particular action produces a particular outcome.[471] The basic assumption of conditioning theory is that certain behaviours can be reinforced, or strengthened, by being associated with primary positive reinforcers (such as food, sleep, water or sex) and inhibited by association with primary negative reinforcers (such as pain or discomfort). However, such associative learning only works because the primary reinforcers are endowed with valence in the first place; in other words, they possess a qualitative nature as better or worse for self, as more or less pleasant.[472] In this sense, the first-order flexibility occasioned by the qualitative nature of inner states (the feeling of what it is like to be satiated or hungry, comfortable or uncomfortable, which determines whether I do one thing or another) is *prior to* and *presupposed by* the second-order flexibility facilitated by associative learning. Elementary consciousness reveals a world imbued with value and significance, a world that is *better for self* or *worse for self*, pleasurable or painful. This world of value is what provides the foundation for associative learning.[473]

Even so, a limited capacity for learning has been found in certain unicellular organisms. We have already come across the 'dietary imprinting' exhibited by *Didinium nasutum* and other ciliates,[474] which may be interpreted as a rudimentary mode of learning to the extent that an organism's present behaviour is determined not just by its inherited constitution but also its (more or less)[475] individual nutritional history. The preferences of such predators, as well as their speed and skill in prey handling, are directly related to their prior dietary experience. In itself, such learning need not be taken to imply consciousness, as the process remains automatic, providing a pre-programmed 'flexibility' that on balance presumably adapts the feeding creature to the nutritional environment most likely to prevail.

One of the most spectacular and least controversial cases of learning is afforded by the filter-feeding trumpet animalcule *Stentor*, which – if persistently molested with noxious particles – will undertake a protracted series of evasive measures before eventually retreating into its tube. Tentatively re-emerging after a while, *Stentor* will start to beat its cilia again so long as the coast is clear, yet if the harassment recommences it will again withdraw into its tube, though this time *immediately*, dispensing with the sequence of avoidance manoeuvres it has gone through before. It has learnt, in effect, that lesser forms of resistance are not worth the trouble. In the end, it will swim away and find itself a new home.[476]

Another early discussion on unicellular learning focused on how quickly paramecia are able to turn round in a capillary tube with a diameter smaller than their own length. This initially takes time, but with practice they come to do it more rapidly and with fewer turns, suggesting that they have 'learnt' to perform the activity with greater agility. Sceptics have countered that the composition of the medium might have changed, or that the creature's pellicle might have become more flexible over the course of the trials.[477] More generally, various unicellular organisms such as the ciliate *Spirostomum* have been found to exhibit non-associative learning in the form of habituation, reducing their response to a stimulus after repeated presentations[478] and thus showing *learnt indifference* to stimuli that prove not to be 'relevant' to self.

Associative learning has been a bone of greater contention. One set of experiments attempted to establish whether paramecia learn to associate bacterial prey with the wire that is used to introduce the prey into the protozoan culture.[479] Another has focused on whether paramecia learn to discriminate between light and dark on the basis of positive reinforcement by 'attractive' cathode stimulation. The idea here is that the paramecia are trained to associate either illumination or its absence with a cathode shock, which has 'attractive' properties (i.e. which they 'like'). During the test sessions, no shock is administered, but the paramecia still 'prefer' the side of the trough they *have learnt to associate* with the cathode shock on the basis of whether it is lit or not.[480] Broad-ranging conclusions are premature given the limited scope of the work carried out, the difficulties of devising, performing and assessing experiments, and the vastness and variety of the realm of single-celled eukaryotes. Yet it would be rash to rule out at least occasional instances of associative learning, possibly also in predator groups other than ciliates.

Knowledge, Thought and Morality

Learning is ultimately secondary to the issue of unicellular consciousness. If present, it may endow it with greater flexibility and versatility, but it need not form a constituent part of it from the outset. Consciousness does not depend upon a creature's ability to associate one thing with another. As such, learning is one of a number of derivative phenomena that are founded upon the intrinsic reflexivity of minimal selfhood and the valenced world that is revealed by consciousness. To conclude this section I shall briefly touch upon some of these features, which are aspects of a more complex 'mental' life that lie *beyond* the elementary consciousness shown by micro-organisms. Though inevitably only scratching the surface of concepts such as knowledge and thought, such an analysis is imperative for a more complete grasp of the *limits* of consciousness in its most fundamental manifestations.

For a start, the claim that an amoeba or dinoflagellate may sometimes be *conscious* of its environment is not necessarily the same as the claim that it is endowed with *knowledge* about its environment. In her Nobel Prize acceptance lecture of 1983, the geneticist Barbara McClintock famously outlined a goal for future generations of biologists: 'to determine the extent of knowledge the cell has of itself and how it utilizes this knowledge in a "thoughtful" manner when challenged'.[481] In fact, the term 'knowledge' requires further specification. A single-celled organism does not have 'knowledge' in the sense of propositional knowledge (knowledge *that*), because it does not have a propositional language at its disposal. However, it does have dispositional knowledge (knowledge *how to*), manifest in its proficiency in identifying, chasing and engulfing a paramecium or diatom and in pursuing its own interests in general. Such an organism should likewise not be understood to have 'self-knowledge' in the sense of an explicit apprehension of its own identity as the subject of a sequence of experiences or as an autobiographical self with a life-story. There are no grounds for believing that a protozoan is blessed with a concept of itself *as* itself. But it does have the pre-reflective self-awareness that has been examined above, embodied in its appetites, its motivations and its bodily self-presence: what we have called its 'tacit selfhood'.

To the extent that the consciousness displayed by predatory protozoans is logically prior to the use of concepts, moreover, such micro-organisms cannot be ascribed a capacity for thought. *Oxyrrhis* and *Didinium* (with all due respect) are not 'thinkers'. Again, the terms in question require further specification. The notion of a 'concept' has itself been understood in different ways by different people. Some regard the possession of concepts as a *linguistic* capacity that consists in an ability to use words correctly in diverse situations according to a meaning established by convention. This 'strong' understanding of concepts unequivocally excludes any creature without a language.[482] A 'weaker' sense of the term equates concept-possession with an ability to recognize or distinguish different categories of entity. Yet this sense seems rather too flimsy, leaving it unclear how the possession of concepts is to be distinguished from mere perception, in that to perceive is already to perceive *as*.[483] In general usage, something more is demanded of a concept.

One option is to characterize concepts as enabling us to *represent* something in its absence, a faculty seemingly denied to protozoans such as *A. proteus*. Or we might expect the possession of concepts to involve an ability to *combine* them – rather like building blocks – into meaningful composites, or thoughts.[484] In contrast with the structural complexity of much human thought, we might concede that the structure of non-human thought need consist of no more than concept A (or B or C) in conjunction or association with concept a (or b or c). In the case of the salt-hungry elephants, for example, we might imagine a concept of 'salt' (A) being combined with a concept of a particular spatial location (a) to produce the thought (Aa). The fact that the concept of 'salt' (A) *could*, in theory at least, be combined with concepts of other spatial locations (Ab or Ac), just as the particular spatial location (a) *could* be combined with other resources or activities such as dust baths or underwater pools (Ba or Ca), is what turns 'salt' and the particular spatial location into concepts, and the composite of the two of them into a thought.

In the case of the prey-hungry amoebae, by contrast, there is a suspicion that 'prey' is *always* 'there' by contrast with 'here', with no further spatial qualification required or possible. This entails that any putative concept of 'prey' is not separable or detachable from its deictic spatial location ('there') and thus incorporates it *as part of* the concept.[485] An item of prey is necessarily 'what is there'; once it is 'here' it has already been ingested, or is on the way to becoming so. The ability of the amoeba to distinguish a paramecium from a diatom is not inconsistent with this, for any such differentiation can be assumed to occur tacitly and without explicit awareness. Once a paramecium is 'there' (i.e. the focus of attention), any diatom that was previously 'there' ceases to be so; it goes off the radar. This leaves us with a solitary, non-combinable concept of 'prey-there', which is about as useful for thought-formation as a single brick for building a house.

Without knowledge, concepts or thoughts, the conscious self of unicellular organisms excludes a self-concept and the power of reflective introspection: the single-celled predator does not 'know' that it is hungry, or entertain thoughts akin to 'I'm *dying for* a paramecium!' More broadly speaking, it necessarily excludes any sort of narrative or autobiographical self. Yet just as significant in comparing protozoan consciousness with less elementary forms of consciousness is the apparent lack of social emotion (perhaps any emotion) and of moral awareness. In this context, of course, the prosocial behaviours of *D. discoideum* farmers – or even slime bacteria[486] such as *Myxococcus xanthus* – raise questions that are as difficult to answer as they are interesting. However, genuine morality is normally deemed to involve two factors that lie beyond the reach of even the most social of microbes: language and the ability to generalize on the one hand, and a 'theory of self' on the other. Language and generalization ground the normative component of morality, allowing the formulation of rules of behaviour that are considered to be applicable in diverse circumstances. Possession of a theory of self, more commonly designated 'theory of mind', is what opens up the world of empathy and shame.[487]

This is the world familiar to socially interacting human selves, a world in which each self no longer operates in splendidly solipsistic isolation, but coexists and interacts with other selves, each one an end in itself. 'Empathy' denotes precisely this recognition by one self that another self is also a *self to itself*, fostering identification with this other 'selfish' perspective on the world and with the interests and points of view of a self other than oneself. 'Shame' stems from the converse. It involves the recognition by one self that it is itself an 'other' to other selves, producing our awareness that we are ourselves objects of perception to those who view us (and judge us) from their own 'selfish' perspective. These two factors, empathy and shame, have been decisive in the development of selves that are motivated – or regard it as in their interest – to behave in the interests of selves other than themselves, i.e. to act in ways that may be held to be moral.

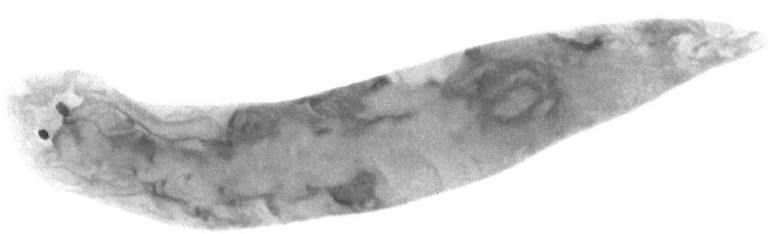

Figure 2: Dugesia tigrina
typically measuring ca. 5–10 mm in length

Figure 3: Oxyrrhis marina
typically measuring ca. 0.02–0.03 mm in length

Figure 4: Stentor
reaching up to 2 mm in length

Figure 5: Tripedalia cystophora
typical bell diameter 7–10 mm

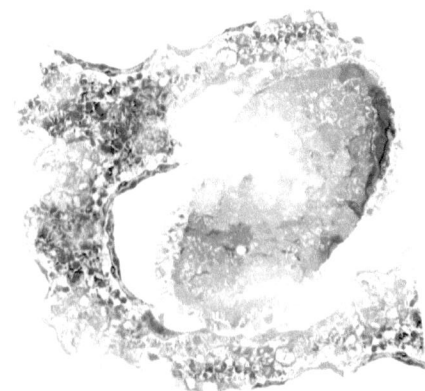

Figure 6: Amoeba proteus
consuming *Paramecium*
typical *A. proteus* measuring
ca. 0.5 mm in length

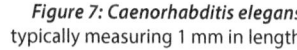

Figure 7: Caenorhabditis elegans
typically measuring 1 mm in length

VII.

Epilogue: Consciousness in Simple Animals

Three Questions

The argument of this book has been that the minimal self, appropriately defined, provides an explanatory foundation for the most elementary forms of consciousness. The idea is that consciousness is logically entailed by certain directional modes of self-moving selfhood. This has been seen to allow for the ascription of consciousness to some free-living protozoans some of the time (though by no means all or always), but it also has similar implications for metazoans that engage in similar activities in similar contexts.

If the preceding argument is on the right lines, there are three sets of questions that need to be asked in order to ascertain whether or not the attribution of consciousness to a particular entity is appropriate. The first set of questions relates to whether the entity in question is a self, as defined in terms of intrinsic reflexivity. This is not merely a matter of whether it shows a capacity to maintain itself, i.e. whether it is a metabolic system that uses an influx of energy or fuel to keep itself going. Equally significant, as we shall see, is whether it displays the intrinsic reflexivity of self-containment, manifest in a capacity to separate self from non-self and in the functional unity and interdependence of its constituent parts.[488] The second set of questions concerns whether the entity genuinely moves itself and, if it does, whether this movement is guided or oriented by external cues: in other words, is it truly directional self-movement as opposed to random locomotion? The third set of questions asks whether the entity's self-propulsion represents an invariable reflex that always occurs in response to a particular external stimulus or whether it depends upon a variable internal state (e.g. hunger as opposed to satiety). Such a dichotomy raises the possibility of it being 'like' something to be such a self in such a situation. This in turn tacitly determines the relationship – predation or sated indifference – between the self in question and the non-self it may or may not pursue.

In the following account I shall touch first and foremost upon just a few categories of animals, or animal-like organisms, considered 'primitive', 'basal' or 'ancestral' in evolutionary terms. In practice, this means that the most recent common ancestor we share with such creatures lived in the depths of the evolutionary past, possibly more than 500 million years ago. Of course, the extant representatives of such lineages have been evolving as we have ever since. By contrast with our cousins the primates or with mammals in general, or even with vertebrates as a whole, however, they are animals with which we are only distantly related. Some of these animals are small, their size overlapping with that of the larger protozoans, but a more prevalent feature is that they are not endowed with a brain, or not much of a brain, at least in comparison with the swollen-headed megacephaly boasted by humans. The focus is thus on animals that are not commonly regarded as conscious. At the same time, it is on animals about which a reasonable amount is known and that can be taken to provide a representative illustration of the main issues.

The first of the three sets of questions – the criterion of self-containing selfhood – rules out of contention certain classes of entities that may be deemed capable of self-movement but that lack other key features of full selfhood. As emerged from the analysis of progressively more sophisticated versions of 'Cugnot's car' in *The Minimal Self*,[489] such considerations apply to the self-steering, self-fuelling drones we are likely to witness in the alarmingly near future. These may well show a self-maintaining 'metabolism' in the form of a capacity to propel themselves to wherever they can procure the energy needed to keep this metabolism running. They may even be said to partake in a manner of 'reproductive symbiosis' that involves satisfying the needs of their human users.[490] At least as conceived in the thought experiment, however, such proto-selves lack the self-containment – the thoroughgoing functional integration – associated with consciousness. This applies especially to the processing of information. More specifically, the information-transmission channels that relay a signal received by a sensor to a motor effector capable of generating appropriate locomotion can be excised from the 'self' as a whole without impairing anything *other* than its self-movement. In the case of living unicellular and multicellular organisms, by contrast, the information-processing circuit is an integrated and inseparable part of the self-maintaining self in its entirety.

The question nonetheless arises whether such self-containment is necessarily an all-or-nothing phenomenon. Would it not be a sufficient level of integration if the information channels were simply to incorporate a link to the drone's internal state, monitoring whether or not it had enough fuel to accomplish its present activity and then locate, reach and tap into a power supply? The signals relayed by the data-transmission channels would thus integrate information generated both by external stimuli, such as the location of a nearby energy source, and internal stimuli, such as the entity's own energy levels (its 'hunger'). It is easy to imagine a drone programmed not only to perform a task unpleasant or dangerous to humans, but also – whenever it was running low on fuel (i.e. 'hungry') – to break off and search for a power line on which to perch and recharge itself by scavenging from the electricity grid.[491] Or perhaps it might even have to chase and catch its power source, like a predator pursuing prey. Such an artefact would certainly *behave* like a rudimentarily conscious self, yet most of us would probably balk at conceding that it might be 'like anything' to be such an entity, dismissing it as a mere 'simulation' of conscious behaviour. And what if *we* were its power source, its prey? Would we still insist on putting the scare quotes around 'hungry'?

That self-containment, and by extension selfhood, is not an all-or-nothing phenomenon is also illustrated by the social amoeba *Dictyostelium discoideum*, individual cells of which can aggregate to form a motile multicellular body called a 'grex' that nonetheless does not belong to the lineage of metazoans.[492] The question here is whether self-containment (with concomitant selfhood) is best ascribed to the individual amoebae, which are membrane-bound and functionally integrated protozoans that eat, grow and reproduce in their own right, or to the slug-like multicellular body that is formed when food runs short and up to two million of them unite in common cause. Indeed, the grex too shows remarkable cohesion in its behaviour, migrating towards heat and light and avoiding repulsive odours such as ammonia. It is physically surrounded and supported by a thin slime sheath; its constituent cells show, at least incipiently, the sort of specialization characteristic of animal bodies; and it even has an immune system designed to distinguish and bar access to forms of non-self such as parasitic conspecifics or pathogenic bacteria.

Whereas the individual cells of stably self-contained complex metazoans never stray from the multicellular body that 'contains' them, however, the individual cells of the *Dictyostelium* grex may be enticed (by cAMP, the very chemoattractant that caused them to aggregate in the first place) to untether themselves from their own multicellular body and join forces with a nearby grex that wanders too close. Any particular grex can be split into two, and two of them can fuse with one another. In this respect, the individual amoebae do not fully subsume their selfhood within an indivisible collective self, and it is *as discrete cells* that they may respond to attractants and repellents in the environment around them. In spite of the adaptive appropriateness of its coordinated self-movement, therefore, the multicellular *Dictyostelium* grex lacks the requisite self-containing unity to be considered a potential candidate for consciousness, *at least as a grex*.

Sponges and Other Filter Feeders

Similar concerns might be raised about what is generally considered to be the most basal metazoan phylum, Porifera, whose members are usually known as sponges. Here too the relationship between the individual self of the constituent cells and the collective self of the organism as a whole is more flexible than in complex metazoans such as humans or insects. Most graphically, the individual cells display a greater capacity to survive autonomously if sundered from one another and from the body they constitute.[493] At the same time, however, the status of the multicellular animal as a self in its own right is emphatically reinforced by the epithelium-like outer layer of flattened cells that holds it together and separates inside from outside. Equally, the animal is protected by a highly developed immune system that includes specialized amoeboid cells known as archaeocytes capable of identifying and engulfing bacterial non-self in the manner of the macrophages of mammalian immune defences.

It is thus for other reasons that sponges are likely to be excluded from the kingdom of consciousness. Above all, Porifera is a class of fundamentally *sessile* filter feeders. Most poriferans consist of a system of chambers that take in water through pores called ostia and expel it from one or more oscula at the top. As the water circulates through the body of the sponge, it encounters a series of progressively finer filters that sift out bacteria, protists and particles of organic matter for engulfment by individual cells through phagocytosis. Mobile archaeocytes subsequently travel through the sponge distributing ingested nutrients to other cells involved in activities such as reproduction or skeleton construction. Yet the sponge as a whole remains immobile, in this sense resembling a plant rather than an animal.

Many species appear all the more plant-like because individual cells host photosynthetic endosymbionts such as cyanobacteria or green algae, which share the energy they harvest from the sun in return for protection and a cosy home. Like plants, moreover, they are able to respond appropriately to a range of environmental stimuli, closing the oscula to stop or diminish the flow of water through the aquiferous system if the suspended particles are too large or densely concentrated, or secreting toxic mucus to ensure that the oscula are not overgrown by corals. Fleeing is not an option in the face of predators, but sponges are afforded special protection by calcareous or siliceous needles and an array of chemicals that are poisonous to animals with a nervous system.[494]

Sponges were traditionally thought to be filter-feeding detritivores, herbivores or bacterivores, 'restricted in their aggressive activities to waging chemical warfare in substrate competition with other sessile organisms and in anti-predatory defence against mobile animals'.[495] This is now known not necessarily to be the case. Deep-sea sponges such as the harp sponge *Chondrocladia lyra* have dispensed with the system of filtering bacteria and microalgae from a throughflow of water, instead adopting a carnivorous lifestyle that involves ensnaring copepods and other small crustaceans that happen to bump into their branching appendages. The captured prey are then gradually engulfed and broken down within a secreted digestive membrane. Clearly distinct from filter feeding, such a strategy recalls the diffusion feeding of unicellular radiolarians, heliozoans and suctorians. Although the manipulation and ingestion of the prey requires work, no genuine locomotion is called for, and as with the above-mentioned protists it seems logically superfluous to posit any consciousness on the part of the predator, whose strategy is essentially a passive assimilation of whatever comes its way.[496]

According to the present argument, the sedentary nature of both diffusion-feeding carnivorous sponges and the filter-feeding bacterivorous variety renders consciousness unnecessary. Yet the phenomenon of filter feeding in particular is diverse in its manifestations. As in the case of unicellulars, there are variations in the amount of work and movement demanded of different types of filter feeder. One relevant factor is whether it is ambient currents that bring the food to be filtered out or whether the flow of water is produced by the organism's own metabolic energy. The flow through the internal chambers of sponges, for example, is at least partially generated by the beating flagella of specialized cells called choanocytes. Sea lilies

– which belong to the phylum of echinoderms – are sessile animals that sit on a stalk, holding five arms outstretched to funnel sinking detritus into their mouth.[497] A less passive strategy is deployed by salps, chordates like us, which vigorously contract their barrel-shaped gelatinous body, using a kind of jet propulsion to power water *through* themselves and trap plankton and organic matter as it traverses a series of internal meshes.[498] Another filter-feeding chordate, the simple, fish-like lancelet (or amphioxus) burrows into the sand in shallow waters, with just its head protruding to sift food from ambient currents.[499]

Varying degrees of metabolic work notwithstanding, none of these filter feeders requires any form of directed self-movement for the acquisition of food, meaning that their eating habits do not *in themselves* provide a foundation for consciousness. This is not to say that an animal such as the lancelet is never conscious; it simply rules out food-seeking, directional locomotion as the root of amphioxus consciousness, if such there is. It is possible that consciousness might emerge for other purposes involving sporadic directional behaviour, such as steering clear of predators or searching for a mate or a suitable place to bury itself in the sediment.

That filter feeding need not be incompatible with the possible occurrence of consciousness is highlighted by examples such as the basking shark, *Cetorhinus maximus*, the second largest of all extant fish. As with unicellular filter feeders such as *Paramecium*, the currents that are filtered are actively generated by the motion of the animal as a whole. In theory, the movement *could* be non-directional to the extent that the feeder simply sweeps through an area rich in nutrients. However, the survival of these gentle leviathans hangs crucially upon their ability to pinpoint the richest possible *patches* of plankton, and this presupposes sensory and decision-making apparatus that dictates not only where to go but how long to stay, in short how to maximize intake and minimize risk. Observations of the feeding behaviour of basking sharks have shown that the time they spend in a particular prey patch is proportional to the density of zooplankton found there. Movements between these patches take one or two days and involve distances of several kilometres. The sharks apparently follow temperature gradients and tidal flows, possibly also sensing the weak electric fields generated by copepod muscle activity or the dimethyl sulphide released when zooplankton graze on phytoplankton.[500] In such circumstances, food-oriented consciousness seems more than plausible, as well as that associated with the range of other activities in which basking sharks engage.

The Non-Directional Movement of Placozoans

The second of the questions outlined at the beginning of this chapter concerns whether the potential candidate for the ascription of consciousness engages in self-movement and, if so, whether this self-movement is genuinely directional. In the case of the sessile filter feeders and diffusion feeders encountered above, the answer is clearly no. However, there is a creature commonly regarded as one of the most ancestral of all metazoans – the placozoan *Trichoplax adhaerens* – that does resort to locomotion in its pursuit of nourishment.[501]

Trichoplax is certainly the simplest known animal in terms of its morphology and organization, lacking organs of any sort, muscle cells and nerve cells. This tiny inhabitant of tropical and subtropical coasts is a more or less flat, disk-shaped agglomeration of cells, measuring up to two or three millimetres in width and just 15 micrometres in height, but with an amoeboid capacity to modulate its seemingly shapeless form. Like other relatively simple metazoans, it has a notable ability to regenerate quickly and effectively after injury, and if one individual is sliced into two, both of the resultant parts may well survive in their own right. This suggests that the factor of self-containment – the functional interdependence among the parts of a unitary whole – is less pronounced than in complex metazoans such as mammals, which tend to perish if any of their constituent parts are removed. Fission also underlies the mechanism of vegetative reproduction by which a mother individual divides into two genetically identical daughters, again recalling the analogy with an amoeba. At the same time, however, the diminutive animal is unambiguously 'contained' by both an upper and lower epithelium, which sandwich a loosely spaced filling of contractile fibre cells. Its movement, which involves either beating its cilia to glide across the substrate or contracting the central layer of fibre cells to modify its body shape, is cohesive and coordinated. In these respects, it is undoubtedly a self.

Trichoplax is blessed with two modes of feeding. Most ingestion seems to take place through the ventral epithelium, i.e. the underside of the organism. When the gliding placozoan reaches a patch of algae, the beating of its cilia ceases and the animal comes to a halt. The digestion is extracellular: secretory cells called lipophils[502] distributed uniformly across the ventral surface release granules whose contents lyse the algae beneath, and the resulting chyme is rapidly absorbed. Once this is done, the beating of the cilia recommences and the animal glides away to new algal pastures. Yet algae and other food particles may also be incorporated through the dorsal epithelium. In this case, the digestion is intracellular and involves a mechanism that has been called 'transepithelial cytophagy',[503] which is to say that the particles pass through the dorsal cell layer on their way to being phagocytosed by fibre cells within. The dorsal epithelium is also believed to permit the expulsion of waste material.

Whereas the dorsal mode of ingestion appears to consist in a somewhat random assimilation of anything edible that comes down from above and adheres to the mucosal layer of the upper epithelium, ventral ingestion is known to be coordinated with movement of the body as a whole. In the absence of food, *Trichoplax* is constantly gliding, rotating and modifying its morphology. As its food increases in abundance, pauses become more frequent and longer-lasting, locomotion becomes slower and the animal becomes flatter, increasing its surface area to facilitate digestion. The simple logic is that movement is neither required nor even desirable in a place that is *good for self* (i.e. rich in nutrients), but is likely to become so once again when the nutrients run out. Even without anything akin to a nervous system, therefore, the placozoan not only senses the presence or absence of food, but is presumed to emit intercellular signals that foster the synchronized modulation of locomotory behaviour, orchestrating the rhythm of the ciliary strokes.[504] Coordinated though it may be, however, its locomotion always remains random. To the extent that the movement is non-directional, it is logically superfluous to posit any consciousness on the part of the placozoan of the world in which it glides or shuffles about. *Trichoplax* remains oblivious to the path that will lead it, or not, to a food-rich environment that is again *better for self*.

'Hungry' Cnidarians

In considering the directionality of movement, there is another phylum of basal metazoans that provides an interesting range of behavioural alternatives. This phylum is Cnidaria, some members of which may moreover be described as displaying physiological states akin to 'hunger' or 'satiety'.[505] Although most cnidarians are obligate predators, not all species are motile.

The sessile sea anemones, for example, depend upon water currents and the unwitting approach of prey to bring potential food items into contact with their tentacles. The tentacles are armed with specialist cells called cnidocytes. Flanked by mechano- and chemosensitive supporting cells, cnidocytes fire the phylum-defining cnidae (or nematocysts) that capture and kill the prey for subsequent conveyance to a centrally located mouth. This in itself raises the knotty question of whether the discharge of a nematocyst – in response to a combination of chemical stimulation, vibration and mechanical contact – is more appropriately likened to a form of directional self-movement (the targeting of a perceived object) or to the thigmonasty of a carnivorous plant such as the Venus flytrap, the rapid shutting of which is a largely invariable reflex. Or perhaps it falls somewhere in between?

The issue is further complicated by studies showing that when sea anemones are 'satiated' or 'fed to repletion' they exhibit a marked reduction both in nematocyst discharge and prey ingestion, whereas prolonged 'food deprivation' leads to increased nematocyst discharge and greater ingestion of prey.[506] Might we – at a stretch – conceive of hunger in these most sedentary of animals? The matter is far from straightforward. For a start, even a well-fed animal continues to fire *some* nematocysts, although these have been found to exhibit a lower 'intrinsic adherence' or holding power than otherwise.[507] This reduction in predatory 'efficiency' could be due to substances exuded by wounded prey or to inhibitory factors derived from the nematocysts themselves.[508] In other words, the decrease in successful prey capture need not reflect an 'inner state' ascribable to the sea anemone (a putative 'sensation' of satiety) but could be the consequence of what appears to be a functional flaw. Perhaps the sea anemone is as relentless an 'eating machine' as single-celled *Vorticella*, its insatiability only curbed by the non-adherence of its nematocysts. Or perhaps both factors are involved, the truth again residing somewhere in between.

Another class of broadly sedentary cnidarian, the hydra, provides an illuminating variation on the theme. Like other basal metazoans, hydras show remarkable powers of regeneration that almost seem to undermine the unity of fully self-containing selfhood. If a hydra is cut in half, for example, the top half will grow its foot back, and the bottom half its head. If both the head and the foot are cut off, the remaining stump retains its original polarity to grow a head at the top and a foot at the bottom.[509] A fragment consisting of just 300 cells is able to reconstitute itself into a complete individual. In their regenerative flexibility hydras resemble sponges,[510] but unlike sponges they have a fully functional nervous system capable of generating a coordinated response to a stimulus. Sensitive to touch as well as to chemicals in the water, their sensory cells transmit impulses to a diffuse nerve net that enables the animal *as a whole* to act as a single, integrated self. This sensitivity applies above all to a chemical identified as glutathione, which has been found to cause the hydra to open its mouth and to induce a characteristic posture in the tentacles around the mouth.

The significance of glutathione is that it tends to be released by dying animals along with the tissue fluids that escape on being punctured by a nematocyst. When a prey animal is captured and injured, the ensuing glutathione concentration gradient not only elicits the posture of 'anticipation' in the hydra, but enables it to locate its potential meal with its mouth, bending in the direction where the gradient is most pronounced. If additional glutathione is mixed into the water (by an interfering experimenter), the gradient is annulled and the ability of the hydra to obtain its food is seriously curtailed. The hydra ends up 'confused' and its coordination impaired.[511] Again, therefore, some degree of directed movement is involved, albeit just a part of the body up a single gradient.

Again, moreover, a dimension of differential 'hunger' or 'satiety' appears to be present, manifest in behavioural variations associated with varying physiological states in the hydra. A well-fed hydra will not react to food that is offered to it but will remain quietly attached to the substrate, only displaying its feeding response if stimulated with an unusually high concentration of glutathione.[512] Once its appetite has returned, it will exhibit a different set of behaviours, contracting and stretching its body and tentacles in new directions as though 'seeking' a quarry. With time (and increasing hunger), the contractions and stretchings increase in frequency and vigour. Eventually, the hydra will move off to a new location, gliding along on the amoeboid cells of its base or performing a 'somersault' that involves bending over, attaching its tentacles to the substrate, loosening its base and then swinging over like a tiny gelatinous gymnast.[513] Such displacements may be random in orientation or in some cases minimally directional, taking advantage of the hydra's photosensitivity to aim for better-lit areas where nutrition tends to be more abundant. In other cases, the hydra simply allows itself to float freely with the currents.

Leaving aside any residual gelatinophobia, one thus wonders whether the sporadic positive phototaxis of a 'hungry' hydra provides grounds for the attribution of elementary consciousness. Is it 'like' anything to be such a hydra as it heads towards what is *better for self*, i.e. the light that signals a more probable presence of food? To the extent that its behaviour is different from the behaviour it shows when it is in a different physiological state ('sated'), the ascription of 'hunger' makes sense. But the recurrent uncertainty is whether we are justified in divesting the 'hunger' and 'satiety' of their scare quotes.

The present argument is that true appetite, in this basalmost context, is what tacitly structures and shapes the consciousness presupposed by flexibly directional self-movement, i.e. by genuine behaviour in the sense of 'action'. If there is no action but only random or invariant locomotion, consciousness and the tacit selfhood that structures it are logically unnecessary: no genuine 'being like' need be inferred, and the attribution of 'hunger' or 'satiety' must remain metaphorical. In the case of our hydra, of course, the motion may be considered directional precisely to the extent that it includes phototaxis alongside sessile and non-directional strategies. Even granting the occasional occurrence of guided locomotion, however, movement up a gradient towards a potential *prey patch* (i.e. an area that is statistically more likely to yield nourishment) perhaps falls short of movement towards an individualized *prey item*, bringing us back to the logical puzzle raised on page 76. We may still be a step or two away from elementary consciousness.

Other cnidarians are more motile, yet not necessarily more likely to be endowed with consciousness. The 'slow swimming' of the feeding jellyfish *Aglantha digitale*, for example, is based upon an initial process of upward propulsion that involves the rhythmic contraction of a conical sheet of muscles and the expulsion of water from within its gelatinous bell. This is followed by a stage of drifting passively downwards and thereby 'fishing' for whatever items of prey happen to be in the way.[514] At the bottom of this descent, the jellyfish realigns itself by means of a set of gravity-sensing statocysts akin to the otoliths of the vertebrate vestibular system to which we owe our sense of balance. Having righted itself in this manner, *Aglantha* can duly propel itself upwards again. Noteworthy is that if its statocysts are removed, the swimming movement of the jellyfish becomes haphazard and aimless. This shows just how reliant the successful feeding movement of *Aglantha* is upon the implicit orientation associated with its statocysts, the prerequisite for an invariant form of 'dumb' but highly effective taxis. Insofar as the directionality of its movement is pre-established and thus unvarying with respect to environmental contingency, consciousness is not in itself entailed by such a strategy.

Still other free-swimming cnidarian medusas appear to possess a greater degree of discernment of their environment. The Caribbean box jellyfish (or cubozoan) *Tripedalia cystophora* (illustration page 161) has aroused particular interest on account of an elaborate visual system comprising 24 eyes of four different kinds.[515] Eight of these eyes are complex, lens-bearing sensory structures morphologically similar to the vertebrate eye, sparking a certain amount of controversy and speculation on their capacity for image-formation and 'crude' forms of vision.[516] Even though the retina of *T. cystophora*'s lensed eyes is commonly thought to lack the resolution needed to generate a focused image, however, the sophistication of the animal's visual system – in conjunction with its ability to modulate the dynamics of bell contraction and to regulate and channel bell outflow – permits it to adjust both the speed and direction of its swimming to suit its needs.[517] By means of rapid phototactic locomotion, it is thus able to navigate towards the vertical light shafts that tend to be populated by the dense swarms of copepods on which it habitually preys. Once located within a light shaft, it maintains its position there by non-directional modifications of its swimming behaviour, reducing its speed, increasing its turning rate, and pivoting abruptly should it happen to stray away. The result is that *Tripedalia cystophora* can discern and target the light shaft even though it does not see the copepods themselves, its swimming behaviour *within* the shaft remaining largely unaffected by the presence or absence of its prey.[518]

There remain important questions pertinent to the possible ascription of consciousness to *Tripedalia*. Is its movement towards light in any way modulated by levels of 'hunger' or 'satiation'? If not, it may be dismissed as an automatic feeder or 'eating machine', its navigation towards light little more than an invariant taxis reminiscent of unicellular *Paramecium*, and its persistence within the light shaft just non-directional kinesis. As with hydra, we may continue to harbour residual doubts about the targeting of a prey *patch* as opposed to an individual *item*.[519] Yet the box jellyfish is perhaps the most likely cnidarian candidate for consciousness on account of the greater motility and more varied behavioural repertoire that set it apart from the largely sedentary hydra. Its multifaceted visual system makes guided locomotion possible in situations other than feeding, enabling it (for example) to avoid obstacles in the water and use visual cues to navigate back – if washed away – to its preferred habitat among the mangrove roots.[520] *Tripedalia* has even been found to exhibit diurnal activity patterns (foraging in the day and resting at night) that may imply a condition in some respects resembling sleep.[521] It would be precipitate to rule out rudimentary consciousness on principle or simply because it is made of jelly and lacks a brain.

Two Worms

So far we have not encountered a phylogenetically basal metazoan that unambiguously fulfils the criteria for consciousness proposed in the present treatise. Even relatively complex self-moving selves can fall short by being automatic feeders (with no distinction between hunger and satiety) or by being restricted to forms of locomotion that are not genuinely directional. Many cnidarians exhibit hunger-like states, yet it is not clear how far their movements – in the non-sessile cases – are more than random wanderings or invariable forms of taxis. I shall conclude by focusing on two of the best-known and most frequently studied classes of worm,[522] one endowed with what is widely considered to be a brain, and the other not. The idea is to ascertain whether either or both of these vermiform groups comply with the criteria.

The first of these classes of worm is the flatworm phylum Platyhelminthes,[523] which is mainly made up of parasitic worms (e.g. liver flukes and tapeworms), but which also includes the non-parasitic class Turbellaria, whose most celebrated representatives are planarians such as *Dugesia*. Much of the fame enjoyed by some planarian species is owed to their powers of regeneration, which are comparable to those of the hydra. If an individual planarian worm is cut in two, for example, each part will develop into a complete new worm within a week, the tail segment engendering a fully functional nervous system and brain. Planarians may be cleft into more than 200 pieces, each resulting portion capable of regenerating to form a complete organism.[524] In itself, this may again be taken to infringe the unitary self-containment of planarian selfhood, implying that the individual cells do indeed retain a greater degree of pluripotency, i.e. a greater capacity to survive autonomously in their own right, separate from the multicellular body that happens to contain them. Yet everything else about such planarians testifies to a high degree of cohesion and functional integration. They possess a range of sensory faculties, enabling them to perform a wide variety of behaviours appropriate to a predatory lifestyle in a fluctuating environment. They have chemosensory organs called 'auricles' that permit them to discern the presence of nutrients and toxins in the vicinity and direct their movements accordingly; they have eye-spots called 'ocelli' as well as 'extraocular' photoreceptors responsible for the negative phototaxis that causes them to shun illuminated places; they are also responsive to touch, appear to be sensitive to gravity (if flipped upside down, they will immediately 'right' themselves), and display positive rheotaxis, i.e. a tendency to move counter to a current of water.[525]

This behavioural repertoire is coordinated and supervised by what is sometimes regarded as the 'first' brain,[526] i.e. a bilobed neural structure that subserves the entire body (as opposed to restricted segments) and has functionally specialized parts.[527] Lacking circulatory and respiratory organs, planarians are restricted to small sizes and flat shapes that permit the diffusion of gases such as oxygen throughout their body. Yet although many species of planarian measure less than a centimetre in length and weigh just one five millionth of an average human adult, the ratio of the planarian brain to its body weight is in fact on a par with that of a rat,[528] with 20,000 to 30,000 neurons in a planarian about eight millimetres long.[529] Such a ratio underscores the significance of planarian cephalization, or at least its relative significance (given that planarians can survive decapitation).

The effects of decapitation on planarian feeding behaviour are particularly revealing. An intact planarian shows a clear differentiation between hunger and satiety, as the following description of *Dugesia tigrina* makes clear:

> *When mosquito grubs were presented to a group of planarians, they began moving on the vessel bottom to approach the victim one or several times before capturing it. This is search for food or the reaction of approaching the food object. ... The sucking of the mosquito grub took 10–15 min. Then the planarians gathered on the vessel walls at the water edges and stayed there for a 24-h period. After that, the planarians descended to the vessel bottom and preferred to hide*

under stones. During the next 24 h, the planarians did not react to a new portion of food. However, [after just] 2 days, when the food appeared again, the planarians repeated, with rare exception, the whole repertoire of their feeding behavior.[530]

The varying 'inner state' of the planarian can easily be distinguished on the basis of the variation in its behaviour in otherwise similar circumstances: when hungry, it performs the work of approaching its prey and activating its pharynx; when sated, it ignores – or fails to perceive – the food and remains quiescent. The satiety of *Dugesia*, which lasts two days, may be associated with the temporary transformation of its intestines into a syncytium,[531] this process possibly signalling repletion and inhibiting feeding behaviour. Subsequently, the intestine structure is restored and the worm regains its appetite. A further consideration is that the planarian lacks a through-gut, its pharynx doubling as an anus.

After decapitation, by contrast, *Dugesia* no longer approaches the mosquito grub,[532] and decerebrate planarians generally show a reduction in guided, organized locomotion. Yet there are some species, such as *Planocera gilchristi*, that continue to engage in feeding activity – albeit lacking in coordination – provided that direct contact is made with the prey item.[533] In these cases the manipulation and ingestion of food can occur even in the absence of a brain. Significantly, satiety no longer inhibits further feeding. So although the distinction between hunger and satiety holds for an intact animal, decerebration seems to turn certain planarians – within their mechanical limitations – into 'eating machines'.[534] An implication of this is that, for planarians at least, the presence or absence of a brain makes the difference between the possible occurrence or otherwise of rudimentary consciousness. Simple rhythmic motions may be feasible without a brain, but not complex, coordinated behavioural sequences attuned to the inner state of the animal.[535]

Other behaviours and abilities evinced by flatworms are also closely associated with consciousness. Though not in themselves sufficient for consciousness to be inferred, such behaviours and abilities add dimensions that may enrich its phenomenology. For a start, planarians periodically display a state of rapidly reversible behavioural quiescence and reduced responsiveness to stimuli that ticks all the boxes to be classed as sleep.[536] The quiescence exhibited by planarians is not always a function of satiety, therefore, but may conform to circadian rhythms, occurring in this form predominantly during the day (not surprisingly, given their aversion to light).[537] Like sleep, this underlying rhythm has been found to persist in conditions of continuous darkness, implying an endogenous origin, and it is homeostatically regulated, with sleep deprivation having to be compensated by a subsequent decrease in activity. Such quiescence usually assumes the form of a typical contracted posture. As in other animals such as humans, moreover, it is regulated by the hormone melatonin, pointing to an evolutionarily shared origin. This distinction between wakefulness and sleep – between endogenously generated rhythms of activity and quiescence – provides further evidence of a differential 'inner' state that has recognizable behavioural or locomotive ramifications, manifesting itself as a disposition to move oneself or not (in a given context).

A capacity for learning, as we have seen, is also commonly identified with consciousness, although it is not essential to its most elementary form. Here too planarians prove to have certain abilities. *Dugesia japonica*, for example, shows non-associative modes of learning such as habituation, responding to water turbulence by coming to a halt, but ceasing to react in this way if the turbulence is recurrent.[538] In the field of associative learning, *Dugesia* is usually deemed rather a dullard, apparently requiring scores of training sessions to relate a particular stimulus (a flash of light) with another stimulus (an electric shock) that follows immediately afterwards.[539] However, there are other contexts in which planarians do demonstrate more of a memory. It has been established that worms that have been fed in a particular environment will subsequently be quicker to start eating in this 'familiar' context than others that have never previously been exposed to the feeding area.[540] Such concepts of environmental familiarity or unfamiliarity clearly imply that the planarian has *some kind of* relationship – albeit implicit – to its relatively distant past and is not wholly swallowed up in its 'present'.

Flatworms also have 'preferences'. Their robust negative phototaxis dictates that they generally eschew well-lit areas. If an enticing drop of liver extract is placed in the middle of an illuminated area, therefore, the planarian must 'overcome' its natural aversion to light – as well as its tendency to hug the edges of containers – in order to venture out to procure its coveted meal.[541] This brings us back to the question of how much discomfort an animal is willing to undergo in order to gain a reward, the phenomenon of 'pleasure' again emerging as the common currency by which motivational drives – attractions and aversions – can be weighed up and a decision taken. Experiments on the planarian *Dugesia japonica* have attempted to ascertain the comparative strengths of chemotaxis, phototaxis, thigmotaxis and thermotaxis in a particular set of experimental conditions.[542] Chemical stimuli were found to be the top priority and light stimuli came second, revealing the capacity of these tiny worms to integrate a wealth of diverse stimuli in such a way, presumably, as to maximize well-being and minimize vexation. The result is a scale of values in which an attractive (probably food-related) smell prevails over an unpleasant light or temperature, but *only up to a point*. Once the glare or the heat becomes too intense, the planarian will make a different choice.

Further light is shed upon planarian preferences and pleasures by the effect that drugs have upon them. A straightforward experimental paradigm called the 'conditioned place preference' protocol – which measures the time that an animal spends in a location associated with a stimulus – has shown that planarian worms develop a preference for an area associated with the administration, for example, of the drug methamphetamine, a dopamine agonist.[543] The place in question, in other words, becomes positively associated with the 'reinforcing properties' produced by the drug applied there. Maladaptive and harmful this may be, but such 'reinforcement' presupposes a world suffused with valence, in which the reinforcers themselves have a qualitative nature as more or less pleasant. We are brought back to the earlier definition of a self-moving self as a *pursuer of pleasure*.[544] Like humans and many other metazoan selves, planarians too are inclined to pursue what feels good rather than bad. And this may not in practice always coincide with what actually *is* good.

*

If the arguments I have put forward are valid, it would be churlish not to admit planarians such as *Dugesia* to the club of (sometimes) conscious organisms. Given that the planarian is the only unequivocally successful metazoan candidate so far, this might be taken to imply that consciousness in animals requires a brain, dependent as it is upon coordinated and directional self-movement attuned to an internal state, say, of hunger or satiety. This in turn would seem to rule out nematodes such as *Caenorhabditis elegans*, a diminutive worm comparable in size to many protozoans (roughly 1.3 mm in length and 80 μm in diameter), the adult hermaphrodite of which has a nervous system with just 302 neurons and some 7,000 connections.[545]

But perhaps this hurried dismissal of what has been described as the 'hydrogen atom of systems neuroscience'[546] is unwarranted. Possessed of neither a circulatory nor a respiratory system, the free-living soil-dweller *C. elegans* is certainly capable of adapting its locomotion in a coordinated and integrated manner to a wide range of sensory stimuli, including odorants, touch, light, temperature and vibration. The head or neck region is equipped with a pair of conspicuous sensory organs known as amphids, each of which contains various chemosensory, mechanosensory and perhaps also thermosensory neurons, making appropriately targeted self-movement feasible at least.[547]

At the same time, the first of our three criteria is certainly met. *C. elegans* is robustly self-containing, in terms both of structural integrity[548] and functional integration. By contrast with planarians, it has only very limited powers of regeneration. Apoptosis, or programmed cell death, is not only a normal feature of its development, but a crucial part of the immune system whereby infected or stressed cells 'sacrifice' themselves for the greater good of the organism as a whole.[549] It is clearly a self. Granted the selfhood of each individual *C. elegans* organism, the aim in the remaining pages is to cast a glance at the other two questions relevant to the possible presence of consciousness: 1) does *C. elegans* display genuinely directional locomotion in its pursuit of nourishment? 2) is its self-movement duly attuned to an inner state, say of hunger or satiety?[550]

Some features of the nematode may suggest that the answer to the first question is no. For a start, *C. elegans* is a bacterivorous filter feeder, taking water with suspended food particles (bacteria) into its pharynx, trapping the particles and then expelling the liquid.[551] In itself, this suggests a measure of passivity and non-discernment in its feeding behaviour insofar as the worm does not strictly 'choose' – i.e. individually pick out and pursue – the food that ends up in its pharynx. To be sure, it is a *self-propelling* filter feeder, which means that the work of locomotion is involved. Like the basking shark considered above, in fact, *C. elegans* has the work both of propelling itself through a prey patch shovelling up whatever food it can, and of finding that prey patch in the first place. Yet it is clear that we are not dealing with a predator that perceives and identifies its prey on a one-by-one basis.

A second doubt is whether the nematode moves by orienting itself in the direction of a gradient (the target being where its next meal is) or adopts an essentially non-directional mode of locomotion, i.e. kinesis. The latter has already been seen to subsume a distinction between orthokinesis and klinokinesis. These strategies involve modulation of the animal's speed and turning rate respectively in response to the relative intensity of some form of stimulation. Similar, non-directional strategies have been ascertained in *C. elegans*. First, the nematode has been found to modulate its locomotory rate in the presence of bacteria, moving more slowly than in their absence.[552] Indeed, researchers have established both a 'basal slowing response' and an 'enhanced slowing response' that are activated according to whether the worm is well-fed or food-deprived.[553] The rationale is that, having found what is *good for self*, it makes sense not to navigate away from it, but rather to tarry where goodness is plentiful.

Secondly, foraging nematodes have also been found to exhibit more frequent high-angled turning – 'reversals' as well as sharp head-to-tail manoeuvres known as 'omega turns'[554] – immediately after an encounter with food, gradually reducing the frequency of such turns as time passes since their last repast.[555] To the extent that the procedure consists simply in modifying the overall frequency and angle of otherwise random turns, it too can be considered non-directional. Yet such a strategy has been shown to be capable of maximizing the time a foraging animal spends in nutrient-rich areas and extending the search further afield once the food supply becomes scarcer.[556] It requires an internal timing mechanism to regulate how long the nematode searches locally before starting to follow a more linear trajectory, i.e. some sort of 'physiological clock that keeps track of time elapsed since the last encounter with food'.[557] This timing mechanism could be physical repletion. However, no consciousness of an external world is called for. In itself, the strategy need imply no more than a correlation between the period of time elapsed since the last ingestion of food and the frequency of high-angled turns.[558]

Yet these are not the only locomotory strategies employed by nematodes, and not all their movement is non-directional. *C. elegans* is also known to exhibit strong chemotaxis towards odours associated with food, in particular with bacteria, as well as with mating partners and habitats. It uses six primary sensory neurons to recognize over 40 volatile attractants and repellents.[559] In addition to chemotaxis, it is guided by thermotaxis to preferred temperatures and by aerotaxis to optimum oxygen levels and low levels of carbon dioxide.[560] Though unconcerned with picking out a particular prey item, *C. elegans* is thus perfectly capable of navigating towards locations where it can flourish, i.e. prey patches where it can sate itself. But is this enough for consciousness to be ascribed? Again, we are confronted with the previously raised objection that such chemotaxis may be a merely gradual progression up a gradient (where each minuscule step promises a slightly more bounteous filter-feeding yield) rather than an authentic targeting of a goal. If so, we may be disinclined to view such movement as providing a foundation for consciousness. Or we might prefer to classify it as a borderline case, situating nematode worms at the *threshold* to consciousness.

Such doubts may be further compounded by qualms about the nature of nematode chemotaxis. Chemotactic locomotion requires the animal in question, whether worm or otherwise, to compare the concentration of a chemical attractant at various points in space in order to establish which way the gradient runs. At least three mechanisms are possible.[561] It can be done, for example, by the simultaneous use of two receptors in distinct positions on the body, located to the right and left or the front and back. Alternatively, one or more receptors might compare concentrations measured successively in time as the animal moves forward, as exemplified by *E. coli*. A third mechanism is klinotaxis, which bases the comparison on the lateral displacement of one or more receptors.

The first strategy has generally been ruled out for *C. elegans*. Although the worm has receptors both on its head (amphids) and tail (phasmids), the latter are not normally used in chemotaxis, precluding a comparison of the concentrations sensed anteriorly and posteriorly. The two amphids are not considered to be far enough apart for a lateral comparison to be feasible (or more accurately a dorsoventral comparison, since *C. elegans* swims on its side). It has commonly been held that nematodes base their chemotactic locomotion upon a form of klinotaxis, displacing their amphids dorsoventrally to compare the stimulus intensity at different points and thus orient themselves within the gradient.[562] Chemotactically moving worms were thought to point 'the tip of the head up the gradient, like a weather vane pointing into the wind'.[563]

Yet the weathervane strategy has in turn been called into question. Rather than following a constant orientation, nematodes ascending a gradient have been observed to intersperse periods of relatively smooth movement known as 'runs' with bouts of frequent turning termed 'pirouettes'.[564] These pirouettes occur after episodes in which the worms have been moving down instead of up the gradient, suggesting that they have drifted off course and are heading the wrong way. In themselves, pirouettes may thus suggest a run-and-tumble strategy akin to that used by *E. coli* and other bacteria.

By contrast with the biased random walk, however, it has been argued that the pirouette functions not by *randomizing* the animal's orientation, but by *correcting* its course. If this is so, a form of error compensation may be achieved by correlating (albeit weakly) the size of the turn with the degree to which the worm has veered off course immediately prior to the pirouette.[565] Nematologists have proposed that *C. elegans* pirouettes may thus represent 'a transitional stage between biased random locomotion and continuous alignment with the direction of the gradient'.[566] In fact, it seems likely that the course-correction and weathervane techniques may function in concert, complementing and reinforcing one another.[567]

These different techniques – run-and-tumble, the pirouette and 'weathervane' continuous alignment – incorporate different levels of randomness and directionality, bringing to light once again that the elementary consciousness with which guided locomotion is associated is unlikely to be an all-or-nothing phenomenon. Even though the question of whether the nematode's self-propulsion is genuinely directional is best left as undecided, however, the question of its attunement to an inner state is much less ambivalent.[568] We have already noted that the reduction in speed shown by *C. elegans* on being presented with a meal of bacteria is modulated by its hunger state. Whereas recently fed worms exhibit a 'basal' slowing response, food-deprived worms show a slowing response that is recognizably 'enhanced'. Whether the nematodes are hungry or satiated thus determines differential behaviour in the face of external stimuli and can be identified as such.[569]

This is not all. A state of satiety in *C. elegans* has been found to express itself as a behavioural 'quiescence' that consists in decreased movement and a gradual cessation of food intake.[570] This quiescence bears a close resemblance to satiety in other animals. For a start, it is brought on by high-quality food,[571] which, unlike low-quality food, induces the worm gradually to stop eating and moving about. It also depends on the worm's nutritional status. Mutants deficient in ingestion (pharyngeal pumping) or nutrient absorption show less quiescence, which is thus assumed to require the appropriate signals from the intestine. Thirdly, worms that have fasted prior to feeding are more likely to reach this state of satiety, a previous period of enforced abstinence thus augmenting subsequent quiescence.[572] Intriguingly, mutants lacking a particular kinase[573] (a protein that among other functions determines locomotor states and body size control) do not show quiescence at all, but constantly move and feed. Failing to attain satiety, it is as though they have been transformed by the loss of a protein into 'eating machines' (à la *Vorticella*), bereft of this fundamental behavioural dichotomy. The regulation of nematode quiescence also involves peptide hormones such as insulin, which control feeding in mammals.[574]

Quiescence is to be distinguished from the two other principal locomotor states known in *C. elegans*, dwelling and roaming.[575] Dwelling involves maintaining low speeds, frequent alternations between backward and forward movement, and little overall displacement; it is sometimes associated with 'browsing'. In spite of the superficial similarity between quiescence and dwelling (in that both entail a reduction in locomotion), quiescent worms cease entirely to move or eat, whereas dwelling worms continue to feed actively. As with quiescence, however, the onset of dwelling – or the suppression of roaming – is believed to be triggered by a metabolic signal that is produced following feeding.[576] On eating high-quality food, an initial phase of dwelling may indeed yield to subsequent quiescence (with insulin signalling contributing to the control of both behaviours), suggesting that these distinct locomotor states may possibly represent responses to different *degrees* of satiation.[577]

Characterized above all by inactivity, nematode quiescence has been likened not only to the satiety common to mammals and other animals, but also to their 'post-prandial sleep',[578] recalling the convergence of states akin to satiation and sleep in our trusty amoeba. However, a different form of quiescence, in a different context, comes even closer – if not all the way[579] – to sleep as generally conceived. *C. elegans* passes through four larval stages on its way to adulthood, shedding its cuticle at each transition. Just prior to moulting, the worm exhibits a two to three-hour period of quiescent, sleep-like behaviour known as *lethargus*.[580] Unlike the circadian sleep of other animals, *lethargus* takes place within an 'ultradian' periodicity of seven to nine hours and is associated with the moulting cycle rather than a 24-hour diurnal rhythm. It has been objected that such quiescence might simply be a result of the mechanical constriction caused by ecdysis, yet there are a number of key affinities between *lethargus* and sleep. Not only is *lethargus* characterized by rapidly reversible behavioural quiescence,[581] a stereotypical (hockey-stick-shaped) posture and periodic reduced responsiveness to mechanical and chemical stimuli, but the nematode timing mechanism also shares molecular homology with the circadian timer found across the animal kingdom.[582] Like the sleep of other metazoans, moreover, nematode slumber is homeostatically self-regulating, with periods of enforced wakefulness subsequently redressed by sleep of heightened depth and duration.[583] Worms that are pestered during *lethargus* (for example, by being kept moving) are quicker to return to a quiescent state of inactivity afterwards and are even less responsive to external stimuli. They are out for the count.

As well as the behavioural modifications (or variations in self-movement) generated by the hunger-satiety dichotomy and circadian-like rhythms, another feature shared by nematodes with planarians and other animals is the possession of 'preferences' that may be modified by experience. *C. elegans* has been found to be capable of a form of associative learning that relates the presence of an odorant such as benzaldehyde – and its familiar cherry-almond smell – to the food content in the area.[584] Naïve worms are innately attracted to benzaldehyde but, as a result of a phenomenon known as olfactory adaptation (a kind of habituation), prolonged exposure to the odorant in a food-deficient environment results in attenuation of this attraction. This suppression of the attraction to benzaldehyde is in turn eliminated, however, if they come across the odorant *paired* with *E. coli*. In effect, the worms learn that benzaldehyde does predict a bacterial meal after all. In another set of experiments, the differential pairing of food with chemoattractants such as sodium or chloride ions has been shown to lead to the formation of a preference for ions recently paired with food over those that have not been paired.[585]

An even more dramatic illustration of the nematode's capacity to form associations is the aversive olfactory learning of which it is capable.[586] Although *C. elegans* feeds on bacteria in its natural environment, some bacteria may be harmful to it, leaving it vulnerable to toxicity or infection. Pathogenic strains of bacteria such as *Pseudomonas aeruginosa* and *Serratia marcescens* – both of which are linked with hospital-acquired infections in humans – are able to proliferate in the nematode gut, resulting in its death within a matter of days.[587] *C. elegans* protects itself from pathogens not only by innate mechanisms akin to immunity (enabling it to withdraw from a lawn of *S. marcescens* recognized as pathogenic),[588] but also by *learning* to avoid the odours of such bacteria after interacting with them, effectively associating these odours with the intestinal distress it has suffered on previous occasions. Such induced avoidance of odours and tastes related with 'feeling bad' – an ability to steer clear of what is identified with discomfort or unpleasantness – is a crucial strategy in the worm's pursuit of what is better rather than what is worse for itself. The concept of 'visceral malaise'[589] used by nematologists is no careless anthropomorphism, but clearly implies that it is 'like something' to be a nematode that has recently grazed on dodgy bacteria. It is in some way different from the normal feeling of satiety. The worm's subsequent behaviour (learning to give such pathogens a wide berth) is an *expression* of what it is like.

Given our nagging doubts regarding the directionality of its locomotion, the consciousness of *C. elegans* is likely to remain a grey area, at least for the present. Yet the complexity of its interactions with food suggests that even this tiny worm may inhabit a world perceived differentially as better or worse for itself, or as more or less pleasurable. Such is the logical origin of consciousness.

Glossary

Actin: microfilament-forming protein, abundant in eukaryotic cells and essential to functions such as locomotion and cell division

Allo-: preface signalling the opposite of *auto-*, i.e. by 'non-self' or 'other': e.g. if *autopoiesis* denotes self-creation, *allopoiesis* is creation by non-self or other; in the present context *allo*-containment is used to denote containment by non-self or other, as opposed to self-containment

Amoebozoa: major clade of single-celled eukaryotes, comprising amoeboid protists

Apoptosis: a highly controlled process of programmed cell death, or cell 'suicide'

Arthropod: member of the phylum Arthropoda ('animals with jointed legs'), which includes insects, spiders, scorpions, crabs and the extinct trilobites; they have an exoskeleton, or external skeleton

ATP: adenosine triphosphate: a molecule that stores and transports the energy required to power living processes

Autotroph: an organism that can produce complex organic compounds from simple inorganic compounds, for example by using the energy from sunlight (photosynthesis)

Bacteriophage/phage: a virus that infects bacteria

Bilateria: the clade of animals characterized by bilateral symmetry at some stage in their life cycle, i.e. possessing a front and a back, a top and a bottom, and a right and a left; it includes the protostomes and the deuterostomes (q.v.), but not sponges or cnidarians such as corals or jellyfish

Cell membrane: see cytoplasmic membrane

Chemotaxis: a form of taxis (q.v.) induced by a chemical stimulus

Chloroplast: organelle within which photosynthesis is carried out

Chordate: member of the phylum Chordata, which includes vertebrates, tunicates (such as salps and sea squirts) and cephalochordates (whose extant representative is the lancelet, also known as amphioxus); they are characterized, among other things, by possession of a notochord for at least part of their life cycle

Ciliate: group of protists whose cell surface features hair-like extensions called cilia; like flagella (q.v.), cilia serve as organelles of motility but they are generally shorter and more numerous than eukaryotic flagella

Cnidaria: a phylum of exclusively aquatic animals that include corals and sea anemones, jellyfish and box jellyfish, freshwater hydras and venomous siphonophores such as the Portuguese man o' war

Cryptobiotic: existing in, or capable of surviving, a state of *cryptobiosis*, or *ametabolism*, i.e. a cessation of metabolism; such a state may be brought on by conditions of extreme cold or desiccation

Cryptomonads: a group of flagellated algae characterized by the presence of a type of extrusome (q.v.) known as an ejectisome

Cyanobacteria: a division of bacteria that derive their energy from photosynthesis in a similar way to chloroplasts

Cytoplasm: the contents of a cell that are outside the nucleus (if there is one) but within the cell membrane

Cytoplasmic membrane, plasma membrane, cell membrane: membrane separating the inside of a cell from the external environment; it consists of a double layer of phospholipid molecules

Cytoskeleton: dynamic protein structure in the cytoplasm of cells, fulfilling a wide range of functions including the maintenance of cell shape, locomotion, intracellular transport and cell division

Deuterostomes: a superphylum of bilaterian animals that includes the chordates (which in turn include the vertebrates), echinoderms and hemichordates; they are opposed to the *protostomes* (q.v.)

Diatoms: group of mainly unicellular photosynthetic algae endowed with glass tests or shells known as frustules; they rank among the world's most abundant aquatic organisms

Dinoflagellates: major category of flagellate, i.e. flagellum-bearing, protist

Endosymbiont: an organism that lives inside the body or cells of another organism in a mutually beneficial relationship of *endosymbiosis*

Epithelium: type of animal tissue, taking the form of one or more layers of cells that cover a body's outer surface and line its cavities

Euglena: a genus of flagellate protist, most species of which have chloroplasts and can photosynthesize but are also able to feed by phagocytosis (q.v.)

Euglyphida: a prominent category of testate, or shell-bearing, amoeba

Eukaryote: an organism whose cells contain their genetic material within a membrane-bound nucleus

Eumetazoa: major subkingdom within Metazoa (q.v.), generally considered to encompass all animals except sponges and sometimes Placozoa (q.v.)

Extrusome: an organelle present in certain eukaryotes that can discharge or 'extrude' its contents in order to capture and kill prey (e.g. trichocysts) or to protect itself (e.g. ejectisomes)

Flagellum (plural: *flagella*): whip-like appendage in certain prokaryotic and eukaryotic cells, used primarily for locomotion in a fluid medium

Foraminifera: class of mainly marine protists with pore-studded tests or shells from which microtubule-reinforced projections emerge

Gastrotricha: a small phylum of microscopic, worm-like, aquatic animals, colloquially known as hairybacks

Gram-negative bacterium/Gram-positive bacterium: two main classes of bacteria, differentiated by their response to a certain staining procedure

Halobacterium: a group of halophilic ('salt-loving') archaea, i.e. archaea that tolerate highly saline conditions

Haptorid: a class of ciliates that includes *Didinium* and *Dileptus*, which capture or kill their prey mainly by firing toxic filaments known as trichocysts

Heterotroph: an organism that requires complex organic molecules as its principal source of food; it contrasts with an autotroph (q.v.)

*HGT, horizontal gene transfer (*also: *lateral gene transfer):* transfer of genes between organisms other than by parent-offspring transmission; it contrasts with *vertical gene transfer,* which is by sexual or asexual reproduction

Infusoria: traditional, taxonomically obsolete term for aquatic micro-organisms such as protozoa and unicellular algae

Interneuron: a class of neuron that conveys information from one neuron to another

Isomerization: process by which one form of a molecule can change into another form with the same atoms but arranged in a different configuration

Isopleth: a line connecting points that register the same amount or ratio of some measurable variable

Kinase: an enzyme that catalyses the addition of phosphate groups to proteins, thus activating protein function; the enzymes that catalyse the removal of phosphate groups and thus the de-activation of protein function are called phosphatases

Klinotaxis: a way of gauging a chemical gradient used by organisms without paired receptor organs; it involves a succession of measurements by sensory receptors that are displaced from side to side

Lipid: any of a large and diverse group of organic compounds that are insoluble in water but soluble in organic solvents such as alcohol, ether and chloroform; examples include fats, oils, waxes and steroids; they are among the main constituents of plant and animal cells

Lipopolysaccharide, LPS: a complex molecule consisting of both lipid and carbohydrate parts, and making up the outer membrane of Gram-negative bacteria (q.v.)

Lysosome: membrane-bound vesicle (q.v.) that contains enzymes capable of digesting food particles and breaking down alien viruses or bacteria

Macrophage: a type of white blood cell whose functions include the phagocytosis (q.v.) of pathogens as part of the immune system

Metazoa: (also known as *Animalia*) the kingdom of multicellular eukaryotic animals

Microaerophilic: describes prokaryotes that require oxygen, but at lower concentrations than present in the atmosphere

Mitochondrion: organelle in eukaryotic cells that uses energy from aerobic respiration to synthesize ATP (q.v.), commonly termed the 'powerhouse' of the cell

Mutagenesis: the production and development of mutations in a genome

Myxobacteria: (also known as 'slime bacteria') a group of bacteria that includes the model organism *Myxococcus xanthus*; noted for travelling as 'swarms' and aggregating as 'fruiting bodies' when nutrients are scarce

Nematoda: the phylum comprising nematodes or roundworms

Organelle: a specialized structure within a eukaryotic cell, examples being mitochondria (q.v.) and chloroplasts (q.v.)

Osmotrophy: a form of nutrition that involves the uptake of small organic molecules by osmosis

Peptide: organic compound consisting of short chains of amino acids

Phagocytosis: process by which a cell engulfs a solid food particle; *phagocytes* are immune cells that ingest potentially harmful non-self in this way

Phagosome: a vesicle (q.v.) formed during phagocytosis (q.v.) when a food particle or prey item is engulfed and internalized by the cell membrane; the phagosome subsequently fuses with a lysosome (q.v.) for digestion to take place

Phenotype: the bodily characteristics of an organism

Phospholipid: one of a class of lipids (q.v.) that includes both a phosphate group and one or more fatty acids

Phototaxis: a form of taxis (q.v.) induced by light

Placozoa: one of the most basal groups of Metazoa, generally considered to consist of a single species, *Trichoplax adhaerens*

Plasma membrane: see cytoplasmic membrane

Platyhelminthes: the phylum of flatworms or platyhelminths, which includes parasitic forms such as tapeworms and flukes but also free-living turbellarians such as planarians

Polymer: a molecule that consists of many repeated elements (monomers): e.g. proteins are polymers of amino acids; DNA and RNA are polymers of nucleotides; *polymerization* is the process by which polymers are formed

Porifera: the phylum of sponges

Prokaryotes: cells that have no membrane-bounded nucleus or membrane-bounded organelles (q.v.) such as mitochondria; they include the bacteria and archaea and are contrasted with the eukaryotes (q.v.)

Proteobacteria: a major group of Gram-negative bacteria that includes the genera *Rickettsia*, *Escherichia*, *Salmonella* and *Buchnera* as well as myxobacteria such as *Myxococcus*

Protist: informal term referring to a diverse group of mainly unicellular eukaryotes

Protostome: a superphylum of bilaterian animals that include the arthropods (q.v.), molluscs, annelid worms and nematode worms

Protozoa: informal term referring to a diverse group of non-photosynthetic unicellular protists such as amoebae and ciliates

Pseudopod, pseudopodium: a temporary protrusion of the cytoplasm (q.v.) of amoeboid cells that is used for locomotion and the capture of prey

Radiolaria: major class of protozoa (q.v.) characterized by a delicate silica skeleton and long thin projecting pseudopods known as axopods

Retroelement, retrotransposon: a genetic element that can multiply its presence within a genome by using an enzyme to turn RNA copies of itself back into DNA, which may then be inserted into the genome

Rhodopsin: a light-sensitive receptor protein

Rotifera: a phylum of mainly microscopic invertebrates

Social amoebae: (also known as 'cellular slime moulds') a class of amoeboid protists that includes the model organism *Dictyostelium discoideum*

Suctoria: a class of ciliate that is sessile in its developed stage and feeds by means of projecting tentacles

T4 phage: virulent phage (q.v.) that infects *E. coli*

Tardigrada: phylum of microscopic invertebrates capable of surviving in extreme conditions, commonly known as water bears

Taxis: directional movement of a motile organism towards or away from a stimulus such as light (*phototaxis*), chemicals (*chemotaxis*), physical contact (*thigmotaxis*) or gravity (*gravitaxis*); it is characterized as positive or negative depending on whether it is 'towards' or 'away from' the stimulus; it is distinguished from *kinesis*, which is a non-directional response to a stimulus

Testate: of amoebae, possessing a shell or test

Thigmonasty: non-directional response of a plant to physical contact

Trophont, trophic stage: the feeding stage of an organism, especially of a ciliate; in other contexts, the term *trophozoite* is sometimes used

Tropism: directional growth or movement, usually of a plant, in response to an external stimulus such as a chemical (*chemotropism*), light (*phototropism*), physical contact (*thigmotropism*) or the position of the sun (*heliotropism*); it has been used in the past to denote what is now designated *taxis* (q.v.); it is characterized as positive or negative depending on whether it is 'towards' or 'away from' the stimulus

Vacuole: a type of vesicle (q.v.), a membrane-bound space within the cytoplasm of a cell, often used for storing food, water or waste

Vesicle: a membrane-bound compartment within the cytoplasm of a cell

Virion: a complete virus particle comprising both the genetic material and the protective capsid

Viroid: a short, circular, infectious, single-stranded RNA molecule that does not code for any proteins and does not have a protective capsid

Warnowiaceae, warnowiids: a family of predatory dinoflagellates (q.v.) endowed with an 'ocelloid', an elaborate organelle akin to a metazoan eye

List of Figures

Figure 1: From: W. McDougall, *An Outline of Psychology* (1923, p. 60) .. 124
Figure 2: *Dugesia tigrina*... 159
Figure 3: *Oxyrrhis marina* 159
Figure 4: *Stentor*... 160
Figure 5: *Tripedalia cystophora* 161
Figure 6: *Amoeba proteus* consuming *Paramecium* 161
Figure 7: *Caenorhabditis elegans* 161

Figures 2 – 7/illustrations by Christina Nath, 2018

Endnotes

1 Glasgow (2017); the book can be downloaded for free from the publisher via the following link: https://nbn-resolving.org/urn:nbn:de:bvb:20-opus-145252.
2 Realistically, the aim is thus not necessarily to serve up all the right answers in this analysis of rudimentary consciousness. Our empirical understanding of (for example) the locomotion of single cells will undoubtedly be fine-tuned with time, and this is likely to have a bearing on some of the conclusions proposed. Rather than providing answers, the objective is – given a particular understanding of 'selfhood' based on intrinsic reflexivity – to unearth the *questions* that are most relevant in considering whether consciousness can be ascribed to a particular form of life. I owe this interrogative approach to W. D. Glasgow, who believed strongly that the purpose of philosophy is not to produce ready-made answers, but to learn how to ask the right questions.
3 The other main approach to the concept of 'selfhood' derives from the emphatic use of the pronoun. On this view, your self is what you are, or perhaps what you *really* are. The implication tends to be that selfhood denotes some kind of timeless essence. Intrinsically reflexive selfhood does not imply an essence, but nor does it preclude the possibility of one.
4 The attribute 'reflexive', based on the term's grammatical use, is to be distinguished from that of 'reflective', which denotes the process of reflection or thought and is here employed primarily in the context of 'pre-reflective self-awareness', a form of awareness that is prior to explicit thought processes or mental representations. 'Reflexive' is also to be distinguished from the notion of a reflex in the sense of an automatic bodily response to a stimulus. Here the adjective used is 'reflex', as in a 'reflex reaction'.
5 On the contrast between self-organization and self-assembly see Glasgow (2017), 63– 64.
6 In fact, the formalism in question is of a rather special kind. Intrinsically reflexive processes are constitutive of a type of entity that in some sense *forms itself*. As proposed in Glasgow (2017; 24), the coinage *self-formalism* captures an important feature of intrinsic reflexivity in marrying formalism with process and change. One might say that – like Aristotle's 'soul' – a self is not just a form, but a

form constantly engaged in and constituted by the process of sustaining itself as the form that it is, as well as adapting this form (within limits) to changing circumstances. This is suggested by Aristotle's notion of *entelechy*, understood as denoting the work of self-maintenance.

7 On the selfish or self-like nature of energy flows and genetic material, see Glasgow (2017), chapters II and III respectively. On the selfhood inherent in organisms and biological individuals, see chapter VI. Forthcoming works, I hope, will look at the selfhood of super-organisms, biospheres and universes.

8 For a discussion of whether 'reproduction' really is 'self-reproduction' and can thus aptly be described in terms of intrinsic reflexivity – in other words, the unanswerable logical quandary thrown up by the question of whether progenitor and progeny really are 'the same' – see Glasgow (2017), 38–45.

9 See Maynard Smith and Szathmáry (1999), 3, according to whom natural selection presupposes a population of entities endowed with the properties of multiplication (or, in intrinsically reflexive terms: self-multiplication), heredity and variation.

10 On the relationship between selfhood and selfishness see Glasgow (2017), 53–56, 101–4.

11 By contrast, the individual cells that make up multicellular bodies such as animals and plants are deemed not to be selves. For an explanation, see the subchapter below on 'Metazoan Cells'.

12 As noted above, the lack of one or more of the three fundamental categories of intrinsic reflexivity results in something that is merely *selfish* or *self-like*. The absence of self-maintenance, for example, is typified by the non-metabolic selfishness characteristic of viruses or virus-like entities. The absence of self-multiplication rules out heredity, variation and the concomitant possibility of evolution by natural selection among a population of entities. In the absence of self-containment, intrinsic reflexivity takes the form of the dissipative structures exemplified by self-organizing flow patterns or self-propagating forest fires, which are unable to channel their energetic flow into the performance of (constructive) work.

13 See Bray (2009), 89–93.

14 Ibid., 6.

15 Jablonski (2006), 17.

16 On *Paramecium*, see Greenspan (2007), 5–21.

17 See Dawkins (2004), 398.

18 On the shadow reflex of barnacles and the molecular basis of photoreception in general see Greenspan (2007), 23–40; on the evolution of sight see Lane (2009), 172–204.

19 *Halobacterium*, for example, uses bacteriorhodopsin to capture light energy and produce a proton gradient across its cell membrane. This proton gradient is then employed to synthesize the energy-carrying molecule ATP and thus power cellular activity.

20 On warnowiids such as *Erythropsidinium*, see Gómez et al. (2009).

21 The restoration of balance is generally not immediate, since time is required for it to take effect. However, it is anticipated by bodily signals of ingestion. See page 95.

22 This is not to say that such 'imprisonment' can never be to the advantage of the 'prisoner', as in

the case of the protection provided by endosymbiosis, which makes self-movement largely pointless. On the endosymbiotic existence of formerly free-living bacteria such as *Buchnera aphidicola*, which are now (more or less) permanent inhabitants of specialized cells in their greenfly hosts, see Glasgow (2017), 182–86.

23 It may be objected that rudimentary consciousness does not in fact presuppose self-reproduction. Indeed, there is a slight asymmetry in the relationship of consciousness to self-maintenance and its relationship to self-reproduction, in that the original function of consciousness is to enable a hungry self to get from 'here' (no food) to 'there' (food) in order to fuel itself and thus *keep itself going*. But this is far from being the only plausible reason for guided self-propulsion. Once sexual reproduction has emerged, it is logically feasible that nutrient uptake might occur purely passively and so necessitate neither movement nor consciousness; consciousness, meanwhile, might arise from a periodic need to find a mate rather than prey, i.e. to get from 'here' (no mate) to 'there' (mate). Even in this scenario, however, the directed self-propulsion here deemed necessary for consciousness *always presupposes energetic self-maintenance*, since the self must have fuelled itself and must have energy surplus to its own immediate metabolic requirements for movement to be possible. If this is so, then consciousness does not logically require full minimal selfhood (i.e. all three forms of intrinsic reflexivity), but merely the quality of being *self-like* (i.e. two out of the three modes of intrinsic reflexivity). As it occurs on our planet, of course, consciousness does seem to coincide with full minimum selfhood, and it is difficult to conceive of the requisite self-containment and self-transcendence occurring in a self that is not itself the product of a process of evolutionary self-transformation through natural selection among a population of self-reproducing selves. Whether this is merely an empirical contingency or reflects a deeper logical limitation may simply be unanswerable at present. An example of a *self-like* entity that has not yet reproduced itself (as far as we know) is the biosphere of our planet. Would we be willing to ascribe consciousness to the biosphere as an entity if we were aware of it 'behaving', i.e. moving itself directionally in relation to non-self, say, by planet-hopping? As it happens, such planet-hopping on the part of the biosphere might even coincide with reproduction.

24 Protozoa may be categorized as flagellated, ciliated or amoeboid, depending respectively on whether they move and feed using flagella, cilia or transient extensions of the cell body called pseudopodia. However, these broad categories may overlap: pelobionts such as *Mastigella*, for example, are amoeboid cells equipped with a flagellum; heteroloboseids such as the facultative pathogen *Naegleria fowleri* have a life cycle incorporating both an amoeboid and a flagellate stage.

25 Throughout this work the terms 'rudimentary' and 'elementary' will be used interchangeably to describe consciousness in its logically minimal or most simple manifestation, whether applied to single-celled or multi-celled organisms.

26 The term 'drive' does not enjoy the best of reputations; it has often been dismissed as speculative, metaphysical or simply vacuous. I here use the term as an alternative to 'appetite', especially in contexts where the object relates to reproduction (or sex) rather than nutrition. Like 'appetite', the concept implies both mechanical and purposive elements, suggesting both a physiological imbalance and

directedness towards a goal object. For a critique of the concept of 'drive', see Peters (1958), 93–129.
27 On the notion of 'structural coupling', see Glasgow (2017), 52; see also Thompson (2007), 45.
28 See Jonas (1966; 2001), 84.
29 See Ari Berkowitz (2016; 85–90) and Rodolfo Llinás (2001; 5–7), who cite in particular the work of the influential physiologist T. Graham Brown on cats in the early part of the 20th century. In most vertebrates, it is the spinal cord rather than the brain that generates such rhythms, functioning rather like a pacemaker.
30 Notably, it is only skeletal muscles – not the cardiac muscles responsible for pumping blood or the smooth muscles responsible for gut movements – that are under voluntary control.
31 The underlying point is that consciousness is presumed, through the evolutionary eons, to have fulfilled a function rather than exist as a mere epiphenomenon, a functionless by-product of cognitive processes or nervous activity. Epiphenomenalism raises the question of why consciousness – if it serves no function – should be associated with nervous or cognitive events and yet not with other physical processes such as photosynthesis or combustion. See Morsella (2005), 1001.
32 Aristotle's notion of 'soul' or psyche is akin to a 'principle of animation' by virtue of which a thing can be said to be living. 'Mind' is a much more problematic term, but happens to be the more common of the two in post-Cartesian philosophy. In what follows, I shall assume that anyone who is prepared to claim that a particular entity has a mind will also be willing to ascribe the possibility of consciousness to that entity. I shall treat the term 'consciousness' as synonymous with 'awareness', but opt for 'self-awareness' over 'self-consciousness' on account of the distracting associations of the latter with undue diffidence or bashfulness.
33 See Glasgow (2017), 89–90.
34 Aristotle, *De Anima*, (Book II.3), 414a–b. See also Aristotle (1986), 162.
35 See Schloegel and Schmidgen (2002), 621.
36 For an account of the 'cellular psychology' of Haeckel, Verworn, Binet and others, see ibid., 622–33.
37 Jennings (1906), 336.
38 See Thompson (2007), 161.
39 This is not the same as what is known as psychological behaviourism, which is a method for the study of human beings and animals and which we shall come across below. However, both behaviourisms share an emphasis on what is accessible to public observation, and the former has been interpreted as providing philosophical vindication for the latter. For an overview of logical behaviourism see Priest (1991), 35–64; see also Shaffer (1968), 14–17.
40 For a start, philosophical functionalism is generally treated as a theory of mind, not of consciousness. Yet in spite of their origins in different realms of discourse, there is substantial concurrence between the two sorts of functionalism in the account I am offering. The adaptive function of consciousness consists precisely in the production of behaviour, where 'behaviour' is understood as a particular sort of guided self-movement undertaken by a self-maintaining self. A functionalist theory of mind also interprets mind in terms of the production of behaviour.

41 Priest (1991), 133 – 49; 136.
42 Ibid., 133.
43 Dennett (1996), 68.
44 Greenspan (2007), 6: Greenspan himself regards consciousness as 'unlikely' in *Paramecium* given what is known of its 'neural' repertoire (ibid., 145). Yet the formulation seems not to exclude the possible existence of other protozoa whose neural repertoire might accommodate consciousness.
45 Fodor (1987), 3.
46 'Tropism' is now generally taken to refer to the growth of a plant in response to an environmental stimulus, whereas 'taxis' denotes the movement of a motile organism in response to a stimulus. However, 'tropism' was the term used in the famous controversy about animal movement between Jacques Loeb and H. S. Jennings in the early 20th century.
47 Fodor (1987), 9: 'what makes a paramecium a nonintentional system is that even if you are prepared to describe things that affect it as "stimuli", and even if you are willing to describe the effects of the soi-disant stimuli as "behavioral responses" and even if you are prepared to describe the causal interaction between stimulus and organism as involving the "detection" of some property in the former by the latter, still, all that happens ... is the lawful co-variation of a property of the stimulus with a property of the response'.
48 See ibid., 21 (n. 7).
49 Ibid., 9 (see note 47 above for full quotation).
50 Without formulating it in terms of selfhood, H. S. Jennings recognized that behaviour is self-movement that has a cause internal to the organism; see for example Jennings (1906), 23 – 24.
51 Descartes' letter to Regius, May 1641, cited in Jonas (1966; 2001), 61 (n. 3).
52 Searle (1992), 69. Or, in other words, 'the relation of mental states to behavior is purely contingent' (23). Formulating the point in this way makes it clear how wrong it is.
53 Such deceit is exemplified by the distraction displays of birds such as piping plovers, which feign injury in order to distract a predator's attention from their own offspring. Even though (attempted) deception is involved, there is a perfectly clear link between a 'mental' phenomenon (an intention) and an action. The interpretative subtleties required to recognize trickery *as trickery* do not uncouple or dismantle the logical connection between conscious mental phenomena and external behaviour. On distraction displays see for example Griffin (1992; 2001), 220 – 25.
54 To the extent that the connection between consciousness and behaviour is indeed taken to be logical or conceptual, complex strategies such as feigned injury or pathologies such as locked-in syndrome or tetraplegia do not invalidate it, although they may encourage us to undertake a re-assessment or re-examination of the concepts in question. Just as the concept of 'behaviour' may be extended to incorporate simulation and dissimulation, it may also be reduced in its range to blinking and vertical eye movements. In the case of locked-in syndrome, this reduction may not be mirrored by a corresponding reduction in conscious activity. However, the fact that an individual is physically incapable of behaving as he or she *would wish to* does not undermine the connection

between consciousness and behaviour. A particular *disposition* to move may fail to be realized; the act of speaking may have to be substituted by a complex pattern of eye movements or by the movement of a cursor on a computer screen. On locked-in syndrome see for example Gazzaniga (2008), 338–39.

55 See Priest (1991), 36.

56 Quoted in Gregory (ed.) (1987), 72.

57 The claim that 'consciousness does not exist' is as metaphysical as the claim that 'God does not exist' and certainly inconsistent with the methodology of psychological behaviourism. Logical behaviourism, by contrast, might have contended that claims about consciousness – including whether or not it exists – are meaningless. This is more in line with Watson's later claim that 'consciousness is neither a definite nor a usable concept'; see Watson (1930; 1970), 2.

58 To the extent that it incorporates a metaphor of 'height' with humans on top, the idea of a scale of phylogeny is utterly and irrevocably misleading. It also tends to be harmfully anthropocentric. All extant organisms constitute a 'pinnacle' on the time axis simply by virtue of being extant.

59 Tye (1997), 289.

60 Ibid., 301–3.

61 In effect, a zombie in the philosophical sense is a being that is capable of normal self-movement or behaviour but is bereft of consciousness.

62 To Michel Cabanac (1999), for example, the signs of emotional tachycardia and elevated body temperatures elicited by gentle handling in reptiles but not in amphibians suggest that the phylogenetic emergence of emotion – which is sometimes taken as a proxy for consciousness – lies between amphibians and early reptiles. However, the narrative of a phylogenetic progression from emotion-less to emotionally endowed animals is problematic. There is increasing evidence of the capacity of fish – though ostensibly more 'primitive' in phylogenetic terms than amphibians and reptiles – to suffer and feel emotion; see Braithwaite (2010), Balcombe (2006), 185–91. On the relationship between emotion and consciousness, see below, chapter IV.

63 On the overlapping size ranges of protozoans and metazoans, see McMahon and Bonner (1983), 1–5, also Patterson and Hedley (1992; 1996), 27–28.

64 For an illustration of *Megaphragma* see Polilov (2012), 30; on the fairyfly see Mockford (1997), 115–20.

65 Jennings (1906), 336–37: 'If [the amoeba] were as large as a whale, it is quite conceivable that occasions might arise when the attribution to it of the elemental states of consciousness might save the unsophisticated human being from the destruction that would result from the lack of such attribution'.

66 Bennett and Hacker (2003), 303. Of course, the question of 'complexity' *is* of some relevance to consciousness. A 'complex' brain may provide increased opportunities for behavioural complexity and flexibility; it may thus have a decisive influence on the *nature* of consciousness.

67 Ibid., 304.

68 Jonas (1966; 2001), 2.

69 Glisson held that the body's natural energy is transformed by irritability into sensation. See Giglioni (2008) for an account of why Glisson's theory of irritability promptly fell into oblivion even

though the concept of irritability was to flourish under the less speculative influence of Albrecht Haller. For Haller irritability was merely a manifestation of mechanical elasticity.
70 Schelling was also influenced by the work of the 18th-century Scottish physician John Brown on 'excitability'.
71 See Binet (1889), 64, 105.
72 Ibid., 106.
73 For an example of this usage, see Llinás (2001), 113: 'we know that single-cell "animals" are capable of irritability, that is, they respond to external stimuli with organized, goal-directed behavior'. Elsewhere (212), Llinás defines 'irritability' as an ability to produce a behavioural response to stimuli consisting of 'either moving away from, or approaching an object or another cell'. This is tantamount to taxis.
74 Bray (2009), 25–26.
75 Some single-celled eukaryotes do indeed show phototactic behaviour. We shall return below (chapter VI) to the question of how far this may be taken to imply vision.
76 For an example of such a theory see Rolls (1999), 244–65.
77 On the term 'feeling', see below, chapter IV.
78 Donald Griffin, cited in Balcombe (2006), 28.
79 See note 4 above on the distinction between 'reflexive' and 'reflective'. Of course, the act of reflecting upon oneself reflecting is itself reflexive insofar as the grammatical subject (the thinker) is the same as the grammatical object (the thinker). In fact, it is doubly reflexive: the thinker is reflecting upon himself, and the reflections are 'about' themselves. Yet in neither respect is the reflexivity intrinsic. The thinker, even qua thinker, is not constituted by this reflexivity, for he can think about other things and he can stop thinking and do other things. Equally, the sequence of reflections may cease to be 'about' the act or process of reflection and instead focus on the thinker's upcoming social commitments, a persistent itch, or the sounds of connubial disharmony from next door. Sometimes the rather vague word 'self-reflection' is used, suggesting both reflection and reflexivity. It is in the nature of reflection that the reflexive relationship between the reflection and what is reflected is extrinsic.
80 See Lurz (2009), 9.
81 See Zahavi (2005), 18.
82 For an exemplary discussion see Zahavi (2005), 17–30.
83 On corollary discharge, see Crapse and Sommer (2008). One of the classic papers is Von Holst and Mittelstaedt (1950), who proposed that the organism sends to the sensory pathway a copy (designated an 'efference copy') of the motor command issued to an effector such as a muscle. This motor copy would then be combined, juxtaposed or in some way compared with the input from the sensory receptors.
84 Merker (2005).
85 Ibid., 93.
86 Of course, one might *imagine* the consciousness of an absolutely stationary self that simply records

its surroundings. But what would such consciousness be for? How could consciousness emerge from such a purely passive process?

87 On the mechanism of corollary discharge in the sea-slug *Pleurobranchaea*, see Crapse and Sommer (2008), 589–90.

88 Thompson (2010), 162.

89 Ibid.

90 Of the four known phyla of deuterostomes, only chordates such as vertebrates have a centralized nervous system. Echinoderms (which include starfish, sea lilies, sea urchins and sea cucumbers), hemichordates (which include acorn worms and pterobranchs) and worm-like *Xenoturbella* have radial or net-like systems. If the last common ancestor of all deuterostomes had a central nervous system, which is believed to be the most parsimonious option, these lineages must have reverted from a central nervous system to a diffuse nervous system. This was presumably because it was better at keeping them alive long enough to reproduce. The deuterostomes constitute the sister clade to the protostomes, which include arthropods (insects, spiders and crustaceans), nematodes, annelids and molluscs. On the phylogeny see Moroz (2009), 184.

91 Llinás (2001), 78.

92 On the capacity of protein networks to transmit and process information, see Bray (2009), 71–88.

93 Wittgenstein (1953), § 281.

94 So what is implied by the distinction between 'naked' amoebae and the 'testate' amoebae that have thrown – or whose ancestors have thrown – a cranium-like exoskeleton around much of their brain-cum-body?

95 See Crick and Koch (1990), esp. 270–72.

96 Penrose (1995), 348–92.

97 Tononi (2004) likewise focuses on the thalamocortical system, arguing that 'the fact that consciousness as we know it is generated by the thalamocortical system fits well with the information integration theory, since what we know about its organization appears ideally suited to the integration of information'.

98 See Morsella (2005), 1010.

99 Chalmers (1995), 204–5.

100 Morsella (2005; 1015) himself notes that 'although intersystem integration could conceivably occur without something like phenomenal states (as in an automaton or in an elegant "blackboard" neural network with all of its modules nicely interconnected), such a solution was not selected in our evolutionary history'. Yet this seems to sever consciousness from any logical connection to its function.

101 As was shown in the final chapter of Glasgow (2017), this 'within' need not imply spatial boundaries, but rather 'belonging to' or being 'a functional part of' the system in question.

102 Tononi (2004), by contrast, equates consciousness with 'the ability of a system to integrate information, whether or not it has a strong sense of self, language, emotion, a body, or is immersed in an environment, contrary to some common intuitions'. The divorce between consciousness and any

sort of environment rather contravenes the thermodynamics of information processing, which relies on an input of energy.

103 We tend to be led astray, again, by the metaphor of mental representations or images. The implication is that they are something the brain has to assemble or put together from a multiplicity of informational components. Yet an amoeba perceiving a paramecium does not sense a mental image of a paramecium; it senses the paramecium. I do not perceive a mental representation of the nut roast on my plate; I perceive the nut roast.

104 See Berkowitz (2016), 121–30, for a fascinating account of how this alignment is brought about in a barn owl.

105 For a discussion of this operation, known as commissurotomy, see Glover (1988), 32–35; see also Gazzaniga (2008), 289–92.

106 See Sass and Parnas (2003), 435 (italics omitted).

107 On schizophrenia and proprioception see ibid., 427–44; on schizophrenia and corollary discharge see Blakemore et al. (2000).

108 Chalmers (1995), 200.

109 Ibid., 215–17.

110 Ibid. Perhaps the most urgent question is whether *all* information has a phenomenal aspect. If it does, then the ubiquity of information entails the ubiquity of consciousness.

111 Nagel (1974).

112 Given the behavioural parallels, the burden of proof for the counterclaim that it is not like anything lies with the counterclaimant. As we have seen, this might be achieved by showing that the movements of a predator, be it macroscopic or microscopic, do not genuinely count as 'behaviour' or 'action'.

113 See Glasgow (2017), 36–37.

114 On *Buchnera* and other such endosymbionts see ibid., 182–86.

115 On the functioning of such genetic circuits see Bray (2009), 179–81.

116 See Xu and Gordon (2003).

117 On *Rhodopseudomonas palustris* see Brüssow (2007), 180–82.

118 Broadly speaking, the four main modes of metabolism are photoautotrophy (deriving energy from light and carbon from carbon dioxide), photoheterotrophy (acquiring energy from light but carbon from organic compounds), chemoautotrophy (using inorganic compounds for energy and carbon dioxide for carbon), and chemoheterotrophy (deriving both energy and carbon from organic compounds). See ibid., 180.

119 Ibid., 181.

120 See Turney (2015), 222–23.

121 Shapiro (2007), 814, 807.

122 Ben-Jacob (1998), 58.

123 The focus is here on appetite rather than aversion. More generally, one should perhaps say that it

is directed *in relation to* meaningful non-self (either towards *or* away from).

124 On the problematic notion of an 'object' see the section 'A World of Objects' in chapter VI.

125 See Rolls (1999), 3: 'a reward is something for which an animal will work'. A reward can likewise be specified in terms of what it is like to receive it (namely: good).

126 See Glasgow (2017), 67–72.

127 Ibid., 70–71.

128 On viruses and viroids see ibid., 147–72; on mobile DNA, see ibid., 127–34.

129 On movement proteins see ibid., 151–52.

130 See Leiman (2003), 2356.

131 As Brüssow (2007; 272) points out, highly complex procedures are required to ensure, for example, that the T4 phage does not inject its DNA into the wrong cell in an environment (the human gut) where statistically only one cell in a million is the right one: 'the phage has only a single shot and therefore it uses multiple sensors that need positive feedback before the attack is launched'. T4 has six tail fibres attached to its baseplate, and these 'recognize' and interact reversibly with bacterial surface receptors such as lipopolysaccharides (LPS). It is not enough for just a single fibre to bind to LPS; at least three of the six fibres probably have to recognize the bacterial LPS before the baseplate attaches itself irreversibly to the host cell.

132 Given this divorce from consciousness, such 'sensing' and 'recognition' are best deemed metaphorical and confined to scare quotes; it is merely *as though* the virus were 'sensing' and 'recognizing' its host.

133 See Glasgow (2017), 169–71.

134 'Candidatus' denotes the provisional taxonomic status of an organism that cannot be cultured as required in order to be established as a new taxon.

135 In fact, such endosymbionts do not lead a life of complete immobility. When it comes to transmission from one generation of host aphids or psyllids to the next, they generally leave the bacteriocytes to enter the germ line. See Thao and Baumann (2004), 3401.

136 Osmotrophy may also refer to the *active* transport of metabolites across the plasma membrane. In such cases work and energy are involved, albeit not the muscular work of the cytoskeleton. Like fungi, bacteria frequently employ an externalized digestion system, secreting extracellular digestive enzymes and then absorbing the dissolved nutrients.

137 See Hansen and Calado (1999), 382–85.

138 Ibid., 387–88.

139 See Llinás (2001), 96–97.

140 Singer (1975; 1995), 235.

141 Leonardo da Vinci (1952), 278.

142 Aristotle, *De Anima (Book II.3)* 414 a–b; see also Aristotle (1986), 162.

143 Ibid. *(Book I.3)* 406 a; see also Aristotle (1986), 139.

144 Ibid. *(Book II.4)* 415 b; Aristotle (1986), 165–66: here Aristotle describes the soul as that 'for the

sake of which' the living body exists, whether a plant or an animal.

145 For a more detailed comparison between Aristotle and Theophrastus in their approach to plants, see Hall (2011), 27–35. Theophrastus not only attributes preferences to plants and trees with regard to their environment, but even a capacity for *enjoyment* as manifest in their tendency to flourish in an optimal, preferred setting.

146 Hegel (1977), 436–37.

147 See Glasgow (2017), 242–44.

148 Matthew Hall (2011; 144), for example, suggests that plant plasticity can be seen as 'the manifestation of a plant's awareness of the environment'.

149 See, for example, Baluška et al. (2009).

150 Hall (2011), 144–45.

151 The terms 'intelligence' and 'consciousness' may coincide, but are far from synonymous. To the extent that 'intelligence' is understood to refer to a capacity to process information, solve a problem or produce an appropriate response in variable circumstances, it is only contingently related to selfhood. In other words, an entity may be intelligent without being a self, as exemplified by increasingly smart domestic appliances. The relationship of intelligence to consciousness is also only contingent. Indeed, an entity may be an intelligent self without being a conscious self. It thus makes sense to speak of the collective intelligence exhibited by a community of bacteria through adaptive mutagenesis or by a colony of termites in adapting their mound optimally in the face of environmental vicissitudes. On the view I am propounding here, however, one would not ascribe consciousness in such cases. Plants too, I believe, may come under the category of 'intelligent selfhood' without manifesting 'conscious selfhood'.

152 See Dennett (1996), 61, on how time-lapse photography can make blossoming flowers seem like intentional agents endowed with a mind, ducking and weaving like boxers in the sun as they pursue their own interests.

153 Another argument against plant intelligence or consciousness has been the modular nature of many plants and the relatively 'fuzzy' selfhood that they embody. In itself, decentralization of this sort undermines neither intelligence nor consciousness – if such there is – provided that there is communication between the modules and coherence in behaviour. The degree of communication and coherence within modular organisms is a matter for empirical study.

154 Jonas (1966; 2001), 101.

155 Ibid., 102.

156 Jonas's proposal certainly contains a considerable element of truth. Yet doubts remain. To the extent that plant chemosensation seems closer to taste than to smell, it raises the question of whether taste *in itself* has to be ruled out as a foundation for consciousness. An animal equipped only with taste would lack perception at a distance; it would be unable to move itself in a self-guided way towards nutrition. But can we really dismiss taste-based consciousness? A viable strategy for nutrient acquisition might involve non-directional movement in the form of chemokinesis in conjunction with gustatory selection: having bumped into an item of food at random, the 'decision' to proceed or not with the work of operating one's mouth might depend on whether what one happened upon tasted 'good' or 'bad'. Would we be unwilling to ascribe consciousness to such a creature? What about a microscopic carnivore such as the tardigrade *Macrobiotus richtersi*, a tactile predator that detects its nematode prey by touching them with the sensory area around its mouth (the circumoral field)? In the absence of eyes, it is uncertain whether chemical cues also provide information to guide it in its nematode harvesting (see Hohberg and Traunspurger (2009)). Or what about the much-discussed star-nosed mole, which likewise makes scarce use of teleception (it has a singular ability to smell underwater but is more or less blind) and whose perception of the world, or at least of its food, appears to be basically tactile or gustatory? This creature's remarkable star-shaped nose is used primarily not for olfaction but for 'touching' its prey as it moves along, employing a mechanical detection system that is more rapid than any known optical system. Believed to be the fastest-eating mammal on the planet, the star-nosed mole takes under a quarter of a second to identify, process and ingest individual food items, its brain deciding in a matter of milliseconds whether they are edible or not. Few would deny some form of consciousness to this breathtakingly efficient forager, especially given that foraging is far from being its only activity. It is thought to live socially in loose colonies within networks of tunnels of its own making, and it partakes in the range of activities associated with sexual reproduction. But would we be so generous with the tiny tardigrade *Macrobiotus*, which has a similarly tactile feeding strategy but may otherwise be more limited in its behavioural repertoire? My feeling is that a system involving only random encounter in juxtaposition with gustatory or mechanical contact-based prey selection would not *in itself* provide the foundation for consciousness. On the foraging speed of the star-nosed mole, see for example Catania and Remple (2005), who describe how, 'in an astounding flurry of star movements and prey captures', a mole locates and eats eight separate prey items in under two seconds (521).

157 Harold (2001), 20.

158 See Rothschild (1989), esp. 280–90. A third term proposed for the microscopic kingdom was 'Protoctista', coined by the naturalist John Hogg and meaning 'first created beings'. In the present context I have often opted for the informal category of 'protozoa' to denote unicellular eukaryotes capable of locomotion.

159 In their book *Free-Living Freshwater Protozoa*, Patterson and Hedley (1992; 1996) thus define plankton in terms not of movement but of where they live, namely in the water column (i.e. above the sediment). Planktonic protists, they point out, may either swim or drift (203).

160 Barnes (ed.) (1998), 63–64.

161 Ibid., 59–60.

162 Money (2014), 61: the phylum of dinoflagellates likewise includes many species considered photosynthetic (about half of those that are known), but also many others that have either lost or never had a chloroplast *and* that feed on diatoms or other living organisms. Many both possess a chloroplast *and* actively ingest prey. These are known as mixotrophs.

Endnotes 213

163 See for example Verity (1991); Jürgens and DeMott (1995); Montagnes et al. (2008).
164 See Barnes (ed.) (1998), 97–100; see Glasgow (2017), 274.
165 See Patterson and Hedley (1992; 1996), 177-79. In the case of the suctorians, each tentacle-cum-mouth terminates in a knob that houses an 'extrusome', i.e. an organelle whose contents can be extruded so as to hold on to the prey as its cytoplasm is extracted. In some cases, the prey may be released (alive) once the suctorian has had its fill. Many suctorians are supported on a stalk and contained within an extracellular lorica (shell).
166 The category of suspension feeding includes filter feeding or sieving on the one hand but also various mechanisms of what is known as 'aerosol' filtration on the other. Aerosol forms of particle capture involve filters that are additionally characterized by adhesive properties. See LaBarbera (1984), 76–81.
167 Ibid., 71–72.
168 See Fenchel (1980).
169 Verity (1991), 70.
170 Ibid.; see Snyder (1991) on the chemoattractive response shown by various bacterivorous ciliates to compounds normally found on the surface of prey cells, suggesting an ability to sense dissolved substances derived from their prey.
171 Verity (1991), 70.
172 See Jennings (1906), 174–79. For accounts of Jennings' work on *Stentor*, see also McDougall (1923), 66–67; Bray (2009), 14–17.
173 Jennings (1906), 185–86.
174 Berger (1980), 402-3.
175 Dusenbery (2009; 152–53) shows that – on account of the laws of small-scale hydrodynamics – random movement does not increase the nutrient encounter rate for a medium-sized bacterium with a diameter of ca. 1 μm feeding by osmotrophy in a uniform environment. In itself, swimming is not worth the trouble. A bacterium of such proportions may as well just rely on encountering nutrition by diffusion. According to Dusenbery's calculations, an organism has to be more than 10 μm in diameter for random locomotion to pay its way by enhancing nutrient uptake.
176 Harold (2001), 28; for a comparison of prokaryotes and eukaryotes see 25–30.
177 The Reynolds number is defined as 'the fluid density times a characteristic length times a characteristic speed divided by the fluid viscosity'. In a given context this means it is a ratio 'between inertial and viscous forces per unit volume'. On the Reynolds number see McMahon and Bonner (1983), 89–97; see also Dusenbery (2009), 41–49.
178 Dusenbery (2009), 44–45.
179 See McMahon and Bonner (1983), 197–98, quoting the physicist Edward Purcell.
180 Ibid., 195–96: 'the stopping distance, expressed as a fraction of the cell's diameter, is one-eighteenth of its Reynolds number based on its diameter and its initial speed. For a bacterium 2 micrometers long swimming at a Reynolds number of 10^{-6}, the stopping distance is about 10^{-7} micrometers'.

181 A further determinant is the reversibility of flow at low Reynolds numbers, as a result of which self-propulsion cannot be achieved simply by moving a rigid, oar-like appendage back and forth, even varying the speed in the two halves of the cycle. This is possible at high Reynolds numbers, endowing bivalve molluscs such as scallops with a rather crude form of aquatic locomotion based on their ability to open their shells slowly and then snap them shut. At a low Reynolds number, however, this would get the scallop nowhere, but merely shift it back and forth. On how flagella and cilia overcome the challenge posed by reversible microscopic flow, see Dusenbery (2009), 198–214.

182 The mechanical efficiency of rotating bacterial flagella has been estimated to be slightly more than 1 %. By comparison, fish are calculated to attain efficiencies of up to 80 % at high Reynolds numbers by pushing against water with their bodies; see ibid., 213–14.

183 Ibid., 4.

184 Ibid., 231.

185 See ibid., 239–42; 248.

186 See ibid., 20, on how the size range for each genus was measured. Dusenbery stresses the strength of this correlation, calculating that if motility and size were distributed independently, the probability that 19 % of the non-motile genera were smaller than the smallest motile genus would be less than two in a million (ibid., 22).

187 See Gitai (2005), 577–78: for example, FtsZ is a bacterial homologue of eukaryotic tubulin, and MreB is a homologue of eukaryotic actin.

188 Norris et al. (1996), 197, define the enzoskeleton as 'the ensemble of proteins (principally enzymes) that interact with one another and with membranes and nucleic acids to form extended structures within the cell'.

189 This is possible because the cellular circuitry consists of proteins which – by means of processes such as phosphorylation and methylation – can flip between two distinct states in accordance with circumstance, functioning as molecular switches able to channel the cellular processes in one direction or another depending on whether they are in state a^1 or a^2.

190 Bray (2009), 117, describes the chemotactic pathway, for example, as being 'small and relatively independent of other processes... but the operative word here is *relatively*. You just have to scratch the surface to uncover a multitude of links to all kinds of other cell processes. The kinase that drives the cascade of chemotactic signals, for example, also plays a part in other signaling pathways, such as responses to osmotic changes and the detection of glucose. Just making the proteins of this pathway and positioning them in the membrane and cytoplasm requires numerous other molecular interactions to be performed'. Ultimately, Bray believes, it would be possible 'to trace connections between chemotaxis and every other function of the cell: no circuit is an island unto itself'.

191 See ibid., 94–96; see also Grebe and Stock (1998).

192 Dusenbery (2009; 124–27) draws an extremely useful distinction between 'causal inputs' and 'informational inputs': causal inputs, he writes, 'are inherently important because of the chemical or physical effects that they exert and the work that they can do. In contrast, informational inputs are

important only because they are associated with some causal input and can be used to predict the occurrence of the causal input at another place or a later time'.

193 Ibid., 125–26; see also Adler (1969).

194 Adler (1969), 1590–93.

195 See Thar and Fenchel (2001; 3299) on the difference between true taxis and chemokinesis.

196 Ibid.

197 Ibid.

198 See ibid.

199 See Dusenbery (2009; 214–16) on the 'fundamental physical tendency for free-swimming objects to move in a helical path'. This can be considered the default option unless sufficiently prejudicial. As Dusenbery writes, 'even if the flagellum does not rotate, the body may be forced into rotation. If a swimming microorganism generates its propulsive thrust along a line that does not pass exactly through its center of frictional resistance, it will cause rotation of the body around a perpendicular axis. ... Since no organism (or machine) is constructed perfectly, some rotation around such an axis is inevitable, unless some other force or feedback system is included to correct for deviations from a particular orientation' (214–15).

200 Thar and Fenchel (2001), 3300.

201 In fact, there is such genetic and phenotypic diversity among the different strains of *O. marina* that it has been suggested they may represent different species. For the sake of simplicity I shall refer throughout to *O. marina* as a single species. See Calbet et al. (2013).

202 Roberts et al. (2011 a), 604.

203 Ibid.

204 See Guo et al. (2013), 39: roughly two per cent of *O. marina* populations are believed to fall back on cannibalism in food-depleted environments.

205 Calbet et al. (2013; 68) note that it is generally found in intertidal pools, salt marshes and embayments, rarely inhabiting open ocean waters.

206 See ibid., 73, 78.

207 Roberts et al. (2011a), 609, 604. See also Guo et al. (2013), 38–40. *O. marina* has further been reported to possess a proton-pump-type rhodopsin, possibly acquired from bacteria by means of horizontal gene transfer. This photosensitive receptor protein may well generate energy directly from light.

208 Roberts et al. (2011 a), 609–10.

209 See Breckels et al. (2011).

210 Again, this difference is anything but absolute: we have seen that bacteria too may be 'misled' by a chemical gradient, even though the information in principle coincides with the nutrition.

211 Jonas's description is couched in terms of animal existence, yet applies verbatim to active protozoan hunters. 'In the motions of animals', he writes, 'we have activity made possible by the surplus from previous metabolism and directed toward safeguarding its future, but itself a free expenditure dissociated from the continuing vegetative activity, and thus action in a radically new sense. ... The outward motion is an expenditure to be redeemed only by the eventual success. But this success is not assured. The external action, in order to be a possibly successful one, must be such that it also can go wrong'. By contrast with the sedentary life of plants, therefore, motile animals and (one might add) active protozoan predators lead an existence that is precarious, exposed and committed to 'wakefulness and effort'. With this active consciousness of one's surroundings there emerges the possibility of pleasure and discomfort: 'pursuit itself may end in the disappointment of failure. In short, the indirectness of animal existence holds in its wakefulness the twin possibilities of enjoyment and suffering, both wedded to effort'. See Jonas (1966; 2001), 104–5.

212 See Boakes et al. (2011), 646–47.

213 This brief account is indebted in large measure to the description of how dinoflagellates use their flagella to swim by Tom Fenchel (2001). Again, microbes are now known to swim in a helical path by default 'because at low Reynolds numbers almost any type of swimming will lead to a rotation as well as a translation of the cell' (330).

214 A more linear path is used when prey concentrations are high, whereas at reduced concentrations the helical component is increased. It is thought that such 'helical walks' optimize random foraging where prey densities are low. See Roberts et al. (2011a), 608.

215 See Montagnes et al. (2008); Roberts et al. (2011a), 610; Roberts et al. (2011b), 834.

216 Breckels et al. (2011), 635.

217 Roberts et al. (2011b), 834.

218 On *Chlamydomonas allensworthii* see Starr et al. (1995); see also Dusenbery (2009), 305–7, who points out that the use of pheromones in mating also occurs in two species of ciliates (*Blepharisma intermedium* and *Euplotes octocarinatus*) but that here the attraction is to groups of organisms rather than to individuals.

219 See Ralt et al. (1994). In the plant kingdom, the occurrence of chemotaxis in ferns is well known. Ancient lineages of gymnosperms (non-flowering seed plants) such as ginkgoes and cycads also have sperm that are flagellated and therefore motile. Renouncing the self-propulsion of sperm, more derived plants rely on the random transportation of pollen by wind and passing animals.

220 Buskey (1997), 77.

221 Ibid. See also Hansen and Calado (1999), 386, who note: 'when in the presence of a large organism, the movement extends from end to end of the prey, as if the dinoflagellate were sizing the potential food item'.

222 See Fenchel (2001), 335, describing the behaviour in *Crypthecodinium*: 'every time the dinoflagellates happen to swim away from the particle, they tend to make a turn and so move back towards the particle. The behaviour is similar to what has previously been described for certain phagotrophic dinoflagellates that ingest large prey. ... In these cases, it superficially appears as if the dinoflagellates gauge the size of their prey before attempting to engulf it; in reality the motile chemosensory behaviour simply forces them to encircle the prey cell until their ventral side makes physical contact to its surface by chance'.

223 Echolocation and electroreception may be assumed to perform a similar function in the identification and localization of objects.
224 See the subchapter 'A World of Objects'.
225 Gibbs and Dellinger (1908), 240.
226 Money (2014), 11: a certain anthropomorphism or rather zoomorphism (or perhaps simply poetic licence) might be detected in the attribution of terror to a 'writhing' bacterium. See the subsequent considerations on fear in unicellular organisms.
227 Ralston et al. (2014).
228 Gibbs and Dellinger (1908), 240.
229 See Kusch (1999), 715–18, who describes the contrasting case of *Lembadion* – 'a fascinating ciliate with a huge oral cavity' – which likewise produces a self-recognition signal to inhibit clonal cannibalism, but limits synthesis of the signal in conditions of starvation (so cannibalism can go ahead if needs must).
230 On the cytoskeleton see Pollard (2003); Fletcher and Mullins (2010).
231 For a critique of models of amoeboid motility based solely on dendritic actin polymerization at the leading edge of the cell, see Kay et al. (2008), who suggest that other factors such as hydrostatic pressure may also play a part. The precise mechanisms involved do not alter the present argument.
232 Harold (2001), 137. Assuming a length of $300\,\mu m$, a speed of $5\,\mu m$ per second would mean that the amoeba is crawling the distance of one body length per minute. In these relative terms, bacteria are very much faster.
233 See Kay et al. (2008), 455, who describe the chemotaxis of crawling cells such as amoebae and neutrophils as 'an extremely slow form of movement'. These authors attribute top speeds of just 10-40 μm per minute to neutrophils, which are amoeboid, phagocytic cells belonging to the immune system: 'a neutrophil that moves at 10 μm per minute covers its own body length in approximately 1 minute, which is equivalent to a human taking an hour to cover 100 metres'.
234 See McMahon and Bonner (1983), 200–1, who point out that most ciliated organisms tend to swim at the same speed on account of the consistency in the length of their cilia and beat frequency. Flagellates too tend to have the same swimming speed, irrespective of their size.
235 Gibbs and Dellinger (1908), 233.
236 Ibid., 236–37. For the *Vorticella* study see Hodge and Aikins (1895), who note that although the cell never normally seems to rest, it does undergo periods of 'enforced' rest in the form of encystment in unfavourable environmental conditions. It also, of necessity, interrupts its ciliary activity during stalk contraction (an aversive reaction), although this does not last long enough to count as a 'period of rest' (ibid., 529).
237 Gibbs and Dellinger (1908), 237.
238 See Brüssow (2007), 689–90, who points out that it is only the egg-laying females that need such a nutritious diet; male mosquitoes, assigned the relatively low-energy business of sperm-production, remain 'lifelong vegetarians'.

239 Or at least *Vorticella* is *seemingly* indefatigable in its feeding behaviour; see note 236. Two further provisos should be made. If suspension-feeding ciliates are subjected to centrifugation or transferred to water at a different temperature or pH level, they may 'lose their appetite'. It may be minutes or even hours before they recover it, and for this time it is as though they are *off their food*. Fenchel (1980, 2) observes that in such conditions the ciliates may 'refuse to feed altogether'. The second qualification is that, like many sessile protozoans, *Vorticella* has a motile life stage. Known as telotroch larvae or swarmers, *Vorticella* daughter cells are concerned solely with finding a place to settle, and no feeding occurs in this phase: nourishment only comes once they have completed their search and settled down. So in this sense, too, there is indeed a contrast between feeding and non-feeding states. This raises questions that will be addressed in the next section. On *Vorticella* see Patterson and Hedley (1992; 1996), 113–14.

240 As Jennings points out (1906; 11, 20), citing the work of the zoologist Ludwig Rhumbler, amoebae can also be brought to interrupt their meal by subjection to strong light, which in general has the effect of interfering with their activities and in this context makes them 'lose their appetite'. Mechanical stimuli such as the shaking of the substrate or contact with a sharp needle can likewise cause amoebae to withdraw their pseudopods and remain immobile – and thus indifferent to the presence of prey – for varying periods of time. In such cases too, the amoebae 'lose their appetite'. See Schönborn (1966), 29, who describes the effects of such disturbances on various testate amoebae such as *Difflugia lobostoma* and *Nebela gracilis*. Whereas the former moves off more or less at once, the latter takes 20 minutes to start moving again.

241 See notes 236 and 239.

242 Quoted in Bray (2009), 136. Darwin suggests that only people with asthma are truly aware of the value of breathing. Mountaineering and diving are activities that foster such awareness. The extremely rare condition known as Ondine's Curse is a failure of the normally automatic regulation of our respiration, resulting in apnoea usually but not always during sleep.

243 The species was classified in the genus *Dileptus* until 2012, when it was moved to its new genus. See Wikipedia: https://en.wikipedia.org/wiki/Pseudomonilicaryon_anser. Both genera belong to the family of dileptids.

244 Patterson and Hedley (1992; 1996), 168.

245 Miller (1968), 313.

246 Ibid., 315.

247 Of course, a systematic answer to this question would require an analysis of the dileptid's hunting strategy, in particular the degree to which its prey are 'targeted' as opposed to merely bumped into.

248 See Jakobsen and Strom (2004), 1918.

249 See ibid., 1915: according to Jakobsen and Strom, circadian rhythms are biological rhythms that are characterized by 24-hour periodicity, endogenously generated (though environmentally modulated), and can be entrained by naturally occurring environmental cycles that also show 24-hour periodicity.

Endnotes 219

250 Ibid., 1919.
251 Patterson and Hedley (1992; 1996), 180; see also note 239.
252 Dickerson and Findly (2014), 291.
253 Ibid.
254 Fenchel (2009).
255 On the six morphotypes see ibid., 280.
256 Ibid., 283.
257 By the same token, one might envision a hypothetical organism that was always 'awake', 'active' and 'hungry' (and in this respect was an 'eating machine'), yet had distinct *modes* of hungry wakefulness, at some times of the day showing an exclusive preference for paramecia and at other times an exclusive preference for diatoms. To the extent that a distinction could thereby be drawn between its *paramecium-hunger* and its *diatom-hunger*, the organism would exhibit the tacit selfhood required as a logical prerequisite for consciousness. It would be different for it to confront a paramecium if it was *paramecium-hungry* from if it was *diatom-hungry*. To the observer, this difference would manifest itself in behavioural variations (pursuit of one type of prey as opposed to the other).
258 Calbet et al. (2013), 73.
259 Jakobsen and Strom (2004), 1918.
260 Jürgens and DeMott (1995).
261 It might be objected that such behavioural tendencies could be caused by the predator sensing the changes in the external food concentration rather than by internal changes in the predator's nutritional status. However, the time lag of between 30 and 60 minutes between the addition of bacteria and the maximum discrimination against beads is taken to suggest that it is variations in nutritional status that produce the effect. In the words of Jürgens and DeMott, the feeding behaviour thus depends on 'gut fullness', 'food vacuole formation', or 'biochemical correlations of hunger and satiation' (ibid., 1505).
262 Ibid., 1503: 'flagellates that were cultured under food-limiting conditions showed a modest but significant preference for beads when both particles were offered simultaneously. However, both flagellates exhibited strong discrimination against the inert beads within 30 – 60 min after the addition of a satiating concentration of live bacteria. As bacterial abundance declined over 24 h, discrimination against the inert beads gradually relaxed'.
263 Ibid., 1506.
264 See Christaki et al. (1998), 463: 'for the ciliates examined, selectivity may not pay when food is plentiful. One possible mechanistic explanation is that the rejection of undesirable particles is much more efficient at the slower swimming speeds characteristic of both ciliates in stationary vs. log-phase cells'. (In modelling bacterial and protozoan growth patterns, the 'log-phase' corresponds to a period of exponential growth, whereas the 'stationary' phase refers to a period in which growth is limited, possibly by nutrient depletion).

265 Miller (1968), 316. Of course, this too may have a mechanical rather than an internal biochemical explanation: it could be that successful prey handling is in some way physically hampered by the organism's state of physical repletion.
266 Matsuoka et al. (2000), 85. This contrasts with the cannibalism shown by various species of the normally bacterivorous filter-feeding ciliate *Blepharisma*. In the latter case, cannibalism is associated with gigantism, and its occurrence seems to depend not on starvation but simply on whether the predator's mouthpart is large enough to engulf its conspecifics; see Giese (1973), 123–34.
267 Guo et al. (2013), 39.
268 Denton (2005), 7.
269 Ibid., 8, citing A. D. Craig.
270 Ibid., 7.
271 Rolls (1999), 60–61.
272 Bennett and Hacker (2003), 199–200.
273 Ibid., 200.
274 As we have seen, Rolls defines what he refers to as 'emotions' – but what I would refer to as 'appetites' – in just such terms.
275 Craig (1918), 91–92, 93.
276 Denton (2005), 127. The equivalent in a unicellular context is a protozoan displaying behaviour associated with satiety as soon as its food vacuoles are full rather than waiting until its inner biochemical balance is restored. Vacuolar distension thus functions *as a signal* for an imminent return to homeostatic equilibrium. This signal may be misleading, as shown by bacterivorous ciliates fed to satiation on latex beads, which behave in the same way as ciliates that have been sated on nutritious bacteria. See Snyder (1991), 210.
277 The implication that reproduction is *good for self* may rankle to the extent that reproduction is often considered to entail the death of the progenitor self and the birth of a new, different self. On the logical implications of viewing self-reproduction as a form of self-perpetuation, see Glasgow (2017), 39–41.
278 Balcombe (2006), 9: Balcombe's work provides a marvellous account of the presence of pleasure in the animal kingdom.
279 Romanes and Darwin (1885), 110–11.
280 See Cabanac (1992), 174.
281 The logical need for a 'common currency' in order to choose which of various behavioural options is 'the best' (for oneself) and should thus be pursued was already recognized by Aristotle. See *De Anima* (Book III.11) 434 a; also Aristotle (1986), 216.
282 Cabanac (1992), 174, 176.
283 The role of outcome expectations further implies a temporal dimension that is absent in reflex behaviour.
284 Ibid., 175, 193: Cabanac points out that it is a matter of 'rationality' not in the philosophical but in the economic sense: 'Maximization of pleasure may thus be the link between physiology and behavior

and give the key to the problem of physiological optimization without the implication of the animal's knowledge and rationality about its physiological state. A working man does not have to know his body temperature, blood oxygen and glucose, muscle glycogen and lactic acid, etc. to take an occasional but necessary break. He just has to "listen to" his sensations and maximize the algebraic sum of pleasures'.

285 On the relationship between selfhood and selfishness see Glasgow (2017), 51–56, 101–4.

286 Balcombe (2006; 37) quotes the veterinarian Jerrold Tannenbaum on the unrelenting harshness of animal life.

287 See Balcombe (2006; 161) for the effects of catnip on felids: 'Under its spell, cats chase and paw at non-existent mice and phantom butterflies. The plant contains nepetalactone, a chemical compound akin to a pheromone in the urine of sexually receptive cats. The solicitous rolling about of female cats under catnip's influence suggests that sexual arousal is a side effect. A cat who has discovered a catnip plant will return to it daily. Ditto cougars, lions, jaguars and leopards'.

288 See ibid., 161–64.

289 It is plausible that the two most rudimentary forms of play – locomotor play and object play – in fact have their evolutionary roots in the pleasures of hunting, searching, foraging and the pursuit of prey or mates, activities that have come to be positively evaluated in themselves in the light of the subsequent reward. In other words, it is not just the final consummation of an appetite that is positively valenced, but the whole process of pursuit and capture. Such 'play' activities may thus seem to be non-functional to the extent that they involve self-movement without the subsequent consummation. However, their occurrence can be explained not only in terms of the proximate causation of sheer pleasure – what the German language refers to as *Funktionslust* – but also the ultimate causation of increased 'fitness' deriving from enhanced locomotive or manipulative skills. As suggested by the *autotelic* nature of play, play exists in a deep relationship with selfhood, which is likewise autotelic by definition. For an exhaustive account of the phylogeny of play see Burghardt (2005).

290 Jennings (1906), 330.

291 Berridge (2003), 108.

292 Ibid., 113-14.

293 See Balcombe (2006), 93; Berridge (2003), 109.

294 See Thorogood et al. (2018). Social transmission of aversions has been observed, for example, in vervet and tamarin monkeys, house sparrows, domestic chicks and great tits.

295 Balcombe (2006), 102.

296 In fact, some protozoans do combine the characteristic features of amoebae and flagellates; see note 24. The so-called pelobionts are amoeboid in shape but also sport a beating flagellum. *Mastigella* and *Mastigamoeba* are two such genera. However, neither of these is known to 'wag' its flagellum specifically in excited anticipation of pelobiont chow. On the pelobionts, see Patterson and Hedley (1992; 1996), 56–57, 100.

297 If my intention in making these claims had been to *explain* motivation by reference to (implicitly anticipated) pleasure, the argument would here be circular in that it affirms that pleasure is ultimately

recognized by the occurrence of motivated behaviour. However, the aim here is not explanation but conceptual analysis. Appetite, motivation and pleasure are viewed as logically or conceptually linked.

298 See McFarland (2008), 118–29, comparing the 'hedonic view' of Cabanac with the 'automaton view' of opponents, who conceive an organism as a type of self-regulating machine.

299 Anyone who believes that a feeling of pleasure necessarily incorporates a conscious thought about this feeling of pleasure will be justified in refusing to ascribe such a state to unicellulars. Yet even though humans are endowed with this capacity to reflect on their pleasures, it does not follow that – in order to experience a pleasure – one needs to be able to reflect on or think about this experience. It goes without saying that the specifically human capacity to contemplate, remember and anticipate one's pleasures adds extraordinary new dimensions to the experience of pleasure.

300 Of course, concepts such as 'perspective' or 'point of view' are misleadingly visual in their implications; the 'point of smell' is more relevant for many animals.

301 Zahavi (2005), 11, quoting from Husserl, *Zur Phänomenologie der Intersubjektivität II*.

302 See Denton (2005), 124–26.

303 As described above, corollary discharge gives rise to our normally unquestioned capacity to distinguish self-caused sensory input from sensory input caused by non-self. Our proprioceptive and kinaesthetic self-awareness is a pre-reflective sense of fluctuating bodily 'hereness' in animals with individuated limbs that can shift in relation to one another. Other aspects of tacit selfhood include equilibrioception (i.e. our sense of balance, mediated in most mammals by the vestibular system), and what is known as self-body-size perception (our dispositional ability to cross gaps and negotiate openings such as doors). To the extent that directional self-movement is what grounds the possibility of consciousness, these factors – coordinating and synchronizing the self-movement of a highly complex body – silently structure consciousness itself. Given the necessarily speculative nature of attempts to ascribe these aspects of tacit selfhood to unicellular organisms, the present discussion will leave these questions unexplored. Yet even though amoebae lack permanent limbs (perhaps unlike ciliates, which have cilia) and a constant body size, their movements are still governed by an overriding need for cohesiveness and coordination.

304 Shoemaker (1968).

305 Bennett and Hacker (2003), 97.

306 For a full discussion of traditional misconceptions regarding pain and its 'privacy', see ibid., 88–97.

307 There is logical redundancy, therefore, in the claim 'I know that I am in pain'; it is enough to say 'I am in pain'. By contrast, there is no logical redundancy in the assertion 'I know that I am RDVG' (I may suffer sporadic amnesia and need to fall back on empirical reassurance to convince either myself or someone else who I am). This is because such an assertion pertains to my narrative or autobiographical self.

308 Damasio (2000), 77, 78.

309 The human affliction known as congenital insensitivity to pain, or congenital analgesia, hints that the connection between pain and consciousness is far from absolute. This genetic disorder, which affects fewer than one in a million people, is not associated with any form of cognitive disorder except an inability to feel pain, leaving sufferers with a diminished awareness of – and an extreme vulnerability to sustaining – bodily damage to themselves. See for example Lane (2009), 250.

310 Smith (1991), 26. For a general discussion of invertebrate and insect pain see also Sherwin (2001), Eisemann (1984).

311 Ammermann et al. (2012). It is also conjectured that the discharged extrusome might prevent the cryptomonads from being ingested by a potential predator, entangling the feeding apparatus.

312 See Craig (1918), 91, who provides a lucid account of the asymmetry in the relationship of appetite and aversion, the former caused by the *absence* of an 'appeted' stimulus, the latter caused by the *presence* of a 'disturbing' stimulus.

313 See Eisemann (1984; 166) on the absence of pain guarding in invertebrates: 'No example is known to us of an insect showing protective behavior towards injured body parts, such as by limping after leg injury or declining to feed or mate because of abdominal injuries. On the contrary, our experience has been that insects will continue with normal activities even after severe injury or removal of body parts. ... Among our other observations are those on a locust which continued to feed whilst itself being eaten by a mantis; aphids continuing to feed while being eaten by coccinellids; a tsetse fly which flew in to feed although half dissected; caterpillars which continue to feed whilst tachinid larvae bore into them'.

314 Sherwin (2001), S113.

315 On octopus pain see Godfrey-Smith (2017), 102, 224, describing recent work by Jean Alupay and her colleagues.

316 See chapter VI.

317 Non-directional learned avoidance is presumably insufficient to suggest consciousness. This has been found to occur in single isolated ganglions of decapitated cockroaches; see below note 473.

318 On the case of fish as the ancestral vertebrate, see Braithwaite (2010).

319 Damasio (2000; 74–75) reports on the effects in one such case. After the operation the patient was a new person, relaxed and happy. When asked about the pain, he replied that 'the pains were the same,' but that he felt fine now. The operation had done nothing to alter the sensory patterns corresponding to the local tissue dysfunction, notes Damasio, but it had abolished the emotional reaction: the suffering had gone.

320 Ibid., 75–76.

321 See Gerber et al. (2014), especially 240.

322 Grandin and Johnson (2005), 189–93. This may sound rather a bold claim. What is meant is that fear has a greater potential to incapacitate an animal: animals in considerable pain can still function, acting as though nothing were the matter; animals in a state of panic cannot function at all (190).

323 Jonas (1966; 2001), 105.

324 As with consciousness in general, there has been a tendency to posit a 'cut-off' point in the phylogenetic 'scale' beneath which it is inappropriate to ascribe emotions to animals. It has been

argued, for example, that amphibians, unlike reptiles, lack emotions in that they do not exhibit changes in heart rate or core body temperature in response to handling stress. The idea has a certain appeal given the apparently expression-less inscrutability of fish and amphibians, deprived as they are of our mammalian dexterity in pulling faces and gesticulating. Although it may seem plausible, however, it can be queried from two angles. First, it is not obvious that there is a *straightforward* correlation between such autonomic responses and 'emotions'. Second, an increasingly substantial body of evidence suggests that even fish are indeed highly susceptible to strain and stress: it has been shown, for example, that it is 48 hours before their hormonal levels return to normal following rough handling. See Balcombe (2006), 186-87; Braithwaite (2010).

325 This classification is indebted to Bennett and Hacker (2003), 199–202, who not only distinguish emotions, agitations and moods, but describe how they may shade off into attitudes that are not emotions (such as liking or disliking) and into character traits (such as benevolence or irascibility). The boundaries between such categories, as the authors concede, are far from sharp.

326 Dennett (1991), 101.

327 For his analysis of *Stimmung* (albeit as a specifically human phenomenon), see Heidegger (1929/30; 1983), 89–103. Heidegger was already developing similar thoughts in his 1919–20 lectures on *The Fundamental Problems of Phenomenology*, where he speaks of the *Irgendwie* (the somehow) and the *Wiegehalt* (the how-content) of experience. The phenomenal world is encountered not just as a manifold of objects, but always *in some way or other*, funnelled through my own particular *Selbstwelt* (self-world). In this fascinating early work Heidegger also elaborates the concept of *Sich-Selbst-Haben* (having-oneself) as a form of pre-reflective self-intimacy (*Vertrautheit mit sich selbst*). See Heidegger (1919/20; 1993).

328 The bristletails, another class of primitively wingless hexapods, also resort to a directionless escape jump. Other insects incorporate varying degrees of directedness into their jumps. Depending on urgency, fruit flies choose between two escape strategies in the face of a 'looming' stimulus. Both these strategies exhibit directionality, involving a sequence of at least four sub-behaviours: freezing, adjusting directional posture, elevating the wings and taking off. The two strategies differ above all in the time spent on wing elevation prior to take-off. The 'short' mode produces a less stable initial flight, but is quicker than the 'long' mode, and tends to be elicited by looming that is more rapid. See von Reyn et al. (2014).

329 The complexities are illustrated by the fast escape responses of fish and crayfish (which are not fish, but freshwater crustaceans). As the neurobiologist Ari Berkowitz reports (2016; 36–38), considerable attention has been paid to a neuron called the Mauthner cell (or M cell) in fish and to the lateral giant neuron in crayfish. These huge neurons, provided with thick axons adept in the expeditious transmission of information, resemble 'command neurons' in that a single neuronal spike is enough to trigger a fast escape movement, a speedily executed tail flip in the case of crayfish or a 'turn and swim' response in fish. Such mechanisms are 'like a push button' (and presumably call for little in the way of consciousness). However, there are other neuronal circuits that come into play if the M cell is put out of action, for example, generating a slower, less stereotypical response. These smaller neurons also contribute to the later stages of normal escape behaviour, 'fine-tuning its trajectory'. In crayfish, such circuits are used when the emergency is somewhat less pressing, producing a sequence of flips more tailored to the specific situation: 'a giant-neuron circuit produces a very stereotypical flip, whereas the nongiant circuits produce a flexible set of slightly different flips, through which movement direction can be better controlled. So if you have some time to collect information and deliberate, you might be better off using a nongiant circuit to make sure you're going off in the best direction, rather than using the eject button'. What initially seems to be an invariant response, therefore, proves on second examination to include a much more adaptable mechanism that may well entail *directionality* and thus some sort of *awareness* of the surroundings. It may also be modulated by factors such as 'social status' (43 – 47), moreover, as determined by the winning or losing of fights against conspecifics. Fight winners have been found to be more likely to employ the non-directional escape triggered by the lateral giant; fight losers tend to make use of the adjustable form of getaway.

330   Romanes and Darwin (1885), 342.
331   Binet (1889), vi.
332   Binet was himself aware of his liability to the charge of anthropomorphism, as shown by his discussion of unicellular choice (see ibid., 62). For his doubts regarding consciousness see ibid., 61.
333   Gibbs and Dellinger (1908), 240 – 41.
334   Bray (2009), 18; on attention in this sense see also Jennings (1906), 331.
335   Jennings (1904), 198.
336   Ibid. Such behaviour seems to be a more general strategy in weaker gradients, where 'cells do not orientate pseudopodia directly up the chemotactic gradient, but instead produce new pseudopodia by splitting existing ones with little reference to the gradient. … Cells then steer by favouring the daughter pseudopod that is up-gradient, which then becomes dominant, and the unsuccessful daughter is retracted'. See Kay et al. (2008), 456.
337   Bray (2009), 18.
338   See, for example, Zahavi (2005), 62– 64.
339   As Alva Noë has shown, this phenomenal background is closely associated with various aspects of our tacit self, namely our dispositional sensorimotor skills and our proprioceptive or kinaesthetic self-awareness. My sense of the perceptual presence of the world in all its detail does not consist in a 'representation' of the minutiae of the world that I encounter, but rather in a selective awareness of certain salient features, together with my possible sensorimotor access to further details by controlled self-movements (a turn of the head, a shift of my eyes, a step forward) and in conjunction with my tacit kinaesthetic self-awareness and understanding of how these movements would produce changes in sensory stimulation. See Noë (2004), 49 – 66.
340   See Bennett and Hacker (2003), 244: 'Transitive consciousness is a matter of being conscious *of* something or other, or of being conscious *that* something or other is thus or otherwise. Intransitive

consciousness, by contrast, has no object. It is a matter of being conscious or awake, as opposed to being unconscious or asleep'.

341 Gibbs and Dellinger (1908), 234.

342 Ibid., 235, 237.

343 Of course, one might equally well speak of degrees of appetite. Again, there need not be a hard-and-fast distinction between appetite and arousal.

344 George Mashour, quoted in Geddes (2011).

345 Roach (2013), 166.

346 See Jakobsen and Strom (2004). Compare Gibbs and Dellinger (1908), 233, who note that the rest periods of *A. proteus* 'apparently have nothing to do with light or darkness, day or night'.

347 On circadian rhythms in general see Greenspan (2007), 77–90. As regards the sleep of fruit flies, Greenspan observes that it is not just that they are inactive when it is dark. If subjected to conditions of constant darkness, they remain active in what would have been the daytime. 'Flies do not snore', Greenspan reassures us, 'or close any of the 1400 ommatidia of their compound eyes. They just stand still (which is not adequate to qualify as sleep). In addition to being quiet, they also are less responsive to stimuli such as light or vibration, and if forced to become active during the nighttime when they would usually be quiet (i.e., [if they] become sleep deprived), they will recover some of the lost sleep during the next day. These are characteristics of sleep' (85).

348 Ibid., 86.

349 See Brüssow (2007), 74–75, 240–41: this temporal compartmentalization consists in limiting oxygenic photosynthesis to daylight conditions and nitrogen fixation to the dark. Other, filamentous cyanobacteria such as *Anabaena* resort to spatial compartmentalization in the form of a multicellular division of labour. A specialist 'heterocyst' cell is used to carry out the nitrogen fixation. This calls for cooperation among a collective of cells.

350 Greenspan (2007), 86.

351 Jakobsen and Strom (2004), 1915.

352 See McClung (2006), 794.

353 See Nath et al. (2017).

354 Ibid., 2984: the state of behavioural quiescence and reduced responsiveness must be 'rapidly reversible' to distinguish it from other immobile states such as coma or paralysis. The link with sleep is corroborated not only by the homeostatic and possibly circadian regulation of this quiescent state but also by the probable role of the highly conserved molecule melatonin in this process (2989).

355 See Puttonen et al. (2016).

356 Sonner (2008), 849–50.

357 See Sanders et al. (2012); Alkire et al. (2008).

358 Kaech et al. (1999), 10433; Penrose (1995), 369.

359 See Alkire et al. (2008); Hudetz (2012), Schrouff et al. (2011).

360 See page 44–45.

361 But see Sonner (2008), 849–50, who suggests that the capacity to modulate ion channels in the unicellular micro-organisms that preceded the emergence of multicellularity may have originally had a beneficial defensive function, preventing the entry of deleterious ions that might have induced 'spurious motile responses' in the cell. Sonner's proposals seek to provide an evolutionary narrative explaining the reaction of present-day organisms to inhaled anaesthetics. His conjecture is that 'organisms today respond to inhaled anesthetics because their ion channels are sensitive to inhaled anesthetics by virtue of common descent from ancestral, anesthetic-sensitive ion channels in one-celled organisms (i.e., that the response to anesthetics did not arise as an adaptation of the nervous system, but rather of ion channels that preceded the origin of multicellularity)'. Sonner's membrane-centred hypothesis thus accounts for the continuity between unicellular and multicellular anaesthesia.

362 See Hameroff (2006), 406.

363 See Kaech et al. (1999).

364 Ibid. As the authors point out, volatile anaesthetics seem not to exert a direct influence on actin dynamics (for example by binding to a hydrophobic site on the actin molecule and interfering with its assembly into filaments), but to have an indirect effect, possibly by interacting with a component of one of the pathways that influence polymerization (10436).

365 See Damasio (2000), 357–58 (endnotes): Damasio describes curare as mimicking locked-in syndrome.

366 Dennett (1978), 209–10.

367 Ibid.: as Dennett points out, 'patients administered our compound, curare-cum-amnestic, will not later embarrass their physicians with recountings of agony, and will in fact be unable to tell in retrospect from their own experience that they were not administered a general anaesthetic. Of course *during* the operation they would know, but would be unable to tell us. At least most of our intuitions tell us that curare-cum-amnestic would not be an acceptable substitute for general anesthesia, even if it were cheaper and safer. But now how do we know that general anesthetics in use today are not really curare-cum-amnestic?' (210).

368 Applewhite and Gardner (1971), 287.

369 See above, page 67.

370 Of course, the work of phagocytosis is required in diffusion feeders, and some prey manipulation may be needed.

371 Denton (2005), 121–23. Having failed to evolve such a strategy since moving onto land, amphibians do not search for water even when severely dehydrated. It seems to have been the first wholly terrestrial vertebrates (reptiles) that evolved an 'appetite' for water, i.e. a capacity to discern its presence and a disposition to undertake motivated behaviour to find and drink it.

372 Jonas (1966; 2001), 116.

373 See Turner (2000), 43–45. Some thinkers suggest that the term 'taxis' is misleading to the extent that the process is not a stimulus-response mechanism but a purely passive phenomenon. See Dusenbery (2009), who notes that 'even microbiologists do not call the movement a taxis when

bacteria sink under the force of gravity' (383; see also 164–65). Dusenbery prefers to call such bacteria 'magnetic' rather than 'magnetotactic'.

374 For an illuminating account of magnetotaxis in a philosophical context, see O'Malley (2014), 25–41.

375 Dusenbery (2009), 164–65.

376 As Dusenbery explains, 'the magnets reduce the movements of the bacteria from three dimensions to one, and ... reduction of dimensionality makes for more efficient guidance'. This permits magnetic bacteria to extend the duration of time over which 'they can maintain their orientation without attaching to the surface of a larger object. This allows them to take as much time as desirable to obtain directional information, without the limitation imposed by rotational Brownian motion. They can then swim forward and backward along this line, in response to chemical stimulation' (ibid., 166–67).

377 On this distinction see Turner (2000), 44. The distinction partly reflects the uncertainty of human investigators as regards the *benefits* of magnetic orientation, which are not as obvious as the benefits of, for example, phototactic orientation. It is perfectly feasible, indeed, that there is an adaptive explanation for magnetosomes that has nothing to do with locomotion or motility. It has been suggested that magnetosomes might serve as a repository for excess iron or play a role in the detoxification of reactive oxygen species such as hydrogen peroxide. On the various possible functions of the magnetosome, see O'Malley (2014), 31.

378 Of course, it *is* self-caused insofar as it depends on the work performed by the organism and thus on the organism being alive and metabolically active rather than dead or in a state of cryptobiosis. Assuming the aliveness of the creature, however, the response is basically fixed or unvarying.

379 By contrast, other ciliates are known to regulate their phototaxis in accordance with how well-fed they are. When undernourished, *Chlamydodon* exhibits positive phototaxis; when satiated, it shows negative phototaxis. Though generally avoiding light and preferring the darkness of the depths, that is, hungry specimens may swim to the water surface in order to feed on the phototrophic prey that frequently accumulate there. See Jékely (2009), 2799, 2802.

380 Villarreal (2009), 111–12.

381 See McDougall (1923), 60–61. A very similar principle – though dispensing even with photoreception – underlay the original conception of phototaxis developed by Jennings's contemporary Jacques Loeb and others. This envisaged the stimulus acting *directly* on the locomotor organs of the creature (e.g. the cilia of a paramecium), causing those on the more strongly stimulated side to contract either to a greater or lesser extent than those on the opposite side. Jennings (1904) showed that the explanation for the movements of ciliates such as paramecia was not as simple as Loeb and colleagues had proposed. The phototactic paramecia and euglenas he observed moved by a process more akin to 'trial and error', which involved turning and trying out a new direction until one was found that worked.

382 See Jékely (2009), who pinpoints four necessary and thus universal features required of an organism for three-dimensional phototaxis to be possible: '(i) polarity and a fixed shape; (ii) spiral swimming with cilia; (iii) photosensory molecules and a phototransductory cascade that affects ciliary

beating; and (iv) a shading or refractive body that ensures the orientation-dependent illumination of the photopigments during axial rotation' (2802). As Jékely notes, the relatively frequent conjunction of these features has resulted in the evolution of phototaxis eight times independently in eukaryotes. Prokaryotes, by contrast, are not able to discriminate the direction of light. Instead, they measure the *intensity* of light and use a biased random walk to negotiate a light-intensity gradient (2795).

383 See Thar and Kühl (2003), 5751. More specifically, the flagella at the end with a rising oxygen concentration increase their rotation speed, whereas those at the end with a falling concentration decrease their speed.

384 See ibid., 5752. The reasonably large size of the bacterium (6 μm) is likely to ensure, note the authors, that 'the flagellar bundles at either end of the cell are controlled only by the local sensor regions'.

385 See Glasgow (2017), 96–98.

386 Tye (1997), 303.

387 Ibid.

388 In fact, the 'satiety' of caterpillars is more associated with the stages of their life-cycle than with reversible, post-prandial 'fullness', recalling to mind some of the questions raised in the section 'Recognizing Hunger: Some Doubts'. Caterpillars generally only cease to eat just before shedding their skin or in the time prior to pupation.

389 See page 30.

390 For other examples of conflicting stimuli, see Jennings (1906), 92–99.

391 On interoception see Damasio (2000), 149–53; 150: 'Under no normal condition is the brain ever excused from receiving continuous reports on the internal milieu and visceral states, and under most conditions, even when no active movement is being performed, the brain is also being informed of the state of its musculoskeletal apparatus. ... The internal milieu and visceral division is in charge of sensing changes in the chemical environment of cells throughout the body. The term *interoceptive* describes those sensing operations generically'.

392 Llinás (2001), 133–34.

393 On cockroaches see Rose (1992), 172; on fruit flies see Greenspan (2007), 93.

394 Bray (2009), 239–40.

395 Bray (ibid.) proposes the centrosome as a possible candidate in animal cells, while acknowledging the conjectural nature of his proposal. The centrosome, or microtubule organizing centre, he writes, 'acts as a seed for microtubules that grow out to other parts of the cell, including its membrane, and thereby influence both the shape of the cell and its movements'. It also plays a central role in mitosis. See also Penrose (1995; 360–61) on the centrosome as the 'focal point' of the cytoskeleton; it is a structure that 'apparently controls the cell's movements and its detailed organization'.

396 Penrose (1995), 358.

397 Hanahan and Weinberg (2000), 61; see Ishizaki et al. (1995), 1443.

398 Both cadherins and integrins are known to be altered in metastatic cells. No longer tethered to

the cells around them, metastatic cells thus reacquire the motility that enables them to spread through the body. See Hanahan and Weinberg (2000), 65.
399 See King (2004), 314.
400 Basal metazoans such as sponges, by contrast, exhibit a more flexible relationship between the individual self of their component cells and the collective self of the organism as a whole. See Epilogue.
401 See Penrose (1995), 371; also 406–7. Penrose remains uncommitted on whether such 'apparent absurdities' will one day come to be accepted. However, he regards the question as scientifically legitimate, its answerability depending on improvements in our understanding of physical nature.
402 Llinás (2001), 218.
403 It is as though one were to deduce the wetness of water molecules from the wetness of water.
404 This is not to mention mobile *germ cells* and the occurrence of sperm chemotaxis. However, spermatozoa can be deemed behaviourally inflexible enough to exclude consciousness, in that their locomotive repertoire consists merely in reaching the oocyte. There is no question of whether or not to stop off for a quick snack on the way.
405 Equally intriguing is the peregrination that even neurons and other bodily cells have to undertake in the course of the development of the embryo. The migration of the embryo's cells is guided, in part at least, by a range of different chemical signals emanating from different tissues in the developing organism. The eventual settling and maturation of a migrating cell is in turn induced by proteins produced by tissues at its final destination. Many cancer cells revert to a migratory mode during metastasis. Unlike animal cells, plant cells – held immobile by their rigid cellulose wall – do not migrate at all. By the same token, plant cancers are not vulnerable to metastasis; nor do plants have mobile phagocytes. For a fascinating account of embryonic cell migration see Davies (2014), 92–105; on plants see Hallé (2002), 130.
406 We have also encountered caterpillars as 'eating machines', although the question of whether they genuinely live up to their reputation for insatiability was left open. A further question mark was left hanging over so-called trophonts, whose non-stop feeding is just a stage in an organism's life cycle. Even the ceaseless feeding of *Vorticella* is just part of its life cycle; see above, note 239.
407 According to the description by Sompayrac (1999, 2008; 16–17), macrophages certainly *seem* to have a fluctuating appetite: in their 'resting' state, they are mainly garbage collectors, responsible for ingesting dead cells; when 'primed' or activated by cytokines such as interferon gamma, they upgrade their activity levels; they may further be 'hyperactivated' by direct bacterial signals such as LPS or mannose. In such circumstances, they grow larger, step up their rate of phagocytosis, and increase their digestive capacity (i.e. the number of lysosomes they harbour). Opsonisation is also described as boosting the 'appetite' of a macrophage. It is notable, however, that these changes in 'appetite' depend on signals that are external to the macrophage itself, though internal to the superordinate system of which it forms a part. Perhaps, after all, the macrophage simply does what the system dictates.
408 At the same time, any such residual selfhood must be tightly reined in; it must *not* be allowed to result in an increased risk of cancer.

409 See note 303.
410 See Proust (2009), 169–70.
411 Thompson (2007), 384.
412 Noë (2004), 66–67.
413 Again, this is to privilege the characteristically human form of teleception over other types, such as echolocation and electroreception.
414 Jonas (1966; 2001), 136. The special relationship between sight and distance is underscored by the fact that 'light travels farther than sound and smell and does not suffer distortion on its way over any distance. Indeed, sight is the only sense in which the advantage lies not in proximity but in distance: the best view is by no means the closest view; to get the proper view we take the proper distance, which may vary for different objects and different purposes, but which is always realized as a positive and not a defective feature in the phenomenal presence of the object' (ibid., 149–50).
415 Land (2014), 52. These differences are based on what is known as retinal disparity, or binocular parallax. This is a consequence of the distance between our eyes, i.e. the fact that each retina registers the same scene from a slightly different angle. The disparity between the two views provides information about the distance of a particular object from us.
416 See ibid., 57–62. Dynamic cues are founded, for example, on principles such as the precept that when we move through the world, nearby objects tend to move across the retina faster than distant ones, whereas objects straight ahead of us tend not to move at all.
417 Ibid., 61.
418 On the shadow reflex see Greenspan (2007), 23–40.
419 Roberts et al. (2011a), 608.
420 Gómez et al. (2009), 440. The precise function of the ocelloid remains an object of speculation. Not all of the proposals are related to vision. Another suggestion is that it functions like a chloroplast, absorbing photons and producing chemical energy, with the lens boosting photosynthetic efficiency. See Money (2014), 57–59, 196.
421 Gavelis et al. (2015), 207.
422 Ibid., 204.
423 Land (2014), 8.
424 Balcombe (2006), 50.
425 Such a representation need not necessarily take the form of a symbolic or isomorphic internal image, although there may be an element of isomorphism between the representation and what it represents. Rather, it is best conceived in causal terms, i.e. as a feature of the 'mind' (if the representation is termed 'mental') or the 'neural circuitry' (if the representation is termed 'neural') that tends consistently to make the organism behave *as though* the represented object were present, or, more basally, that induces the organism *to strive to make it present*, i.e. to look or hunt for it.
426 Noë (2004), 22, 234: Noë cites Rodney Brooks' claim that the world serves as its own best model.
427 Jennings (1904), 196–97; (1906), 13–14.

428 Jennings (1904), 197.
429 Ibid. (italics in original).
430 Jennings (1906), 24.
431 Jennings's constant awareness of the threat of anthropomorphism comes to light in the conditionality with which he expresses his impressions: 'one seems to see...'; the observer can 'hardly resist the conviction', etc. It is a temptation that he himself struggles to resist, pointing out that 'the scene could be described in a much more vivid and interesting way by the use of terms still more anthropomorphic in tendency' (1904; 197).
432 Ibid.: 'after Amoeba b has escaped completely and is quite separate from Amoeba c, the latter reverses its course and recaptures b. ... What determines the behavior of c at this point? ... One who sees the behavior as it occurs can hardly resist the conviction that the action at this point is partly determined by the changes in c due to the former possession of b, so that the behavior is not purely reflex'.
433 A distinction should perhaps be drawn between genuine biochemical preferences (i.e. the role played by chemosensation in feeding selectivity) and mechanical or geometrical biases. Many species of suspension-feeding ciliates, for example, can only retain and ingest particles that fall within a particular size spectrum determined by the morphological properties of their own mouth apparatus. Size and shape can thus be regarded as 'first-order determinants' of prey selection (establishing the limits of mechanical possibility), whereas chemoreception is more akin to 'taste' (in its various senses of gustation, discernment and preference).
434 See Roberts et al. (2011a), 606–7: a well-documented case of intra-species selectivity involves the grazing of *O. marina* on the photosynthetic flagellate *Isochrysis galbana*, which ceases if the prey cells become depleted in nitrogen (suggesting that the carbon-nitrogen ratio might be an index of prey quality). *O. marina* has also been shown to feed preferentially on the cryptomonad alga *Rhodomonas salina* if the latter is rich in phosphorus.
435 See Jürgens and DeMott (1995).
436 Berger (1980). In general, *Didinium* overwhelmingly prefers 'bleached' paramecia, which do not contain the algal symbiont. Normal paramecia take longer to handle and are more likely to cause regurgitation or premature defecation. Among other things, the zoochlorellae can thus be assumed to perform a protective function in paramecia by repelling potential predators.
437 See Sherwin (2001), S110–11; Balcombe (2006), 224–25.
438 A limitation to work as a criterion for measuring preferences and pleasure is that work itself – through its association with the subsequent reward – may come to be positively evaluated and thus experienced as pleasurable. This comes to light, for example, in the general pleasure of the chase, hunt or pursuit, and in elementary forms of play based on object manipulation and locomotor activities.
439 Balcombe (2006), 96.
440 See Schleyer et al. (2013), esp. 50.
441 Jonas (1966; 2001), 3.

442 See Glasgow (2017), 182–86.

443 But see note 379 on ciliates such as *Chlamydodon*, which modulate the sign of phototaxis in accordance with their nutritional state, i.e. how 'hungry' they are.

444 Ridley (1999), 313.

445 On the relationship between selfhood and ownership, see Glasgow (2017), for example 241, 354 (note 794). It is clearly 'ownership' in the sense of functional integration (i.e. belonging together) rather than proprietorship or possession that is at issue here.

446 The ritual death of *sallekhanā* is a renunciation of the most fundamental act of self-maintaining, self-perpetuating selfhood: nutrition. As an expression of reverence and non-violence towards other living selves, it is strictly differentiated from other forms of self-destruction (*ātmaghāta*), which are strongly condemned as expressions of violent passion. On *sallekhanā* see Chapple (1993), 99–100.

447 One can freely choose to be unfree, yet unfreedom may also be collectively enforced, as occurs in various forms of totalitarianism. The point about *multicellularity* as a manifestation of higher-order selfhood is that the transition from a unicellular to a multicellular life-form was an evolutionary one, a 'choice' taken not by the individual cells in our body but by the lineage. None of our bodily cells has had anything akin to a say in the matter. It is questionable whether the collective selfhood of social amoebae or hymenopterans allows of 'freedom' among its constituent organisms.

448 As well as the above quotation from Ridley, see also Cabanac (1992), 197. It does not have to be *uniquely* one's own way. Freedom is not synonymous with uniqueness.

449 Husserl played a major role in drawing attention to this threefold structure of consciousness, which incorporates not only what he termed the 'primal impression' but also 'retention' and 'protention'. These three factors operate in conjunction and ground our sense of 'now' as spanning a temporal width. As structural features of consciousness per se, they are not to be confused with specific, explicit instances of recollection or anticipation. See Thompson (2007), 317–28.

450 We have seen that – by contrast with the dinoflagellate *Oxyrrhis marina* – for *E. coli* the chemical gradient is only 'metaphorically' distanced from the reward, insofar as the gradient from less to more glucose or aspartate comprises both the nutrition and the information signalling the nutrition. This may be taken to imply immediacy. Yet it is the information, not the nutrition, that spurs *E. coli* to undertake its pursuit.

451 Jennings (1906), 19, citing observations by Rhumbler.

452 Hansen and Calado (1999), 386–87.

453 Gazzaniga (2008), 388.

454 See Baumeister et al. (1998): the paper, which is entitled 'Ego depletion: is the active self a limited resource?', argues that 'because much of self-regulation involves resisting temptation and hence overriding motivated responses, this self-resource must be able to affect behavior in the same fashion that motivation does. Motivations can be strong or weak, and stronger impulses are presumably more difficult to restrain; therefore, the executive function of the self presumably also operates in a strong or weak fashion, which implies that it has a dimension of strength. An exertion of this strength in self-

control draws on this strength and temporarily exhausts it' (ibid., 1253). In one of the experiments, people who had resisted the temptation to eat chocolates but instead made themselves eat radishes were shown subsequently to be much quicker to give up in their attempts to solve a brain-teaser.

455 See also Kahneman (2011), 43.

456 See Gazzaniga (2008), 314.

457 See Emery and Clayton (2004), Emery and Clayton (2001).

458 Kabadayi and Osvath (2017).

459 Balcombe (2006), 223: if the hens in question took a food reward straightaway, no more was given to them, but if they waited for 22 seconds they got the 'jackpot': they were found to hold out for the jackpot 90 % of the time. See Abeyesinghe et al. (2005).

460 See Brock et al. (2011). On *Dictyostelium discoideum* in general, see Bonner (2009), also Glasgow (2017), 244–47. See ibid., 256, for a brief account of their 'agricultural' activities.

461 Brock et al. (2011), 393.

462 See Denton (2005), 75–80.

463 Quoted in ibid., 49: Koch continues: 'if the organism's performance is only marginally affected by the delay, then the input must have been stored in some sort of intermediate short-term buffer, implying some measure of consciousness. If the subject can be successfully distracted during this interval by a suitable salient stimulus (e.g. flashing lights) it would reinforce the conclusion that attention was involved in actively maintaining information during the delay period'.

464 Neuser et al. (2008) have shown that *Drosophila melanogaster* indeed possesses what is termed a 'spatial working memory': during locomotion, in other words, flies can be distracted from a target for several seconds and yet subsequently resume their former trajectory.

465 Crick and Koch (1990; 265, 269–70) stress the intimate connection between consciousness and working memory and point out that no case has ever been reported of a person 'who is conscious but has lost all forms of short-term memory' (270). However, human consciousness is not to be equated with consciousness in its minimal or basalmost manifestation. If there is absolutely no memory, of course, the pursuit of prey seems reduced to a 'mindless' ascent of a gradient, yet even here the organism has to *perceive* this gradient and it has to be *motivated* to ascend it given that the reward is not immediate.

466 According to the present argument, the concept of a philosophical zombie (a hypothetical being that is physiologically and behaviourally indistinguishable from a human being but without any sort of consciousness) is logically incoherent. Non-philosophical zombies of the sort that lumber through horror films can perhaps be conceived as 'eating machines', which therefore know neither satiety nor hunger. In fact, however, they may be 'choosy', preferring the taste of some anatomical parts over others.

467 See Hofstadter (1980), 360.

468 See note 151.

469 A third category is noise, although here the concept of 'variability' rather than 'flexibility' seems more apt, since flexibility connotes variability that is adaptive as opposed to random. Variations in responses to sensory stimuli may thus result from the noise that is inevitable in sensory systems operating near detection thresholds, and noise may affect signal transmission at any point between sensory input and motor output. See Globus et al. (2015), 215.

470 For Rolls (1999; 266–67), by contrast, all behaviour that does not involve operant learning is mere taxis, with only 'a fixed response available for the stimulus'.

471 As Dennett points out (1996; 88), such trial-and-error learning is just fine as long as an early error does not lead to an early demise. More complex forms of mentality make it possible for the trials to be carried out 'in one's head', permitting – in Karl Popper's words – 'our hypotheses to die in our stead'.

472 See Bermúdez (2000), 194–95.

473 Strictly, the foundation for associative learning is provided not by *consciousness* (which presupposes directional self-movement) but by *value*. This is why even a single isolated insect ganglion – as demonstrated in decapitated adult male cockroaches – is capable of avoidance learning. Non-directional movement can thus be learnt without consciousness needing to be posited. On the avoidance learning shown by an insect ganglion see Eisenstein and Cohen (1965).

474 Berger (1980).

475 Berger (1980; 401) himself notes the possibility of dietary imprinting persisting 'through successive asexual generations'.

476 See Jennings (1906), 174–79, who concludes: 'the same individual does not always behave in the same way under the same external conditions, but the behavior depends upon the physiological condition of the animal. The reaction to any given stimulus is modified by the past experience of the animal, and the modifications are regulatory, not haphazard, in character. The phenomena are thus similar to those shown in the "learning" of higher organisms, save that the modifications depend upon less complex relations and last a shorter time' (179).

477 See Applewhite (1979).

478 Applewhite and Gardner (1971), 285: the ciliate is found to habituate to a series of mechanical shocks 'so that it no longer contracts to the stimulus; after several minutes the organisms have returned to their pre-stimulus level of sensitivity'.

479 Applewhite (1979), 347.

480 Armus et al. (2006).

481 McClintock (1993), 193.

482 For a discussion see Bennett and Hacker (2003), 339–41.

483 One possible distinction might be that concepts involve more *abstract* categories of entity than do percepts. Honey bees, for example, have been shown to be able to differentiate not only patterns, but also distinct *classes* of pattern, discriminating symmetrical from asymmetrical patterns or even patterns that are 'the same' from ones that are 'different'. Such bees might thus be said to have a 'concept' of symmetry or sameness. On the capacity of honeybees for abstract categorization see Giurfa et al. (2001); see also Greenspan (2007), 132–36.

484 This paragraph and the next are indebted to a reading of Carruthers (2009), who establishes the following constraints on the possession of concepts: 'in order to count as having concepts, a creature needs to be capable of thinking. And that means, at least, that it must possess distinct belief states and desire states, which interact with one another (and with perception) in the selection and guidance of behavior. In addition, the belief states need to be structured out of component parts (concepts) which can be recombined with others to figure in other such states with distinct contents' (90–91). Carruthers argues that many invertebrates, including honey bees, satisfy these constraints, as suggested by their 'flexible use of spatial information in the service of a multitude of goals'.

485 See ibid., 97.

486 'Slime bacteria' or myxobacteria are noted for their cooperative activity. This includes travelling in 'swarms' and forming 'fruiting bodies' when nutrients are scarce; on the model organism *Myxococcus xanthus* see Strassmann (2000).

487 Much has recently been written on the theory of mind. On empathy, for example, see Thompson (2007), 382–411; on shame see Rochat (2009).

488 For the question of whether the third form of intrinsic reflexivity required for full minimal selfhood (i.e. self-reproduction) is also presupposed by consciousness see above, note 23.

489 See Glasgow (2017), 96–98.

490 Ibid., 93–94: in these terms, the intrinsic reflexivity of their 'self-reproduction' can be understood to be *indirect* insofar as successful models *get themselves reproduced* (by the humans whose needs they satisfy). The marketplace is the driver of 'natural selection'.

491 See ibid., 94-96, 322. On small drones see Hambling (2015), esp. 126-37.

492 On *Dictyostelium discoideum* as a compromise between unicellular and multicellular forms of self-containment, see Glasgow (2017), 244-247; in general see Bonner (2009).

493 On sponge self-containment see Glasgow (2017), 236, 265–66.

494 On the feeding biology of sponges see for example Brüssow (2007), 330–36.

495 Lee et al. (2012), 259.

496 On the carnivorous sponges see Vacelet and Boury-Esnault (1996), Vacelet (2006), Lee et al. (2012).

497 On sea lilies see Brüssow (2007), 381.

498 On salps see ibid., 428.

499 On lancelets see ibid., 363–64.

500 On basking sharks see ibid., 431.

501 On *Trichoplax* see Schierwater (2005), Schierwater et al. (2010), Wenderoth (1986), Smith et al. (2015), Ueda et al. (1999) and Kuhl and Kuhl (1966). Despite such work, placozoans remain relatively little studied by comparison with other animals. Future studies of *Trichoplax* may throw up surprises yielding as yet unsuspected insights into the question of consciousness in simple animals.

502 Smith et al. (2015).

503 Wenderoth (1986).

504 Smith et al. (2015) suggest that such behavioural coordination might be attributed to either of two mechanisms: the release of neuropeptides by secretory 'gland cells' also found in the ventral epithelium or possible electrical signalling among fibre cells.

505 I could just as well have chosen to focus on the phylum Ctenophora, commonly known as the comb jellies. This phylum is believed by some biologists to be phylogenetically even more ancestral than the cnidarians. Yet it is a much smaller phylum, comprising just a few hundred species, and so offers rather less in the way of behavioural variety. Ctenophores were traditionally regarded as automatic feeders or 'eating machines' and thus not susceptible to states of hunger or satiety. In fact, they are now known to exert a remarkable degree of control over their prey capture and ingestion, adjusting the area of their food-collection surfaces in accordance with their nutritional state. Over a period of six hours, starved ctenophores have been found to ingest about twice as much as previously fed ctenophores when exposed to the same food density. According to Reeve et al. (1978; 744), 'the initial feeding rate of starved animals can be five times higher at first, decreasing to the pre-fed rate gradually over six hours. This pattern is also affected by the duration of starvation'.

506 On the relationship between nematocyst discharge and prey capture and ingestion in sea anemones see Thorington et al. (2010).

507 Ibid., 123.

508 Ibid., 130.

509 Glauber et al. (2010).

510 Pagán (2014), 127–28.

511 Loomis (1955), 221.

512 Ibid., 219.

513 On the hydra see Buchsbaum et al. (1987).

514 On *Aglantha digitale* see Greenspan (2007), 41–58. Greenspan compares the slow, rhythmic swimming behaviour characteristic of feeding with the much faster escape response triggered by contact with a predator or a bite from a mackerel.

515 On the visual capacities of the cubozoan *Tripedalia cystophora* see for example Buskey (2002), Garm et al. (2007) and Petie et al. (2011).

516 See Buskey (2002), 225–26, 230.

517 Petie et al. (2011).

518 See Buskey (2002), 230.

519 Andrew B. Barron and Colin Klein (2016; 4905) cite the decentralized organization of the cubozoan behavioural control system as a key argument for refusing to grant them any capacity for subjective experience. I am not convinced that the *centralized* organization of information-processing is a significant factor. Information from both internal and external sources must be integrated, of course, but it is not obvious why one cannot take the unitary self *as a whole* (i.e. the organism insofar as it behaves coherently and in its own interests) to be the relevant unit of integration. Barron and Klein dismiss box jellyfish as 'nothing more than simple decentralized stimulus-response systems'

(4905), yet this is only the case if there is no interoception, i.e. no internalized distinction between starvation and satiety. If their appetite is variable, however, the jellyfish will sometimes do one thing (move towards a shaft of light) and sometimes another (say, remain stationary or drift about at random). Barron and Klein also pinpoint a capacity for 'representation' in the sense of a spatial simulation or model of the world as an ineluctable criterion for the possibility of consciousness, which is why they rule out consciousness in the nematode *Caenorhabditis elegans*. Though a key feature of human consciousness and crucial to our *conception* of our own consciousness, it is not self-evident that 'spatial simulation' is a defining characteristic of consciousness *as such*.

520 Petie et al. (2011), 2809.

521 See Garm et al. (2012). Whereas *T. cystophora* is active during the day and inactive at night, another species of box jellyfish, *Copula sivickisi*, shows the converse behaviour, resting during the day and actively foraging and mating at night. This difference between the two species reflects the separate ecological niches they occupy, each corresponding to the activity cycles of their respective prey. Other species of box jellyfish are believed to be active both day and night. Significantly, the activity pattern of *T. cystophora* seems to follow the light regime rather than obeying an endogenous circadian rhythm.

522 All worms are characterized by a body exhibiting bilateral symmetry with a head at one end, yet the distinct groups of worms are only distantly related. Today the three main groups are the segmented annelids, the flatworms or platyhelminthes, and the roundworms or nematodes. The former two groups are more closely related to molluscs, whereas nematodes are positioned nearer to arthropods on the 'tree' of life. Other phyla include Priapulida (penis worms), Xenacoelomorpha (see following note) and Hemichordata, which comprise acorn worms and semi-sessile, tube-dwelling, mainly colonial animals called pterobranchs.

523 The phylum Platyhelminthes was for a long time thought to include members of what is now regarded as distinct phylum, Xenacoelomorpha, which comprises the classes Acoela and Nemertodermatida and the species *Xenoturbella*. These simple animals lack a brain, a circulatory system and a through-gut (i.e. an anus), and are fascinating in their own right. The question of just how 'primitive' they are, phylogenetically speaking, is hotly contested. I shall leave them out of account partly out of ignorance and partly to avoid making the final chapter longer than the rest of the book together. For an overview see Achatz et al. (2013), Nakano (2015), Nakano et al. (2013) and Cannon et al. (2016).

524 On planarian powers of regeneration see Pagán (2014), 127–32.

525 Ibid., 102–7.

526 Ibid., 160.

527 See Buttarelli et al. (2008; 400), who list six features that distinguish a brain from a ganglion, also including the presence of a greater number of interneurons than primary motor or primary sensory neurons and a predominance of multisynaptic over monosynaptic circuits.

528 Sarnat and Netsky (1985), 297.

529 See Inoue et al. (2015), 2.

530 Sheiman et al. (2002), 414–15.

531 Ibid., 417.

532 Ibid., 416. The animal may preserve a minimal motor response in the pharynx, which is located in the central part of the animal's underside. This is a local motor reaction that requires nothing more than mechanosensory contact of the worm with its prey. In the case of *Dugesia*, no ingestion takes place.

533 See Gruber and Ewer (1962), 461.

534 Ibid.: 'Once an intact animal has fed, no further response to food or food extract may be elicited for about another 24 hr. All components of the feeding pattern are apparently inhibited. The response is gradually re-established over a few days until, following defaecation, the complete pattern may be again obtained. With a decerebrate animal there is no such inhibition and the animal will continue to accept food indefinitely even if it is mechanically unable to take it into the pharynx'.

535 Ibid., 460: *Planocera*, for example, normally swims or crawls by means of muscular contractions. Without its brain, it makes greater use of the cilia of its ventral surface to glide. Muscular contractions also occur, but the movements are disorganized.

536 See Omond et al. (2017), whose study focuses on the free-living species of dugesiid flatworm, *Girardia tigrina*.

537 Ibid. *G. tigrina* also appears to be a keen practitioner of the midnight siesta: although its inactivity mainly occurs during the day, it also displays several hours of reduced activity in the middle of the dark phase of the photoperiod. This has been likened to the (midday) siesta shown by male fruit flies.

538 Pagán (2014), 169–70.

539 Ibid., 172. Some of the early work on the capacity of planarians for associative learning – and whether such memory survives regeneration after decapitation – was controversial. For a more recent analysis see Shomrat and Levin (2013).

540 On familiarization in planarians see Shomrat and Levin (2013), 3800.

541 Ibid., 3803.

542 See Inoue et al. (2015).

543 See Kusayama and Watanabe (2000), Buttarelli et al. (2008).

544 See page 98.

545 Gordus et al. (2015), 215. On the phylum Nematoda see Nielsen (3rd ed. 2012), 276–85. As Nielsen points out, it is a characteristic feature of some species of nematodes that the number of cells appears to be genetically determined. In the case of *C. elegans*, the total number of cells is 959 in an adult hermaphrodite and 1031 in an adult male. Most *C. elegans* individuals are hermaphrodites.

546 Bryden and Cohen (2008), 339, quoting Thomas C. Ferrée.

547 See Nielsen (3rd ed. 2012), 279.

548 As well as an epidermis, it has a thick elastic cuticle that helps maintain a high internal turgor pressure to provide a form of hydrostatic skeleton; see ibid., 276.

549 See Arvanitis et al. (2013): for example, intestinal cells infected by *Salmonella* have been shown to engage in apoptosis; *C. elegans* also has a p53-like tumour suppression protein that triggers cell death in response to DNA damage.

550 For the sake of simplicity and brevity I shall here focus on solitary rather than social behaviour in nematodes. Social feeding is thought to be a response to stressful conditions such as crowding or a shortage of food. On social feeding in *C. elegans* see, for example, de Bono et al. (2002), Sokolowski (2002), Artyukhin et al. (2015).

551 Avery and Shtonda (2003). Most filter feeders separate nutrients from medium by passing the suspension though a mesh that traps the food particles. In the case of *C. elegans*, there is no obvious filter. Instead, it seems to be by means of the differential timing of various pharyngeal muscle contractions that the nematode succeeds in sweeping the food particles backwards into its intestine while ejecting the liquid from its mouth.

552 Sawin et al. (2000). By contrast, *C. elegans* does not modify its velocity in response to gradients of chemoattractants such as salt; see Iino and Yoshida (2009), 5373. Also noteworthy is that this slowing response in the presence of bacteria is exhibited by solitary strains only. Social strains of *C. elegans* do not decelerate in this way; see de Bono et al. (2002), 899: 'natural isolates of the soil nematode *C. elegans* feed on bacteria either alone or in groups. Solitary feeders such as the standard N2 strain reduce locomotory activity and disperse on encountering bacterial food. By contrast, social feeders such as strain CB4856 continue moving rapidly on food and aggregate together'.

553 Sawin et al. (2000).

554 See Hills et al. (2004), 1219.

555 This strategy is sometimes referred to as 'area-restricted search'; see also Hills (2006). It is thought to be optimally adaptive when resources are distributed in a 'clumpy' or 'patchy' as opposed to a homogeneous way. Since 'clumpiness' tends to prevail in biological environments, the best place to look for resources is in the close vicinity of where they have just been found.

556 Ibid.

557 Ibid., 9.

558 Of course, possible variations in the degree to which the randomness of the turns is constrained or controlled in response to external factors may suggest varying gradations of directionality in the animal's movement.

559 Nuttley et al. (2002), 12449; see also Bargmann and Horvitz (1991), 729: '*C. elegans* can chemotax toward the peak of a gradient of a number of small molecules, including positively charged ions such as Na^+ and K^+, negatively charged ions such as Cl^- and SO_4^{2-}, basic pH, and several small organic molecules, including cAMP, cGMP, lysine, cysteine, and histidine'.

560 See Lockery (2011).

561 On nematode chemotaxis see Ward (1973), 820.

562 Ibid., 821.

563 Pierce-Shimomura et al. (1999), 9568.

564 Ibid., 9561: a pirouette may refer either to a bout of two or more sharp turns in quick succession or to a single sharp turn: it is defined as 'a series of one or more sharp turns separating consecutive runs'.
565 Ibid., 9568. Iino and Yoshida (2009), by contrast, regard the pirouette strategy as a form of 'biased random walk'. However, this klinokinetic strategy, they agree, is combined with the klinotactic strategy of weathervane orientation. Computer simulations suggest that neither the pirouette mechanism nor the weathervane mechanism alone achieves the efficiency attained by real worms, but the two mechanisms together combine to produce effective chemotaxis.
566 Pierce-Shimomura et al. (1999), 9568.
567 Ibid.: 'We cannot rule out the possibility … that a weak weather vane strategy operates in parallel with the course-correction model, making runs better oriented than they might otherwise have been. … We also cannot rule out the possibility that the weather vane strategy exists as a default mechanism when the course-correction strategy is inactivated or when animals are in steeper gradients'. See also Iino and Yoshida (2009); Lockery (2011).
568 See for example Globus et al. (2015), who trace some of the neural interactions by which sensory information may be integrated within the underlying dynamics of the interneuronal network, generating 'different behaviors under different feeding states' (223).
569 See Sawin et al. (2000), 627.
570 On the quiescence of nematodes, see You et al. (2008).
571 You et al. (2008; 249) define 'food quality' operationally in terms of an ability to support growth. The *E. coli* strain HB101 is considered high-quality, whereas the strain DA837 is regarded as low in quality.
572 Ibid., 250.
573 Ibid., 252: the kinase in question is the protein kinase G (PKG), EGL-4.
574 Ibid., 251.
575 See You et al. (2008), Ben Arous et al. (2009).
576 Ben Arous et al. (2009).
577 Ibid.
578 Gallagher et al. (2013), 9716.
579 See Trojanowski and Raizen (2016) on the arguments for referring to *lethargus* as 'sleep' rather than merely 'sleep-like'. In addition to the developmentally timed sleep of *lethargus*, *C. elegans* also exhibits a non-circadian 'stress-induced' sleep in response to environmental trauma. This likewise manifests itself as a cessation of feeding and locomotion and reduced responsiveness. Though behaviourally similar, *lethargus* and stress-induced sleep are two physiologically distinct sleep states.
580 On *lethargus* see also Raizen et al. (2008), Iwanir et al. (2013).
581 Again, the criterion of 'rapid reversibility' is required to be able to differentiate the state from pathological forms of quiescence.
582 See Trojanowski and Raizen (2016): the *C. elegans* gene *lin-42* is a homologue of the gene that regulates circadian rhythms in other animals such as mammals; the *lin-42* gene product cycles its

expression in phase not with circadian time but with moulting time.
583 On the homeostatic self-regulation of sleep see Raizen et al. (2008), 570; Iwanir et al. (2013), 393.
584 See Nuttley et al. (2002).
585 Wen et al. (1997).
586 On aversive olfactory learning in *C. elegans* see Zhang et al. (2005).
587 Ibid., 179.
588 See Pujol et al. (2001) on how the Toll signalling pathway enables the nematode to recognize pathogenic *S. marcescens* and then undertake the appropriate strategy of behavioural avoidance, leaving the bacterial lawn. Such recognition may come about when a protein akin to the Toll-like receptors in vertebrate innate immunity binds to the pathogen's characteristic LPS structure or its bacterial flagellin, the primary protein component of the flagellum (818).
589 Zhang et al. (2005), 179.

Bibliography

ABEYESINGHE, S. M., NICOL, C. J., HARTNELL, S. J. & WATHES, C. M. (2005) 'Can domestic fowl, *Gallus gallus domesticus*, show self-control?' *Animal Behaviour* 70(1), 1–11

ACHATZ, J. G., CHIODIN, M., SALVENMOSER, W., TYLER, S. & MARTINEZ, P. (2013) 'The Acoela: on their kind and kinships, especially with nemertodermatids and xenoturbellids (Bilateria incertae sedis)'. *Organisms, Diversity & Evolution* 13(2), 267–286

ADLER, J. (1969) 'Chemoreceptors in bacteria'. *Science* 166(3913), 1588–1597

ALKIRE, M. T., HUDETZ, A. G. & TONONI, G. (2008) 'Consciousness and anesthesia'. *Science* 322(5903), 876–880

AMMERMANN, S., SCHNEIDER, T., WESTERMANN, M., HILLEBRAND, H. & RHIEL, E. (2013), 'Ejectisins: tough and tiny polypeptides are a major component of cryptophycean ejectisomes'. *Protoplasma* 250(2), 551–563

APPLEWHITE, P. B. AND GARDNER, F. T. (1971) 'Theory of protozoan habituation'. *Nature* 230(17), 285–287

APPLEWHITE, P. B. (1979) 'Learning in protozoa', in M. Levandowsky and S. H. Hutner (eds), *Biochemistry and Physiology of Protozoa*, vol. 1. New York: Academic Press

ARISTOTLE (1931) *The Works vol. III: De Anima,* trans. J. A. Smith. Oxford: Clarendon Press

ARISTOTLE (1986) *De Anima (On the Soul)*, trans. H. Lawson-Tancred. London: Penguin

ARMUS, H. L., MONTGOMERY, A. R. & JELLISON, J. L. (2006) 'Discrimination learning in paramecia *(P. caudatum)*'. *The Psychological Record* 56(4), 489–495

ARTYUKHIN, A. B., YIM, J. J., CHEONG, M. C. & AVERY L. (2015) 'Starvation-induced collective behavior in *C. elegans*'. *Scientific Reports* 5

ARVANITIS, M., LI, D.-D., LEE, K. & MYLONAKIS, E. (2013) 'Apoptosis in *C. elegans*: lessons for cancer and immunity'. *Frontiers in Cellular and Infection Microbiology* 3(67)

AVERY, L. AND SHTONDA, B. B. (2003) 'Food transport in the *C. elegans* pharynx'. *The Journal of Experimental Biology* 206(14), 2441–2457

BAGORDA, A. AND PARENT, C. A. (2008) 'Eukaryotic chemotaxis at a glance'. *Journal of Cell Science* 121(16), 2621–2624

BALCOMBE, J. (2006) *Pleasurable Kingdom: Animals and the Nature of Feeling Good*. London: Macmillan

BALUŠKA, F., MANCUSO, S., VOLKMANN, D. & BARLOW, P. (2009) 'The "root-brain" hypothesis of Charles and Francis Darwin: Revival after more than 125 years'. *Plant Signaling & Behavior* 4(12), 1121–1127

BARGMANN, C. I. AND HORVITZ, H. R. (1991) 'Chemosensory neurons with overlapping functions direct chemotaxis to multiple chemicals in *C. elegans*'. *Neuron* 7(5), 729–742

BARNES, R. S. K. (ed.) (1998) *The Diversity of Living Organisms*. Oxford: Blackwell Publishing

BARRON, A. B. AND KLEIN, C. (2016) 'What insects can tell us about the origins of consciousness'. *Proceedings of the National Academy of Sciences* 113(18), 4900–4908

BAUMEISTER, R. F., BRATSLAVSKY, E., MURAVEN, M. & TICE, D. M. (1998) 'Ego depletion: is the active self a limited resource?' *Journal of Personality and Social Psychology* 74(5), 1252–1265

BEN AROUS, J., LAFFONT, S. & CHATENAY, D. (2009) 'Molecular and sensory basis of a food related two-state behavior in *C. elegans*'. *PLoS ONE* 4(10), e7584

BEN-JACOB, E. (1998) 'Bacterial wisdom, Gödel's theorem and creative genomic webs'. *Physics A: Statistical Mechanics and its Applications* 248(1), 57–76

BENNETT, M. R. AND HACKER, P. M. S. (2003) *Philosophical Foundations of Neuroscience*. Oxford: Blackwell Publishing

BERGER, J. (1980) 'Feeding behaviour of *Didinium nasutum* on *Paramecium bursaria* with normal or apochlorotic zoochlorellae'. *Journal of General Microbiology* 118(2), 397–404

BERKOWITZ, A. (2016) *Governing Behavior: How Nerve Cell Dictatorships and Democracies Control Everything We Do*. Cambridge, Mass.: Harvard University Press

BERMÚDEZ, J. L. (2000) 'Consciousness, higher-order thought, and stimulus reinforcement'. *Behavioral and Brain Sciences* 23(2), 194–195

BERRIDGE, K. C. (2003) 'Pleasures of the brain'. *Brain and Cognition* 52(1), 106–128

BINET, A. (1889) *The Psychic Life of Micro-Organisms: A Study in Experimental Psychology*, trans. T. McCormack. Chicago: Open Court Publishing

BLAKEMORE, S. J., SMITH, J., STEEL, R., JOHNSTONE, E. C. & FRITH, C. D. (2000) 'The perception of self-produced sensory stimuli in patients with auditory hallucinations and passivity experiences: evidence for a breakdown in self-monitoring'. *Psychological Medicine* 30(5), 1131–1139

BOAKES, D. E., CODLING, E. A., THORN, G. J. & STEINKE, M. (2011) 'Analysis and modelling of swimming behaviour in *Oxyrrhis marina*'. *Journal of Plankton Research* 33(4), 641–649

BONNER, J. T. (2009) *The Social Amoebae: The Biology of Cellular Slime Molds*. Princeton, N. J.: Princeton University Press

BRAITHWAITE, V. (2010) *Do Fish Feel Pain?* Oxford: Oxford University Press

BRAY, D. (2009) *Wetware: A Computer in Every Living Cell*. New Haven and London: Yale University Press

BRECKELS, M. N., ROBERTS, E. C., ARCHER, S. D., MALIN, G. & STEINKE, M. (2011) 'The role of dissolved infochemicals in mediating predator-prey interactions in the heterotrophic dinoflagellate *Oxyrrhis marina*'. *Journal of Plankton Research* 33(4), 629–639

BROCK, D. A., DOUGLAS, T. E., QUELLER, D. C. & STRASSMANN, J. E. (2011) 'Primitive agriculture in a social amoeba'. *Nature* 469(7330), 393–396

BRÜSSOW, H. (2007) *The Quest for Food. A Natural History of Eating*. New York: Springer

BRYDEN, J. AND COHEN, N. (2008) 'Neural control of *Caenorhabditis elegans* forward locomotion: the role of sensory feedback'. *Biological Cybernetics* 98(4), 339–351

BUCHSBAUM, R., BUCHSBAUM, M., PEARSE, J. & PEARSE, V. (3rd ed. 1987) *Animals without Backbones*. Chicago: University of Chicago Press

BUCK, R. (2000) 'Conceptualizing motivation and emotion'. *Behavioral and Brain Sciences* 23(2), 195–196

BURGHARDT, G. M. (2005) *The Genesis of Animal Play: Testing the Limits*. Cambridge, Mass.: MIT Press

BUSKEY, E. J. (1997) 'Behavioral components of feeding selectivity of the heterotrophic dinoflagellate *Protoperidinium pellucidum*'. *Marine Ecology Progress Series* 153, 77–89

BUSKEY, E. J. (2003) 'Behavioral adaptations of the cubozoan medusa *Tripedalia cystophora* for feeding on copepod (*Dioithona oculata*) swarms'. *Marine Biology* 142(2), 225–232

BUTTARELLI, F. R., PELLICANO, C. & PONTIERI, F. E. (2008) 'Neuropharmacology and behavior in planarians: translations to mammals'. *Comparative Biochemistry and Physiology, Part C: Toxicology & Pharmacology* 147(4), 399–408

CABANAC, M. (1992) 'Pleasure: the common currency'. *Journal of Theoretical Biology* 155(2), 173–200

CABANAC, M. (1999) 'Emotion and phylogeny'. *Journal of Consciousness Studies* 6(6–7), 176–190

CALBET, A., ISARI, S., MARTÍNEZ, R. A., SAIZ, E. ET AL. (2013) 'Adaptations to feast and famine in different strains of the marine heterotrophic dinoflagellates *Gyrodinium dominans* and *Oxyrrhis marina*'. *Marine Ecology Progress Series* 483, 67–84

CANNON, J. T., VELLUTINI, B. C., SMITH, J. ET AL. (2016) 'Xenacoelomorpha is the sister group to Nephrozoa'. *Nature* 530(7588), 89–93

CARRUTHERS, P. (2009) 'Invertebrate concepts confront the generality constraint (and win)', in R. W. Lurz (ed.) *The Philosophy of Animal Minds*. Cambridge: Cambridge University Press

CATANIA, K. C. AND REMPLE, F. E. (2005) 'Asymptotic prey profitability drives star-nosed moles to the foraging speed limit'. *Nature* 433(7025), 519–522

CHALMERS, D. J. (1995) 'Facing up to the problem of consciousness'. *Journal of Consciousness Studies* 2(3), 200–219

CHAMOVITZ, D. (2012) *What a Plant Knows*. London: Oneworld

CHAPPLE, C. K. (1993) *Nonviolence to Animals, Earth, and Self in Asian Traditions*. Albany: State University of New York Press

CHRISTAKI, U., DOLAN, J. R., PELEGRI, S. & RASSOULZADEGAN, F. (1998) 'Consumption of picoplankton-size particles by marine ciliates: effects of physiological state of the ciliate and particle quality'. *Limnology and Oceanography* 43(3), 458–464

CRAIG, W. (1918) 'Appetites and aversions as constituents of instincts'. *The Biological Bulletin* 34(2), 91–107

CRAPSE, T. B. AND SOMMER, M. A. (2008) 'Corollary discharge across the animal kingdom'. *Nature Reviews Neuroscience* 9(8), 587–600

CRICK, F. AND KOCH, C. (1990) 'Towards a neurobiological theory of consciousness'. *Seminars in the Neurosciences*, vol. 2. Saunders Scientific Publications

DAMASIO, A. (2000) *The Feeling of What Happens: Body, Emotion and the Making of Consciousness*. London: Vintage Books

DAVIES, J. A. (2014) *Life Unfolding: How the Human Body Creates Itself.* Oxford: Oxford University Press

DAWKINS, R. (2004) *The Ancestor's Tale: A Pilgrimage to the Dawn of Life*. London: Weidenfeld and Nicolson

DE BONO, M., TOBIN, D. M., DAVIS, M. W., AVERY, L. & BARGMANN, C. I. (2002) 'Social feeding in *Caenorhabditis elegans* is induced by neurons that detect aversive stimuli'. *Nature* 419(6910), 899–903

DENNETT, D. C. (1978) *Brainstorms: Philosophical Essays on Mind and Psychology*. Hassocks, Sussex: The Harvester Press

DENNETT, D. C. (1991) *Consciousness Explained*. Harmondsworth: Penguin

DENNETT, D. C. (1996) *Kinds of Minds: Towards an Understanding of Consciousness*. London: Weidenfeld and Nicolson

DENTON, D. (2005) *The Primordial Emotions: The Dawning of Consciousness*. Oxford: Oxford University Press

DICKERSON, H. W. AND FINDLY, R. C. (2014) 'Immunity to *Ichthyophthirius* infections in fish: a synopsis'. *Developmental and Comparative Immunology* 43(2), 290–299

DUSENBERY, D. B. (2009) *Living at Micro Scale: The Unexpected Physics of Being Small*. Cambridge, Mass. and London: Harvard University Press

EISEMANN, C. H., JORGENSEN, W. K., MERRITT, D. J. ET AL. (1984) 'Do insects feel pain? – A biological view'. *Cellular and Molecular Life Sciences* 40(2), 164–167

EISENSTEIN, E. M. AND COHEN, M. J. (1965) 'Learning in an isolated prothoracic insect ganglion'. *Animal Behaviour* 13(1), 104–108

EMERY, N. J. AND CLAYTON, N. S. (2001) 'Effects of experience and social context on prospective caching strategies by scrub jays'. *Nature* 414(6862), 443–446

EMERY, N. J. AND CLAYTON, N. S. (2004) 'The mentality of crows: convergent evolution of intelligence in corvids and apes'. *Science* 306(5703), 1903–1907

FENCHEL, T. (1980) 'Suspension feeding in ciliated protozoa: functional response and particle size selection'. *Microbial Ecology* 6(1), 1-11

FENCHEL, T. (2001) 'How dinoflagellates swim'. *Protist* 152(4), 329–338

FENCHEL, T. (2010) 'The life history of *Flabellula baltica* Smirnov (Gymnamoebae, Rhizopoda): adaptations to a spatially and temporally heterogeneous environment'. *Protist* 161(2), 279–287

FLETCHER, D. A. AND MULLINS, R. D. (2010) 'Cell mechanics and the cytoskeleton'. *Nature* 463(7280), 485–492

FODOR, J. A. (1987) 'Why paramecia don't have mental representations'. *Midwest Studies in Philosophy* 10(1), 3–23

GALLAGHER, T., KIM, J., OLDENBROEK, M., KERR, R. & YOU, Y.-J. (2013) 'ASI regulates satiety quiescence in *C. elegans*'. *The Journal of Neuroscience* 33(23), 9716–9724

GARM, A., O'CONNOR, M., PARKEFELT, L. & NILSSON, D.-E. (2007) 'Visually guided obstacle avoidance in the box jellyfish *Tripedalia cystophora* and *Chiropsella bronzie*'. *The Journal of Experimental Biology* 210(20), 3616–3623

GARM, A., BIELECKI, J., PETIE, R. & NILSSON, D.-E. (2012) 'Opposite patterns of diurnal activity in the box jellyfish *Tripedalia cystophora* and *Copula sivickisi*'. *The Biological Bulletin* 222(1), 35–45

GAVELIS, G. S., HAYAKAWA, S., WHITE III, R. A. ET AL. (2015) 'Eye-like ocelloids are built from different endosymbiotically acquired components'. *Nature* 523(7559), 204–207

GAZZANIGA, M. S. (2008) *Human: The Science behind What Makes Your Brain Unique*. New York: Harper Perennial

GEDDES, L. (2011) 'Banishing consciousness: the mystery of anaesthesia'. *New Scientist 2840*

GEHRING, W. J. (2014) 'The evolution of vision'. *Wiley Interdisciplinary Reviews: Developmental Biology* 3(1), 1–40

GERBER, B. AND HENDEL, T. (2006) 'Outcome expectations drive learned behaviour in larval *Drosophila*'. *Proceedings of the Royal Society of London B: Biological Sciences* 273(1604), 2965–2968

GERBER, B., YARALI, A., DIEGELMANN, S., WOTJAK, C. T., PAULI, P. & FENDT, M. (2014) 'Pain-relief learning in flies, rats and man: basic research and applied perspectives'. *Learning & Memory* 21(4), 232–252

GIBBS, D. AND DELLINGER, O. P. (1908) 'The Daily Life of Amœba Proteus'. *The American Journal of Psychology* 19(2), 232–241

GIESE, A. C. (1973) *Blepharisma: The Biology of a Light-Sensitive Protozoan*. Stanford: Stanford University Press

GITAI, Z. (2005) 'The new bacterial cell biology: moving parts and subcellular architecture'. *Cell* 120(5), 577–586

GIURFA, M., ZHANG, S., JENETT, A., MENZEL, R. & SRINIVASAN, M. V. (2001) 'The concepts of "sameness" and "difference" in an insect'. *Nature* 410(6831), 930–933

GLASGOW, R. D. V. (2017) *The Minimal Self*. Würzburg University Press

GLAUBER, K. M., DANA, C. E. & STEELE, R. E. (2010) 'Hydra'. *Current Biology* 20(22), R964–R965

GLOVER, J. (1988) *I. The Philosophy and Psychology of Personal Identity.* London: Allen Lane
GODFREY-SMITH, P. (2017) *Other Minds: The Octopus and the Evolution of Intelligent Life.* London: William Collins
GÓMEZ, F., LÓPEZ-GARCÍA, P. & MOREIRA, D. (2009) 'Molecular phylogeny of the ocelloid-bearing dinoflagellates *Erythropsidinium* and *Warnowia* (Warnowiaceae, Dinophyceae)'. *Journal of Eukaryotic Microbiology* 56(5), 440–445
GORDUS, A., POKALA, N., LEVY, S., FLAVELL, S. W. & BARGMANN, C. I. (2015) 'Feedback from network states generates variability in a probabilistic olfactory circuit'. *Cell* 161(2), 215–227
GRANDIN, T. AND JOHNSON, C. (2005) *Animals in Translation: The Woman Who Thinks Like a Cow.* London: Bloomsbury
GREBE, T. W. AND STOCK, J. (1998) 'Bacterial chemotaxis: the five sensors of a bacterium'. *Current Biology* 8(5), R154–R157
GREENSPAN, R. J. (2007) *An Introduction to Nervous Systems.* Cold Spring Harbor, N.Y.: Cold Spring Harbor Laboratory Press
GREGORY, R. L. (ed.) (1987) *The Oxford Companion to the Mind.* Oxford: Oxford University Press
GRIFFIN, D. R. (1992; 2001) *Animal Minds: Beyond Cognition to Consciousness.* Chicago and London: University of Chicago Press
GRUBER, S. A. AND EWER, D. W. (1962) 'Observations on the myo-neural physiology of the polyclad, *Planocera gilchristi*'. *Journal of Experimental Biology* 39(3), 459–477
GUO, Z., ZHANG, H., LIU, S. & LIN, S. (2013) 'Biology of the marine heterotrophic dinoflagellate *Oxyrrhis marina*: current status and future directions'. *Microorganisms* 1(1), 33–57
HALL, M. (2011) *Plants as Persons: A Philosophical Botany.* Albany: State University of New York Press
HALLÉ, F. (2002) *In Praise of Plants*, trans. D. Lee. Portland and London: Timber Press
HAMBLING, D. (2015) *Swarm Troopers: How Small Drones Will Conquer the World.* Archangel Ink
HAMEROFF, S. R. (2006) 'The entwined mysteries of anesthesia and consciousness: is there a common underlying mechanism?' *Anesthesiology* 105(2), 400–412
HANAHAN, D. AND WEINBERG, R. (2000) 'The hallmarks of cancer'. *Cell* 100(1), 57–70

HANSEN, P. J. AND CALADO, A. J. (1999) 'Phagotrophic mechanisms and prey selection in free-living dinoflagellates'. *Journal of Eukaryotic Microbiology* 46(4), 382–389

HAROLD, F. M. (2001) *The Way of the Cell: Molecules, Organisms and the Order of Life*. Oxford: Oxford University Press

HAYAKAWA, S., TAKAKU, Y., HWANG, J. S. ET AL. (2015) 'Function and evolutionary origin of unicellular camera-type eye structure'. *PLoS ONE 10*(3): e0118415

HEGEL, G. W. F. (1977) *Phenomenology of Spirit*, trans. A. V. Miller. Oxford: Oxford University Press

HEIDEGGER, M. (1919/20; 1993) *Grundprobleme der Phänomenologie (1919/20)*. Frankfurt am Main: Klostermann

HEIDEGGER, M. (1926; 1986) *Sein und Zeit*. Tübingen: Max Niemeyer Verlag

HEIDEGGER, M. (1929/30; 1983) *Die Grundbegriffe der Metaphysik: Welt – Endlichkeit – Einsamkeit*. Frankfurt am Main: Klostermann

HEISENBERG, M. (2013) 'The origin of freedom in animal behaviour', in A. Suarez and P. Adams (eds) *Is Science Compatible with Free Will?: Exploring Free Will and Consciousness in the Light of Quantum Physics and Neuroscience*. New York: Springer

HEISENBERG, M. (2015) 'Outcome learning, outcome expectations, and intentionality in *Drosophila*'. *Learning & Memory 22*(6), 294–298

HILLS, T. T., BROCKIE, P. J. & MARICQ, A. V. (2004) 'Dopamine and glutamate control area-restricted search behavior in *Caenorhabditis elegans*'. *The Journal of Neuroscience 24*(5), 1217–1225

HILLS, T. T. (2006) 'Animal foraging and the evolution of goal-directed cognition'. *Cognitive Science 30*(1), 3–41

HODGE, C. F. AND AIKINS, H. A. (1895) 'The daily life of a protozoan: a study in comparative psycho-physiology'. *The American Journal of Psychology 6*(4), 524–533

HOFSTADTER, D. R. (1980) *Gödel, Escher, Bach: An Eternal Golden Braid*. Harmondsworth: Penguin

HOHBERG, K. AND TRAUNSPURGER, W. (2009) 'Foraging theory and partial consumption in a tardigrade-nematode system'. *Behavioral Ecology 20*(4), 884–890

HUDETZ, A. G. (2012) 'General anesthesia and human brain connectivity'. *Brain Connectivity 2*(6), 291–302

IINO, Y. AND YOSHIDA, K. (2009) 'Parallel use of two behavioral mechanisms for chemotaxis in *Caenorhabditis elegans*'. *Journal of Neuroscience 29*(17), 5370–5380

INOUE, T., HOSHINO, H., YAMASHITA, T., SHIMOYAMA, S. & AGATA, K. (2015) 'Planarian shows decision-making behavior in response to multiple stimuli by integrative brain function'. *Zoological Letters* 1(7)

ISHIZAKI, Y., CHENG, L., MUDGE, A. W. & RAFF, M. C. (1995) 'Programmed cell death by default in embryonic cells, fibroblasts, and cancer cells'. *Molecular Biology of the Cell* 6(11), 1443–1458

IWANIR, S., TRAMM, N., NAGY, S. ET AL. (2013) 'The microarchitecture of *C. elegans* behavior during lethargus: homeostatic bout dynamics, a typical body posture, and regulation by a central neuron'. *Sleep* 36(3), 385–395

JABLONSKI, N. G. (2006) *Skin: A Natural History*. Berkeley: University of California Press

JAKOBSEN, H. H. AND STROM, S. L. (2004) 'Circadian cycles in growth and feeding rates of heterotrophic protist plankton'. *Limnology and Oceanography* 49(6), 1915–1922

JÉKELY, G (2009) 'Evolution of phototaxis'. *Philosophical Transactions of the Royal Society B: Biological Sciences* 364(1531), 2795–2808

JENNINGS, H. S. (1904) *Contributions to the Study of the Behavior of Lower Organisms*. Washington, D.C.: Carnegie Institution

JENNINGS, H. S. (1906) *Behavior of the Lower Organisms*. New York: Columbia University Press (London: Macmillan)

JONAS, H. (1966; 2001) *The Phenomenon of Life: Toward a Philosophical Biology*. Evanston: Northwestern University Press

JÜRGENS, K. AND DEMOTT, W. R. (1995) 'Behavioral flexibility in prey selection by bacterivorous nanoflagellates'. *Limnology and Oceanography* 40(8), 1503–1507

KABADAYI, C. AND OSVATH, M. (2017) 'Ravens parallel great apes in flexible planning for tool-use and bartering'. *Science* 357(6347), 202–204

KAECH, S., BRINKHAUS, H. & MATUS, A. (1999) 'Volatile anesthetics block actin-based motility in dendritic spines'. *Proceedings of the National Academy of Sciences* 96(18), 10433-10437

KAHNEMAN, D. (2011) *Thinking, Fast and Slow*. London: Penguin

KAY, R. R., LANGRIDGE, P., TRAYNOR, D. & HOELLER, O. (2008) 'Changing directions in the study of chemotaxis'. *Nature Reviews. Molecular Cell Biology* 9(6), 455–463

KELLY, I., HOLLAND, O. & MELHUISH, C. (2000) 'Slugbot: a robotic predator in the natural world'. *Proceedings of the Fifth International Symposium on Artificial Life and Robotics for Human Welfare and Artificial Life Robotics*. 470–475

KING, N. (2004) 'The unicellular ancestry of animal development'. *Developmental Cell* 7(3), 313–325

KUHL, W. AND KUHL, G. (1966) 'Untersuchungen über das Bewegungsverhalten von *Trichoplax adhaerens* F. E. Schulze (Zeittransformation: Zeitraffung)'. *Zoomorphology* 56(4), 417–435

KUSAYAMA, T. AND WATANABE, S. (2000) 'Reinforcing effects of methamphetamine in planarians'. *Neuroreport* 11(11), 2511–2513

KUSCH, J. (1999) 'Self-recognition as the original function of an amoeban defense-inducing kairomone'. *Ecology* 80(2), 715–720

LABARBERA, M. (1984) 'Feeding currents and particle capture mechanisms in suspension feeding animals'. *American Zoologist* 24(1), 71–84

LAMING, D. R. J. (2000) 'On the behavioural interpretation of neurophysiological observation'. *Behavioral and Brain Sciences* 23(2), 209

LAND, M. F. (2014) *The Eye: A Very Short Introduction*. Oxford: Oxford University Press

LANE, N. (2009) *Life Ascending: The Ten Great Inventions of Evolution*. London: Profile Books

LEE, W. L., REISWIG, H. M., AUSTIN, W. C. & LUNDSTEN, L. (2012) 'An extraordinary new carnivorous sponge, *Chondrocladia lyra*, in the new subgenus *Symmetrocladia* (Demospongiae, Cladorhizidae), from off of northern California, USA'. *Invertebrate Biology* 131(4), 259–284

LEONARDO DA VINCI (1952) *The Notebooks of Leonardo da Vinci*, ed. I. A. Richter. Oxford: Oxford University Press

LLINÁS, R. R. (2001) *I of the Vortex: From Neurons to Self*. Cambridge, Mass.: MIT Press

LOCKERY, S. R. (2011) 'The computational worm: spatial orientation and its neuronal basis in *C. elegans*'. *Current Opinion in Neurobiology* 21(5), 782–790

LOOMIS, W. F. (1955) 'Glutathione control of the specific feeding reactions of hydra'. *Annals of the New York Academy of Sciences* 62(1), 211–227

LURZ, R. W. (2009) 'The philosophy of animal minds: an introduction', in R. W. Lurz (ed.) *The Philosophy of Animal Minds*. Cambridge: Cambridge University Press

MCCLINTOCK, B. (1993) 'The significance of responses of the genome to challenge', in J. Lindsten (ed.) *Nobel Lectures, Physiology or Medicine 1981–1990*. Singapore: World Scientific Publishing

MCCLUNG, C. R. (2006) 'Plant circadian rhythms'. *The Plant Cell* 18(4), 792–803

MCDOUGALL, W. (1923) *An Outline of Psychology*. London: Methuen

McFarland, D. (2008) *Guilty Robots, Happy Dogs: The Question of Alien Minds*. Oxford: Oxford University Press

McMahon, T. A. and Bonner, J. T. (1983) *On Size and Life*. New York: Scientific American Library

Matsuoka, K., Cho, H.-J. & Jacobson, D. M. (2000) 'Observations of the feeding behavior and growth rates of the heterotrophic dinoflagellate *Polykrikos kofoidii* (Polykrikaceae, Dinophyceae)' *Phycologia* 39(1), 82–86

Maynard Smith, J. and Szathmáry, E. (1999) *The Origins of Life: From the Birth of Life to the Origins of Language*. Oxford: Oxford University Press

Merker, B. (2005) 'The liabilities of mobility: A selection pressure for the transition to consciousness in animal evolution'. *Consciousness and Cognition* 14(1), 89–114

Miller, S. (1968) 'The predatory behavior of *Dileptus anser*'. *Journal of Eukaryotic Microbiology* 15(2), 313–319

Mockford, E. L. (1997) 'A new species of *Dicopomorpha* (Hymenoptera: Mymaridae) with diminutive, apterous males'. *Annals of the Entomological Society of America* 90(2), 115–120

Money, N. P. (2014) *The Amoeba in the Room: Lives of the Microbes*. Oxford: Oxford University Press

Montagnes, D. J. S., Barbosa, A. B., Boenigk, J. et al. (2008) 'Selective feeding behaviour of key free-living protists: avenues for continued study'. *Aquatic Microbial Ecology* 53(1), 83–98

Moroz, L. L. (2009) 'On the independent origins of complex brains and neurons'. *Brain, Behavior and Evolution* 74(3), 177–190

Morsella, E. (2005) 'The function of phenomenal states: supramodular interaction theory'. *Psychological Review* 112(4), 1000–21

Nagel, T. (1974) 'What is it like to be a bat?' *Philosophical Review* 83(4), 435–450

Nakano, H., Lundin, K., Bourlat, S. J. et al. (2013) '*Xenoturbella bocki* exhibits direct development with similarities to Acoelomorpha' *Nature Communications* 4(1537)

Nakano, H. (2015) 'What is *Xenoturbella*?' *Zoological Letters* 1(22)

Nath, R. D., Bedbrook, C. N., Abrams, M. J. et al. (2017) 'The jellyfish *Cassiopea* exhibits a sleep-like state'. *Current Biology* 27(19), 2984–2990

Neuser, K., Triphan, T., Mronz, M., Poeck, B. & Strauss, R. (2008) 'Analysis of a spatial orientation memory in *Drosophila*'. *Nature* 453(7199), 1244–1247

Nielsen, C. (1995; 3rd ed. 2012) *Animal Evolution: Interrelationships of the Living Phyla*. Oxford: Oxford University Press

Noë, A. (2004) *Action in Perception*. Cambridge, Mass.: MIT Press

Norris, V., Turnock, G. & Sigee, D. (1996) 'The *Escherichia coli* enzoskeleton'. *Molecular Microbiology* 19(2), 197–204

Nuttley, W. M., Atkinson-Leadbeater, K. P. & van der Kooy, D. (2002) 'Serotonin mediates food-odor associative learning in the nematode *Caenorhabditis elegans*'. *Proceedings of the National Academy of Sciences* 99(19), 12449–12454

O'Malley, M. A. (2014) *Philosophy of Microbiology*. Cambridge: Cambridge University Press

Omond, S., Ly, L. M. T., Beaton, R. et al. (2017) 'Inactivity is nycthemeral, endogenously generated, homeostatically regulated, and melatonin modulated in a free-living platyhelminth flatworm'. *Sleep* 40(10)

Pagán, O. R. (2014) *The First Brain: The Neuroscience of Planarians*. Oxford: Oxford University Press

Patterson, D. J. and Hedley, S. (1992; rev. ed. 1996) *Free-living Freshwater Protozoa: A Colour Guide*. London: Manson Publishing

Penrose, R. (1995) *Shadows of the Mind: A Search for the Missing Science of Consciousness*. London: Vintage

Petie, R., Garm, A. & Nilsson, D.-E. (2011) 'Visual control of steering in the box jellyfish *Tripedalia cystophora*'. *The Journal of Experimental Biology* 214(17), 2809–2815

Pierce-Shimomura, J. T., Morse, T. M. & Lockery, S. R. (1999) 'The fundamental role of pirouettes in *Caenorhabditis elegans* chemotaxis'. *The Journal of Neuroscience* 19(21), 9557–9569

Polilov, A. A. (2012) 'The smallest insects evolve anucleate neurons'. *Arthropod Structure and Development* 41(1), 29–34

Pollard, T. D. (2003) 'The cytoskeleton, cellular motility and the reductionist agenda'. *Nature* 422(6933), 741–745

Priest, S. (1991) *Theories of the Mind*. Harmondsworth: Penguin

Proust, J. (2009) 'The representational basis of brute metacognition: a proposal', in R. W. Lurz (ed.) *The Philosophy of Animal Minds*. Cambridge: Cambridge University Press

Pujol, N., Link, E. M., Lui, L. X., Kurz, C. L., Alloing, G. et al. (2001) 'A reverse genetic analysis of components of the Toll signaling pathway in *Caenorhabditis elegans*'. *Current Biology* 11(11), 809–821

Puttonen, E., Briese, C., Mandlburger, G. et al. (2016) 'Quantification of overnight movement of birch *(Betula pendula)* branches and foliage with short interval terrestrial laser scanning' *Frontiers in Plant Science* 7(222)

Raizen, D. M., Zimmerman, J. E., Maycock, M. H. et al. (2008) 'Lethargus is a *Caenorhabditis elegans* sleep-like state'. *Nature* 451(7178), 569–572

Ralston, K. S., Solga, M. D., Mackey-Lawrence, N. M., Bhattacharya, A. & Petri Jr, W. A. (2014) 'Trogocytosis by *Entamoeba histolytica* contributes to cell killing and tissue invasion'. *Nature* 508(7497), 526–530

Ralt, D., Manor, M., Cohen-Dayag, A. et al. (1994) 'Chemotaxis and chemokinesis of human spermatozoa to follicular factors'. *Biology of Reproduction* 50(4), 774–785

Reeve, M. R., Walter, M. A. & Ikeda, T. (1978) 'Laboratory studies of ingestion and food utilization in lobate and tentaculate ctenophores'. *Limnology and Oceanography* 23(4), 740–751

Ridley, M. (1999) *Genome: The Autobiography of a Species in 23 Chapters*. London: Harper Perennial

Roach, M. (2013) *Gulp: Adventures on the Alimentary Canal*. W. W. Norton & Company

Roberts, E. C., Wootton, E. C., Davidson, K. et al. (2011a) 'Feeding in the dinoflagellate *Oxyrrhis marina*: linking behaviour with mechanisms'. *Journal of Plankton Research* 33(4), 603–614

Roberts, E. C., Legrand, C., Steinke, M. & Wootton, E. C. (2011b) 'Mechanisms underlying chemical interactions between predatory planktonic protists and their prey'. *Journal of Plankton Research* 33(6), 833–841

Rochat, P. (2009) *Others in Mind: Social Origins of Self-Consciousness*. Cambridge: Cambridge University Press

Rolls, E. T. (1999) *The Brain and Emotion*. Oxford: Oxford University Press

Romanes, G. J. and Darwin, C. (1885) *Mental Evolution in Animals*. London: Kegan Paul, Trench & Co.

Rose, S. (1992) *The Making of Memory*. London: Bantam Press

Rothschild, L. J. (1989) 'Protozoa, Protista, Protoctista: what's in a name?' *Journal of the History of Biology* 22(2), 277–305

Sanders, R. D., Tononi, G., Laureys, S. & Sleigh, J. W. (2012) 'Unresponsiveness ≠ unconsciousness'. *Anesthesiology* 116(4), 946–959

Sarnat, H. B. and Netsky, M. G. (1985) 'The brain of the planarian as the ancestor of the human brain'. *The Canadian Journal of Neurological Sciences* 12(4), 296–302

Sass, L. A. and Parnas, J. 'Schizophrenia, consciousness, and the self'. *Schizophrenia Bulletin* 29(3), 427–444

SAWIN, E. R., RANGANATHAN, R. & HORVITZ, H. R. (2000) '*C. elegans* locomotory rate is modulated by the environment through a dopaminergic pathway and by experience through a serotonergic pathway'. *Neuron* 26(3), 619–631

SCHIERWATER, B. (2005) 'My favorite animal, *Trichoplax adhaerens*'. *Bioessays* 27(12), 1294–1302

SCHIERWATER, B., EITEL, M., OSIGUS, H.-J. ET AL. (2010) '*Trichoplax* and Placozoa: one of the crucial keys to understanding metazoan evolution', in R. DeSalle and B. Schierwater (eds) *Key Transitions in Animal Evolution*, CRC Press

SCHLEYER, M., DIEGELMANN, S., MICHELS, B., SAUMWEBER, T. & GERBER, B. (2013) '"Decision-making" in larval *Drosophila*', in R. Menzel and P. Benjamin (eds) *Invertebrate Learning and Memory*. London: Academic Press

SCHLOEGEL, J. J. AND SCHMIDGEN, H. (2002) 'General physiology, experimental psychology and evolutionism: unicellular organisms as objects of psychophysiological research, 1877-1918'. *Isis* 93(4), 614–645

SCHÖNBORN, W. (1966) *Beschalte Amöben (Testaceae)*. Wittenberg Lutherstadt: Ziemsen

SCHROUFF, J., PERLBARG, V., BOLY, M., MARRELEC, G. ET AL. (2011) 'Brain functional integration decreases during propofol-induced loss of consciousness'. *Neuroimage* 57(1), 198–205

SEARLE, J. R. (1992) *The Rediscovery of the Mind*. Cambridge, Mass.: The MIT Press

SHAFFER, J. A. (1968) *Philosophy of Mind*. Englewood Cliffs, N. J.: Prentice-Hall

SHAPIRO, J. A. (1998) 'Thinking about bacterial populations as multicellular organisms'. *Annual Reviews in Microbiology* 52(1), 81–104

SHAPIRO, J. A. (2007) 'Bacteria are small but not stupid: cognition, natural genetic engineering and socio-bacteriology'. *Studies in History and Philosophy of Science Part C: Studies in History and Philosophy of Biological and Biomedical Sciences* 38(4), 807–819

SHEIMAN, I. M., ZUBINA, E. V. & KRESHCHENKO, N. D. (2002) 'Regulation of the feeding behavior of the planarian *Dugesia (Girardia) tigrina*'. *Journal of Evolutionary Biochemistry and Physiology* 38(4), 414–418

SHERWIN, C. M. (2001) 'Can invertebrates suffer? Or, how robust is argument-by-analogy?' *Animal Welfare* 10, S103–S118

SHOEMAKER, S. S. (1968) 'Self-reference and self-awareness'. *The Journal of Philosophy* 65(19), 555–567

SHOMRAT, T. AND LEVIN, M. (2013) 'An automated training paradigm reveals long-term memory in planarians and its persistence through head regeneration'. *The Journal of Experimental Biology* 216(20), 3799–3810

SINGER, P. (1975; 1995) *Animal Liberation*. London: Pimlico

SMITH, C. L., PIVOVAROVA, N. AND REESE, T. S. (2015) 'Coordinated feeding behavior in *Trichoplax*, an animal without synapses'. *PLoS ONE* 10(9), e0136098

SMITH, J. A. (1991) 'A question of pain in invertebrates'. *ILAR Journal* 33(1–2), 25–31

SNYDER, R. A. (1991) 'Chemoattraction of a bactivorous ciliate to bacteria surface compounds'. *Hydrobiologia* 215(3), 205–213

SOKOLOWSKI, M. B. (2002) 'Social eating for stress'. *Nature* 419(6910), 893–894

SOMPAYRAC, L. (1999; 3rd ed. 2008) *How The Immune System Works*. Oxford: Blackwell Publishing

SONNER, J. M. (2008) 'A hypothesis on the origin and evolution of the response to inhaled anesthetics'. *Anesthesia and Analgesia* 107(3), 849–854

STARR, R. C., MARNER, F. J. & JAENICKE, L. (1995) 'Chemoattraction of male gametes by a pheromone produced by female gametes of *Chlamydomonas*'. *Proceedings of the National Academy of Sciences* 92(2), 641–645

STRASSMANN, J. E. (2000) 'Evolution: bacterial cheaters'. *Nature* 404(6778), 555–556

THAR, R. AND FENCHEL, T. (2001) 'True chemotaxis in oxygen gradients of the sulfur-oxidizing bacterium *Thiovulum majus*'. *Applied and Environmental Microbiology* 67(7), 3299–3303

THAR, R. AND KÜHL, M. (2003) 'Bacteria are not too small for spatial sensing of chemical gradients: experimental evidence'. *Proceedings of the National Academy of Sciences* 100(10), 5748–5753

THOMPSON, E. (2007) *Mind in Life: Biology, Phenomenology and the Sciences of Mind*. Cambridge, Mass. and London: Harvard University Press

THORINGTON, G. U., MCAULEY, V. & HESSINGER, D. A. (2010) 'Effects of satiation and starvation on nematocyst discharge, prey killing, and ingestion in two species of sea anemone'. *The Biological Bulletin* 219(2), 122–131

THOROGOOD, R., KOKKO, H. & MAPPES, J. (2018) 'Social transmission of avoidance among predators facilitates the spread of novel prey'. *Nature Ecology and Evolution* 2(2), 254–263

TONONI, G. (2004) 'An information integration theory of consciousness'. *BMC Neuroscience* 5(42)

TROJANOWSKI, N. F. AND RAIZEN, D. M. (2016) 'Call it worm sleep'. *Trends in Neurosciences* 39(2), 54–62

Turner, J. S. (2000) *The Extended Organism: The Physiology of Animal-Built Structures.* Cambridge, Mass. and London: Harvard University Press

Turney, J. (2015) *I, Superorganism: Learning to Love Your Inner Ecosystem.* London: Icon Books

Tye, M. (1997) 'The problem of simple minds: Is there anything it is like to be a honey bee?' *Philosophical Studies* 88(3), 289–317

Ueda, T., Koya, S. and Maruyama, Y. K. (1999) 'Dynamic patterns in the locomotion and feeding behaviors by the placozoan *Trichoplax adhaerens*'. *BioSystems* 54(1), 65–70

Vacelet, J. (2006) 'New carnivorous sponges (Porifera, Poecilosclerida) collected from manned submersibles in the deep Pacific'. *Zoological Journal of the Linnean Society* 148(4), 553–584

Vacelet, J. and Boury-Esnault, N. (1996) 'A new species of carnivorous sponge (Demospongiae: Cladorhizidae) from a Mediterranean cave'. *Bulletin de l'Institut Royal des Sciences Naturelles de Belgique* 66, 109–115

Verity, P. G. (1991) 'Feeding in planktonic protozoans: Evidence for non-random acquisition of prey'. *Journal of Eukaryotic Microbiology* 38(1), 69–76

Villarreal, L. P. (2009) *Origin of Group Identity: Viruses, Addiction and Cooperation.* New York: Springer

Von Holst, E. and Mittelstaedt, H. (1950) 'Das Reafferenzprinzip'. *Naturwissenschaften* 37(20), 464–476

Von Reyn, C. R., Breads, P., Peek, M. Y., Zheng, G. Z., Williamson, W. R. et al. (2014) 'A spike-timing mechanism for action selection'. *Nature Neuroscience* 17(7), 962–970

Ward, S. (1973) 'Chemotaxis by the nematode *Caenorhabditis elegans*: identification of attractants and analysis of the response by use of mutants'. *Proceedings of the National Academy of Sciences* 70(3), 817–821

Watson, J. B. (1930; 1970) *Behaviorism.* New York: W. W. Norton & Co.

Wen, J. Y. M., Kumar, N., Morrison, G. et al. (1997) 'Mutations that prevent associative learning in *C. elegans*'. *Behavioral Neuroscience* 111(2), 354–368

Wenderoth, H. (1986) 'Transepithelial cytophagy by *Trichoplax adhaerens* F. E. Schulze (Placozoa) feeding on yeast'. *Zeitschrift für Naturforschung C*, 41(3), 343–347

Wittgenstein, L. (1953) *Philosophical Investigations,* trans. G. E. M. Anscombe. Oxford: Blackwell

You, Y.-J., Kim, J., Raizen, D. M. & Avery, L. (2008) 'Insulin, cGMP, and TGF-β signals regulate food intake and quiescence in *C. elegans*: a model for satiety'. *Cell Metabolism* 7 (3), 249–257

ZAHAVI, D. (2005) *Subjectivity and Selfhood: Investigating the First-Person Perspective.* Cambridge, Mass. and London: The MIT Press
ZHANG, Y., LU, H. & BARGMANN, C. I. (2005) 'Pathogenic bacteria induce aversive olfactory learning in *Caenorhabditis elegans*'. *Nature* 438(7065), 179–184

*

www.ingramcontent.com/pod-product-compliance
Lightning Source LLC
Chambersburg PA
CBHW021351300426
44114CB00012B/1177